"This is an extraordinary testimony to the power of beauty in a broken and fragmented world. It is extraordinary not simply because of its unusually direct and winsome style, but because of what the author brings to his theme: a professional expertise in neurobiology. More than a testimony, it is also an invitation: to have our deepest desire set alight, our desire for the One from whom all beauty springs."
Jeremy Begbie, Duke University

"Curt Thompson's previous work on shame has been life-transforming for numerous readers. Here he continues his interdisciplinary exploration of one of the elemental human experiences that founds our sense of self—the desire to see and to share beauty. Disarmingly self-disclosing, deeply in touch with Scripture and classic Christian sources, and engagingly conversant with the advances and insights of current neuroscientific research, this book beckons us to a deeper, healing knowledge of ourselves and, ultimately, of God."
Wesley Hill, associate professor of New Testament at Western Theological Seminary

"*The Soul of Desire* by Curt Thompson is a deep and edifying book that emphasizes that we are people created with a fundamental desire or longing for beauty, goodness, and truth related to healing and wholeness. He helps us to take time to dwell, gaze, and inquire of the Lord to fulfill our desire for beauty in the context of community, as well as sharing our grief and suffering, preparing and practicing for heaven to come. Highly recommended!"
Siang-Yang Tan, senior professor of clinical psychology at Fuller Theological Seminary and author of *Counseling and Psychotherapy: A Christian Perspective*

"'An artist and a psychiatrist get into a car . . .' sounds like the start of a joke, yet this is actually how I met Curt Thompson. And as unlikely a pairing as we appear on paper, *The Soul of Desire* seems like an equally absurd mash-up of ideas. But I am happy to say that we became fast friends, and this book, too, turns out to be a wonderfully balanced amalgamation of neuroscience, aesthetics, and Christian faith. Allow this book to help you let go of shame, put yourself in the path of oncoming beauty, and begin imagining that life can be lived as an expression of God's artistry."
Ned Bustard, author and illustrator of *Saint Nicholas the Giftgiver* and creative director for Square Halo Books

"In his previous books, *The Soul of Shame* and *Anatomy of the Soul*, Curt Thompson integrated neuroscience and theology seamlessly, cheering us on in a hopeful, unhurried journey toward healing. In Curt's new book, *The Soul of Desire*, he brings it all back to the start, setting us right in the path of God's beauty. With the skillfulness of a therapist and the earnestness of an evangelist, Curt Thompson implores us to see how God desires for us to create beauty in the context of confessional community— that our lives would be authentically generative, like works of art."
Sandra McCracken, singer-songwriter and author of *Send Out Your Light*

"I am drawn to Curt Thompson because, like our Creator, he accounts for and carefully tends to the whole person in his work. With the wisdom of a master therapist and the heart of a well-formed disciple, Curt helps us see how our God-given desire can enrich our community and lead us deeper into the heart of Christ. If you are looking for a trustworthy guide to mentor and guide you along this life-giving path, I cannot recommend *The Soul of Desire* more highly to you."

Scott Sauls, senior pastor of Christ Presbyterian Church and author of *Jesus Outside the Lines*

"In *The Soul of Desire*, Curt Thompson shares a profound and uplifting message about what makes beauty simultaneously spiritual and human. This wonderful book will enrich the faith of readers as they seek meaning and purpose in the turmoil of life."

Arthur C. Brooks, professor at Harvard Kennedy School and Harvard Business School, author of *Love Your Enemies: How Decent People Can Save America from the Culture of Contempt*

"Everything Curt writes is life changing for me, and *The Soul of Desire* is no different. He connects the dots between science and faith through the lens of beauty and relationships. Further, the more you understand why you long for intimacy, the more empowered you become to receive it. We were never meant to live alone. You'll love this empowering book!"

Rebekah Lyons, author of *Rhythms of Renewal* and *You Are Free*

"Curt's latest book is really his most hopeful book, a challenge to cultivate the kind of imagination and embodied practice that shifts us from brokenness to beauty. But it's as much Curt's character as it is his wisdom that draws me to this. A remarkable life, a remarkable book!"

Chuck DeGroat, professor of pastoral care and Christian spirituality at Western Theological Seminary, senior fellow at Newbigin House of Studies

"Curt Thompson is a master of integrating themes that invite us to a place of deeper connection with God, ourselves, others, and the world around us. The combination of his expertise in interpersonal neurobiology, his therapeutic work with groups and individuals, and his passion for the beauty of the gospel brings a fresh gaze to the topics of desire, longing, and healing. It's a perfect companion piece to *The Soul of Shame*."

Jill Phillips, singer-songwriter

"Curt Thompson has a keen eye for seeing beauty in the ashes. He's convinced me that beauty is an essential criterion for truth, a path into deep-level healing, and a sign of transformation. I'm grateful for his uncanny ability to integrate these insights as he walks clients and readers from alienation to belonging and community. Masterful!"

Bradley Jersak, dean of theology and culture at St. Stephen's University, New Brunswick

"Reading this wonderful, deep, and engaging book helped me to see and understand the deep longing I have always felt in my soul as God's factory-equipped desire for beauty, and ultimately for God. Dr. Thompson is once again a doctor of our souls, but in this book his prescription for our healing is to gaze upon, and to make, beauty. Beauty is captivating, and this book captivated me—because it is a beautiful book. I highly recommend you read it, not once but over and over again. This book will no doubt shape many conversations about the care and cure for our souls."

James Bryan Smith, author of *The Good and Beautiful God*

"There's something profoundly disarming and inviting about the way Curt writes *The Soul of Desire*. In its pages we encounter the mind of a biblical scholar, the wisdom of a psychiatrist, and the heart of a pastor. Drawing on sweeping biblical narratives, deeply tender stories of the human experience, and yes, neuroscience, Curt reminds us that even in a broken world we are people of desire with a longing to be deeply known. He boldly declares that beauty is integral for our healing, our transformation, and our flourishing, then shares—testifies!—on the power of a vulnerable community in earthing these realities in our everyday lives. I closed this book challenged, changed, and in awe of God's beauty."

Jo Saxton, speaker, leadership coach, and author of *Ready to Rise*

"What if the glory of God can be revealed in our places of shame? And what if we say yes to the generative work of creating beauty, even in our broken relationships? In *The Soul of Desire*, Curt Thompson names our fears, taps our deepest longings, and engages our imagination, inviting us to consider how beauty emerges from places of trauma and how God works through authentic and vulnerable community to make all things new. This is a timely, inspiring, and beautiful book."

Sharon Garlough Brown, author of *Shades of Light* and the Sensible Shoes series

"*The Soul of Desire* is a feast of new creation hope. Weaving together wisdom from Scripture, insights from neurobiology, and stories of broken lives incrementally made whole, Curt Thompson offers much-needed guidance to those beset by grief, trauma, and shame. His daring proposal is that beauty isn't a luxury but a necessity for our healing, and that this transformative beauty is best encountered and created in the context of vulnerable community. As a pastor, I'm eager to see this profound, even heavenly vision unleashed upon the church. As a person seeking to overcome trauma and shame myself, I'm deeply grateful for Curt's compassion for hurting people and his unmistakable love for the God of beauty to whom this book ultimately points."

Duke Kwon, lead pastor of Grace Meridian Hill and coauthor of *Reparations: A Christian Call for Repentance and Repair*

"Curt Thompson's *The Soul of Desire* is a book full of beauty and delight that reveals the secrets of healing and tending to wounded souls. This is a remarkable book that weaves biblical narrative together with neurobiological insight and the arts to help us pursue answers to the profound questions of desire. With a disarming wit and sobering honesty, Thompson grapples with weighty truths, all the while grounding his integration in the redemptive work of a risen Savior. The author skillfully and tenderly walks the reader through stories—biblical, clinical, and poetic—that reawaken our sense of grief, revealing the imprints of trauma that have distorted and corrupted desire. He invites us to learn what is at play in our bodies, spirits, and relationships through the context of what he calls 'confessional communities.' A confessional community 'creates a space in which we gather to name our desires, lament our griefs and traumas—all acts of prayer—and out of them become outposts of beauty and new creation in the other domains of our lives.' Thompson is hoping not simply to awaken our minds but also our creative spirits as we hunger for the dawning of a new creation. At the heart of this book he desires that we come to know the G-d who deeply knows us: the one who would soothe us and redeem the stories we've been living and co-creating. This book will inspire you to risk desire, that your life can become a thing of beauty and goodness, even from what is a story of grief and despair."

J. Derek McNeil, president and provost of the Seattle School of Theology and Psychology

"Pick up this book and read it slowly. *The Soul of Desire* will help you uncover the ways you've built up walls around the deeper places in your soul. With Curt's help, you will see firsthand what beauty can do for the human heart."

Jennie Allen, author of *Get Out of Your Head* and founder and visionary of IF:Gathering

"Curt Thompson's *The Soul of Desire* is a superb example of the integration of theology, psychology, psychiatry, and neurobiology on an applied level. The wisdom he shares penetrates powerfully as it emerges in the lives and stories of real people in safe and transformative communities. Within a few pages, I was eager to reread this book, and I have already begun it again. My guess is many of Thompson's readers will do likewise—desiring, as I do, to live into its depth of insights and practices."

Mark Labberton, president of Fuller Theological Seminary

The SOUL of DESIRE

DISCOVERING *the* NEUROSCIENCE *of*
LONGING, BEAUTY, *and* COMMUNITY

CURT THOMPSON, MD

FOREWORD BY *MAKOTO FUJIMURA*

An imprint of InterVarsity Press
Downers Grove, Illinois

InterVarsity Press
P.O. Box 1400, Downers Grove, IL 60515-1426
ivpress.com
email@ivpress.com

InterVarsity Press® is the book-publishing division of InterVarsity Christian Fellowship/USA®, a movement of students and faculty active on campus at hundreds of universities, colleges, and schools of nursing in the United States of America, and a member movement of the International Fellowship of Evangelical Students. For information about local and regional activities, visit intervarsity.org.

While any stories in this book are true, some names and identifying information may have been changed to protect the privacy of individuals.

The publisher cannot verify the accuracy or functionality of website URLs used in this book beyond the date of publication.

Interior art: John—In the Beginning: *copyright © 2010 Makoto Fujimura*
        Golden Sea: *copyright © 2011 Makoto Fujimura*
        Charis—Kairos (The Tears of Christ): *copyright © 2010 Makoto Fujimura*
        New Wine: *copyright © 2018 Makoto Fujimura*

Cover design and image composite: David Fassett
Interior design: Jeanna Wiggins
Images: organic watercolor doodle: © beastfromeast / Digital Vision Vectors / Getty Images
        orange textured background: © enjoyz / iStock / Getty Images Plus
        yellow abstract: © Jose A. Bernat Bacete / Moment / Getty Images
        white paper texture: © Katsumi Murouchi / Moment / Getty Images
        SEM neurons cells: © koto_feja / iStock / Getty Images Plus
        blue abstract: © Nath Chokh Perm Thnaraks' / EyeEm / Getty Images
        colorful leaves watercolor: © Yifei Fang / Moment / Getty Images

ISBN 978-1-5140-0210-0 (print)
ISBN 978-1-5140-0211-7 (digital)

Printed in the United States of America ∞

Library of Congress Cataloging-in-Publication Data
A catalog record for this book is available from the Library of Congress.

P 25 24 23 22 21 20 19 18 17 16 15 14 13 12 11 10 9 8 7 6 5 4 3 2

Y 42 41 40 39 38 37 36 35 34 33 32 31 30 29 28 27 26 25 24 23 22 21

For

RICH AND JANELLE BUTTERWORTH,

BYRON AND KRISTIN LIST,

and

NEAL AND KENDRICK SMITH

Who, individually and

communally,

have created the beauty and goodness and truth

in which, over the last

three decades,

it has been my joy

to dwell,

to gaze,

and

to inquire of the Lord.

■ ■ ■

CONTENTS

FOREWORD

Makoto Fujimura

*That I may dwell in the house of the LORD all the days
of my life, to gaze on the beauty of the LORD.*

PSALM 27:4

"GOOD LITERATURE," DR. CURT THOMPSON WRITES, "like all meaningful art, helps us access the beauty of what it means to dwell in the house of the Lord all the days of our lives."

In *The Soul of Desire* Curt directs and redirects us, as a good therapist always does, to help us understand how to live a life defined by the psalmist's longing to "dwell in the house of the LORD . . . to gaze on the beauty of the LORD." But such journeys have to start first by recognizing the underlying misalignment of our assumptions, the false prejudgments we make of ourselves and others, and how we are often unable to name our own desires and articulate them clearly. This intimate journey of hope, complex and daunting as it may be, has specific names in this book—names such as Aaron, Carmen and Graham, Tara, Hudson, and Charlotte. Curt tells us their precious and sacred stories. This is a journey toward a community of authentic hope, healing, and tears.

"Psychotherapy provides a setting in which shame is deconstructed through and in the presence of a properly boundaried, empathic relationship, and in which movement toward secure attachment is initiated and sustained," Curt writes.

Curt's other important work *The Soul of Shame* has been a guide book for my own healing over the years. Curt is an expert guide into the dark and cold caves of shame. When I was going through a severe "dark night of the soul" several years back, a dear friend (also a therapist and an author) told me that my "cave of shame" was off limits. He simply forbade me to go there. It was Curt's work that helped me to see the anatomy of my own shame and massage the shame toxins out of my system in order to stay out of such disastrous darkness.

It was then that I also began to fully understand *Kintsugi*, a craft tradition of Japanese refinement that I was introduced to earlier in my life as a national scholar at Tokyo University of Art in Nihonga. Kintsugi, a venerable Japanese tradition of mending broken pottery with lacquer and powdered gold, is a path toward seeing the fractures and fragments as something to be highlighted (with gold), thereby making the resulting mended object more valuable than the original—as valuable as the original may have been before it was broken. As we gaze upon the broken body and beauty of Christ, Curt notes, we are in "intimate contact with [Jesus's] wounds." The post-resurrection body of Christ still bears the nail marks, and "by his wounds we are healed" (Isaiah 53:5).

What is remarkable is that the wounds of Christ represent Jesus' decision to stay human after the resurrection: God chooses to keep the wounds and therefore be fully human—fully alive *in his wounds* after the full suffering as a human. For Curt, this reality of the new creation is amply evident in his journey as a psychiatrist. He then helps us to journey into our shame and pain, only to have the Master Kintsugi Artist, the Creator God, mend to make us new.

This book in itself is a work of art to behold, to gaze upon, to commune with. This is a manual on how a community may become a "Kintsugi community" for generations to come.

INTRODUCTION

"**Are you serious?** You want me to look at a painting every day for the next six weeks? I don't have time for that. And besides, what on earth does that have to do with my life? I'm in trouble here, man. You're a doctor, not a museum guide. I don't need some three-hundred-year-old picture—I need help!"

My patient was a man in his early forties who was about to lose both his marriage and the career he had so arduously established over two decades. He was saturated with anxiety and covered in shame.

"I know you want help," I told him. "But the help you believe you need is not what you're most longing for. Maybe you're not ready to hear this yet, but you want more than simply to be free of your anxiety or to have your marriage fixed and your company restored."

Here was a man of action, on whom the reality was gradually, painfully dawning that the kind of action he was used to taking was only making him more anxious. More afraid. More cut off from himself and those he loved and was terrified of losing. And lose them he would if something didn't change.

After meeting with him several times and encountering his resistance to virtually all my suggestions, I pointed to the painting on my office wall. It was Rembrandt's *Return of the Prodigal Son.* "What do you see?" I asked.

"What do you mean, 'What do you see?'" he scoffed. "I see a painting."

Working to regulate my own impatience, I pressed on. "What do you feel when you look at it?"

He looked at the painting, his exasperation unhidden. "Okay. I see four men. No—five. And one is embracing another." He looked at me impatiently, waiting, as if he had answered my question, nonverbally conveying, "Can we move on?—to solving my problems?" He was unaware that he had *not* in fact answered my question. There was a great deal he was still unaware of, not least the number of characters in the painting.

And so it is that, like my patient, we move about on the earth not so much in the land of the living as in the land of the anxious—the traumatized walking dead. We try to contain our pain and brokenness—from the micromoments of self-flagellation to the macromoments of the violence of politically charged slander, racial bigotry, sexual predation, and emotional abuse. It's our practice of remaining unaware of the way we pay attention to ourselves and to the world that leads to virtually all of our traumatic desolation and injustice for which we seek diagnoses and treatment for our personal and social pathologies.

As I write this we are entering the thirteenth month of the Covid-19 pandemic. It has both revealed and contributed to the traumatic isolation that has become the defining social malignancy of our time. But our isolation is not new. It is as old as humanity; the pandemic has only highlighted and reinforced it. And evil has taken advantage of it, using trauma and shame to disintegrate us as individuals and communities.

Most of our well-intentioned attempts to counter the storms of our inner and outer lives involve identifying our problems and devising solutions for them. But in our hurry to diagnose and treat our diseases of the soul, we're often outrun by the very fear that is driving us to identify and resolve them. And this is often as true for people of faith as anyone else. What are we to do? What, indeed, is my patient—along with all of those who are paying a price for their life choices—to do?

This book offers a response to those questions by inviting you to pay attention to the world in a different way—one in which we have little practice. It invites you to live into the biblical narrative of new creation by focusing first *not* on the surface, on what is obvious, and *not* first on our souls' identifiable diseases—as important as that is to do. Instead, it invites you to look below all of this, at the desire—the longing, the depth of eternity that God has placed in our hearts (Ecclesiastes 3:11).

To consider and answer Jesus' question in John 1:38, "What do you want?" is a life-altering practice, for it opens our minds to the reality that Jesus is keenly interested in *what we want*—our desire. In fact, that question lies at the ground of our being, for it lies at the center of the triune God in whose image we have been made. Jesus' question eventually draws our attention to our deep longing to be known for the purpose of creating beauty in the world, in those very places—our politics, our ethnic identities, our painful marriages, our sexual encounters, our histories of interpersonal and social abuse—where it might seem impossible to imagine it could emerge. Our isolation not only compounds our affliction, but it does so by distracting us from true desire and our longing for beauty.

You might be suspicious that desire has much good to offer us, considering how often our desire can go awry—how often we move from desiring to devouring the very beauty for which we so hunger and thirst. Given how our culture has trampled on or exploited the notion of beauty over the years, you could hardly be blamed for thinking that a book that brings together neuroscience and beauty is barking up the wrong tree. What on earth can they have to do with each other? Sure, the brain is incomprehensibly elegant in its structure and function—beautiful by any measure. But isn't beauty itself an add-on in God's creation economy? A luxury? Something we can consider only if and when we have time in the course of all our effort to fix the problems of our anxiety-ridden lives?

What does putting ourselves in the path of oncoming beauty have to do with the healing of our minds, the changing of our brains—and the transformation of our world's most troubled systems? And how does that depend on our living in the context of a vulnerable community? What does it mean, in other words, for my patient mentioned above to spend time contemplating *The Return of the Prodigal Son* over the course of several weeks when he resolutely resisted other suggestions I had made that seemed more concrete and accessible?

I hope to persuade you that beauty is not only *not* a luxury; it is a necessity. A necessity not merely for flourishing but for our very survival. It is not something we only want to create and experience—it is something we long to become, beauty arising out of our "slight momentary affliction [that] is preparing for us an eternal weight of glory beyond all measure" (2 Corinthians 4:17 NRSV). Beauty for which we were destined before the foundation of the world. Beauty that begins and ends with God and our relationship with him and each other. As Simone Weil said, "In all that awakens within us the pure and authentic sentiment of beauty, there is, truly, the presence of God. There is a kind of incarnation of God in the world, of which beauty is the sign."[1]

For my patient, what began as a tenuous, six-week exercise in "simply" sitting in the presence of one of the world's most beautiful paintings extended into a months-long journey that first required his willingness—his initial reluctance notwithstanding—to look at the painting every day and to practice being curious about the kinds of things we will explore in this book. Along the way, he eventually found himself in a confessional community, a gathering of people that we form in our practice (and with which you will soon become familiar) that provides the crucible in which the same beauty found in the artistic expressions of Rembrandt, Emily Dickinson, Gustav Holst, and Makoto Fujimura is revealed and formed in and out of their own lives, not least those parts of their stories that they often hate the most. And as my patient became woven into that group, the healing of Jesus—found in the presence of the body of Jesus through that community—made its way to, in, and through him. But that beauty did not remain there. Eventually it found its way into his marriage and his work in ways that would have been unimaginable before.

The enterprise that led to my patient's restoration is grounded in the tenets of interpersonal neurobiology, held in the light of the gospel of Jesus. Our trouble is that, like my patient in the early weeks of our relationship, we are so often straitjacketed by our fear and shame that answering Jesus' question, "What do you want?" not only seems unhelpful—it barely makes sense.

But if you're willing, answering that question in the context of a vulnerable community intent on practicing for heaven changes everything.

And so I invite you to join me and to discover and acknowledge that you are a person of deep desire. You desire to be known in the deepest recesses of your story so that you will be liberated to become an outpost of new creation—of beauty and goodness—even as you create that same beauty and goodness yourself, as you practice for the kingdom of God that is here and is surely coming.

DESIRE

A People of Longing

"**WHAT DO YOU WANT?**" **I ASKED.**

A blank stare, just short of quizzical, was the response I got. This was not the question Aaron had anticipated. His was a troubled life, and he thought he had made those troubles plain to me. He thought he knew what his problems were. He was practiced in naming them. He could identify what he perceived to be wrong with his life.

But now words failed him. As he later told me, he could not recall the last time—let alone the first time—anyone had asked him that question apart from ordering in a restaurant. All he could think of—but wasn't able to say at the time—was that he wanted to be relieved of the symptoms that were swallowing his life.

Aaron had not considered that his desire—what he wanted, what he longed for—was central to his experience of depression and intermittent panic. Once he gathered himself, he answered, "I don't know what I want."

It was not difficult for me to see what he meant. Several months earlier Aaron had ended an affair that had nearly devoured his marriage. The work he was doing with his wife to repair the cavernous rupture remained tenuous, and he still struggled to refrain from entertaining fantasies of his experience with the other woman.

What Aaron "wanted," in his view, was the collection of sensations, images, feelings, thoughts, and actions he had immersed himself in over the course of the affair—a state of mind to which he turned his attention whenever he needed relief from anxiety (the equivalent of an addiction). Consequently, to name what he "really" wanted was to evoke great conflict: the comfort and relief offered by images of the affair juxtaposed with feelings of guilt, shame, and despair when he thought about the effort involved in renewing his marriage. Desire mocked him, his mind seemingly lashed to something outside the boundaries of his covenant with God, his wife, and his community.

It never occurred to him that behind his choices lay his most primal desires—indeed, his most holy longings. In fact, these desires were contributing antecedently to everything he judged dysfunctional and shameful about his life.[1] Little did he know that desire was far more than just the source of his affliction (as he presumed); it was in fact the very element that could lead him to a life of beauty, goodness, and joy.

We are people of desire. We want things. We long for things. It is primal to our nature to yearn. As Saint Augustine reflected, "The whole life of the good Christian is a holy longing. . . . That is our life, to be trained by longing."[2] We have been at it as a race for as long as we have been on the planet.[3]

We begin at birth with our embodied desires for breath, nourishment, warmth, and physical security. These are linked to an emotional desire for nurture that begins in childhood, extends through adulthood, and is mediated both interpersonally and neurobiologically—that is, it is felt, sensed, and acted on in our relationships with others and within our own brains. These early longings form the hard deck upon which others stand as a child matures. It doesn't take much to see the breadth of our desire (we modernists want a *lot*, both significant and trivial) or the depth of our desire—although the true nature of this is often outside our conscious understanding.

We are told by many wise guides that this desire begins and ends with God—God's desire for us to desire unity with him. The idea is not for us to be dissolved into God (losing ourselves) but to be unified with him so that the more connected we are to him, the more we become distinctly our-selves. Christian anthropology reveals, perhaps somewhat counterintui-tively, that the depth and intensity of our desire for and unity with God directly and proportionately mirror the degree to which we become the truest versions of our individual selves. And our Scriptures bear this out. Along with expressions of praise and gratitude (which occupy their own place of prominence), we read a vast number of stories of people who desire help from God—who long for guidance, wisdom, and courage. We are a wanting people. Even the prayer Jesus gave his disciples, the Lord's Prayer, is filled with requests. Beyond hallowing the Father's name, all else is an expression of what we want as an extension of what we most deeply need.

James K. A. Smith has shed important light on this, reminding us of the biblical framework within which to approach the nature of desire. Within that frame, he persuasively and constructively explores the an-thropological, philosophical, and theological underpinnings of the nature and role of desire in our status as image bearers of God.[4] Smith, much in the spirit of Augustine, invites his readers to contend with the reality that desire is innate, and simultaneously, it is invariably formed.[5] Desire does not exist merely as some independent phenomenon to which we respond; it is also something that, like any good gardener knows, must be pruned. It must be shaped and will be shaped by whatever practices, habits, or (in Smith's language) liturgies we develop—liturgies we practice whether we know it or not.

Smith lays a foundation that I would have readers of this book presume as well: that a biblical understanding of what it means to be human cen-trally locates desire in love—to use Smith's words, we are what we love.[6] Moreover, we are desiring creatures; we are created, not self-made, and we are made with the intention to love—to desire.

Furthermore, our behavior is far more powerfully driven by the habits we form in our embodied movements than by what we "think."[7] Before we are thinking creatures, we are desiring and then habit-forming crea-tures. This is not to suggest that we are *only* desiring creatures and that rational processing is somehow a subordinate function of our minds or that we are not formed by our thoughts—far from it. If I cannot reason about the order of actions needed to change a flat tire on my car, it doesn't matter how much I desire for it to change. However, it is my desire to drive the car on four air-filled tires so that I can meet my wife at the airport that engages my "thinking" brain to change the tire in the first place. Eventually, we will see how this biblical approach to desire is reflected in the interpersonal neurobiological features that make us human. We will also examine how the work we do in vulnerable community creates space in which to participate in the work of the Spirit, who awakens us and shapes our desires as we practice for heaven—as we form habits, or liturgies, of relational creativity.

All well and good, then, is desire. But I have to admit, this whole notion of desiring God more than anything else can be tricky for me. If my desire begins with God's loving desire for me and ends with finding its consummation in God, the road in between seems anything but straightforward or easy. This despite my awareness that as a follower of Jesus, only God am I made to love—to desire—with all my heart, mind, soul, and strength (Deuteronomy 6:5; Mark 12:30). Frankly, it's easy for me to desire just about anything that is pleasurable, good, or beautiful far more than I desire God. I mean, everything else is right in front of me. I can touch it or feel it—or at least construct it in the recesses of my mind's imagined, disembodied self.

If it's really true that, as Augustine wrote, my heart remains restless until it finds its rest in God,[8] then why, oh why do other things compete so readily for my heart's attention? Why do I long so deeply for the idealized woman or work or status? Why do I yearn so hungrily for food or financial security or simply the absence of suffering or emotional pain? I am reminded of Walker Percy's *Love in the Ruins*, in which we hear the words of Dr. Tom More: "I believe in God and the whole business," More admits, "but I love women best, music and science next, whiskey next, God fourth, and my fellowman hardly at all."[9]

Still, my difficulty in directing my desire, my love, toward God is not completely mysterious. As René Girard points out, no small part of why

I desire something is envy. Human behavior that is intentional is primarily learned through mimicry, by watching the intentional behavior of others. Our desires are no different, as they are expressions of our intention. Therefore, I want something because you want it. And if you're a person of authority in my world, one whose admiration and affection I long for, I will tend to want the things you want.[10] As a result, a great deal of what and how I desire has less to do with the object of my desire and more to do with being able to compete in my world, with being adequate and acceptable. Indeed, my desire is not so much about an object as it is about the condition of my relationality, with whom and how I am living relationally. Thus, when I "hunger and thirst [desire] for righteousness [right relationality]," I will be filled (Matthew 5:6). Not after I "acquire" an object—even if that object is a relationship. And as I have explored in *The Soul of Shame*,[11] my need to have what you have is itself a way for me to defend against my shame of not being enough, shame that finds its way into my life and my soul early and often.[12]

It is helpful to know that much of my desire is related to envy. What I really long for, it turns out, is for God to show up and compete (if indeed I am created to long for him like I long for nothing else as an expression of being loved by and loving him). I want him to appear in an embodied way in my life now (not just two thousand or so years ago) and give me a genuine experience that will persuade me to want him more than anything else. I want him to draw me to himself in some imagined loving, irresistible way such that I won't simply *want* to want him but will actually want relationship with him more than anything else. More than arousal or sex. More than power. More than wealth. More than knowing all the things I want to know so that I won't have to worry about making mistakes and disappointing people who will leave me as a result. I plead in anguish with God, as does John Donne, to "Take me to you, imprison me, for I, / Except you enthrall me, never shall be free, / Nor ever chaste, except you ravish me."[13]

Perhaps I don't desire God like I desire those other things because no one else possesses him like they possess anything else either. To desire

God, it turns out, would have to entail shame being so far outside my life that it wouldn't interfere with my wanting him. But shame is in my life, so evil can use it to leverage my desire for things I can see with my own eyes, things other people have that I don't.

If I asked you the same question I asked my patient Aaron—"What do you want?"—and you could for a moment put aside the predictable anxiety that comes with it, I'm confident that at some point in your reflection you would move beyond the banal and become aware that what calls to you from the depths of your soul, what you most achingly long for, is that which is beautiful, good, true, and joyful. It is not difficult to identify beauty, goodness, and truth found in objects or experiences outside ourselves (e.g., the Grand Tetons, Beethoven's Piano Concerto no. 5, *The Shawshank Redemption*). But we ultimately long to discover and become these things in the context of embodied relationships. Our hearts, minds, and souls most desperately want to love and be loved by real people in real time and space, not the fantasized, virtual people who make up the vast majority of our mental narratives. You know the ones— the imagined stories we tell much of every waking hour that either demonize or idealize our friend or enemy, our spouse or child, as well as the story we tell about ourselves that is laden with shame and so distorts our perspective, making it difficult to receive in an equally integrated way the wild, deep love of God. We want all of that in an embodied fashion. Real. It needs to have color and sound and a pulse. If we can't feel it in our bones and blood, there's little use pursuing it any further.

The evidence of our longing is writ large in our culture, from U2's "I Still Haven't Found What I'm Looking For" to Rembrandt's *Return of the Prodigal Son* to Gabriel Axel's *Babette's Feast* to the words of the New Testament, where we read that "the creation waits in eager expectation for the children of God to be revealed. . . . Not only so, but we ourselves, who have the firstfruits of the Spirit, groan inwardly as we wait eagerly for our adoption to sonship, the redemption of our bodies" (Romans 8:19-23). It is not just we humans who long for things. We do so in concert with the entire material world.

What's more, we don't desire just anything. We aren't interested in the dull or painful. We don't eagerly anticipate the adequate. We don't long to get the flu. We don't hope to be more ashamed by the end of the day. No. We long for a world of goodness and beauty, of biblical justice, of putting all things right. We long for a world in which our relationships with those of the other gender, ethnic people group, and political party, as well as with the material world, are governed by kindness and honesty. Our artifacts and our relationships repeatedly remind us that desire is active, whether it be out in the open, swimming just below the surface of our consciousness, or submerged fathoms below. And, as with Aaron, it is also something to which we pay little proper attention.

Speaking of relationships, we want them to be robust and soaked with kindness. We long for—whether we know it or not—deep connection with friends or the one we want to marry or the one we are married to and have sex with and make a life with. We want to engage in work we find meaningful and that requires the sort of effort that lets us know we have left a part of ourselves in it while expanding our sense of ourselves in the process. We want to partake in creating artifacts—whether they be legal briefs or hikes in Glacier National Park or furniture or music or middle school graduates—that are marked by, literally and nothing less than, beauty.

We want to enjoy our embodied presence on the earth. Who actually wants to be unfit? Who wants heart disease, diabetes, cancer, knee replacements, obesity, or any of the other medical and psychiatric maladies that plague us? We want our bodies to reflect the same goodness and beauty that we long for in any other domain of our lives. We hunger and thirst for a physical engagement with our world that leaves us unworried about the mud God's breath suffuses (Genesis 2:7).

We regularly long for an adventure in nature or human creativity that leaves us speechless, where we know by its depth of profundity that we can't clutch it, despite our inclination to do so. Who doesn't want to be there when the sun rises on El Capitan in Yosemite Valley or can tear their eyes away from van Gogh's *Starry Night*? We want springs, summers, autumns,

and winters that live into their fullness, and we want to be resilient enough
to abide in them with gratitude and wonder, faithfully cultivating the land
and tending the creation in such a way that we live to see the climate
changing—moving, eventually, in a different direction.

We want the joy of others'—not least God's—utter delight at being in
our presence. We long to encounter and be encountered by others
without exploitation on anyone's part. Even when it comes to death, as
much as it is not the way it is supposed to be, we long to die well. When
we are not distracted by our fickle and feckless nature, we can name any
number of things we want at the center of our souls—things we know
require time, energy, and committed relationships to create, things that
reflect, when we truly see it, the world "charged with the grandeur of
God."[14] In a portion of John O'Donohue's "For Longing" the poet expresses much of what echoes in our hearts:

> Blessed be the longing that brought you here
> And quickens your soul with wonder. . . .
>
> May you come to accept your longing as divine
> urgency.
>
> May you know the urgency with which God longs
> for you.[15]

Again—we have been created as people of desire, in the image of the
triune Desirer.

DESIRE AND SEX—A BRIEF NOTE

Unsurprisingly, whenever we bring the topic of desire into view, our
imaginations easily wander in the direction of sex, which can be as dis-
comforting as it is arousing—but it is certainly not irrelevant. Visual and
musical artists rightly draw our attention and give expression to this part
of our lives not only because of the energy surrounding it but also because of the role it plays physically and emotionally, representing some
of the most vulnerable and creative features of our human experience.

And no wonder, given the placeholder sexuality is for the intersection of our desire for beauty and goodness.

But I want to invite you to consider that the beauty, energy, and vulnerability bound up and often expressed in our sexuality often points to something that is deeper and beyond sex itself. It is easy for our imaginations—and hence the rest of our lives—to atrophy (and so they have) if the ultimate endpoint of all desire is orgasm. Because as we know, once it's over, it's over. But we don't want it to be over. We want something more—something eternal. Hence true desire encompasses much more than sex and sexuality.

THE "PROBLEM" OF DESIRE

Let us not assume that human desire is a neutral phenomenon or is always directed toward goodness and beauty—quite the contrary. There is not space here to properly explore a theology of desire; rather, we are focusing on its interpersonal neurobiological features. But to speak of desire necessarily invokes theological and anthropological implications that are worthy of acknowledgment. Indeed, it is my intention for theology and anthropology to set the conditions for our exploration of interpersonal neurobiology, not the other way around. Plausibility structures matter and are in play whether we're aware of them or not.[16] The church fathers consistently acknowledged the beauty and goodness of desire (e.g., Augustine, above), but they were not naive to the potential for desire to be bent by sin. They knew that our longing for an ever-growing relationship with God—one that leads to loving others, ourselves, and the world deeply—could easily be turned to desiring objects for their own sake. Instead of experiencing joy in relationship with God and others, we desire to become God and to possess others and the objects they love.

Moreover, when I cannot have what I desire, I often respond with envy. Again, as Girard has pointed out, although the Tenth Commandment is the last, in many ways it is the source of why I so easily break the first nine.[17] Theologically, then, desire, like all human behavior, is subject to what we call sin and therefore at all times must be held up to the light of the work of the Spirit.[18] I easily attest that in my own life there is nothing I do that is not tainted with mixed motives, laced with some latent urge to own, clutch, consume, or become master of the universe. To be God. Only not God like God is but like the devil would be if he were in charge.

So it's important to be aware of that thread of our desire that seeks not beauty or goodness but rather their devouring. This again is what Girard emphasizes in his work; we must be aware that desire, on shame's terms, is primarily about envy.[19] And envy's source is shame. This is why so much of our desire is channeled in ways that are, to use the language of interpersonal neurobiology, disintegrating. This was what led to Aaron's affair.

But herein lies the goodness and beauty of the gospel. God's desire for us to live in communion with him and steward the earth was so deep that it seemingly outweighed his awareness of what we would do to him and each other after he created us in the first place. It is God's desire for us, his love for us, that leads him to call to our desire, imperfect as our responses may be. He is well aware that I am still quite capable of desiring things in a way that leads only to harm. We read in Genesis 3 that the woman's desire would be for her husband, in Genesis 4 that sin was crouching at Cain's door and its desire was for him. When desire is bent by our sense that the world is one of scarcity, it devolves into devouring.

No one is more aware of the depth of our sin, nor takes more seriously our penchant for devouring, than Jesus. At the same time, he is not worried about it, nor does it prevent him from doing the work of the Father in redeeming and then using our desire to enable us to practice for God's heaven that is surely coming. It is desire—ultimately our desire for him—that God has placed in the very center of our being and that he is counting on to energize our relationship with him and others.

DESIRE AND DEVELOPMENT

Desire is something no child has to be taught. Early in the developmental process, most of a child's desires center around physical needs being met or objects that attract interest. If a child is securely attached to her parents, she will readily and without guile ask for or tell them what she wants, either with nonverbal cues or words. The general posture of children is to name what they want: unvarnished, uncalculated, and unambiguous. Their repertoire expands as their parents (hopefully) guide and direct the energy behind it. In general, securely attached children don't worry about managing others' emotional needs when naming what they want. They don't feel compelled to parent their parents or their siblings. Moreover, good parenting involves acknowledging and validating a child's desires even while setting limits on them.

Desire is part of what it means to be a child, as implied in Jesus' words to his disciples when he tells them, "Truly I tell you, unless you change and become like little children, you will never enter the kingdom of heaven" (Matthew 18:3). If we aren't careful, we can too easily assume that all children want is for their own personal needs to be met; we interpret this energy of desire in a theological framework that categorizes it as sinful or not depending on how unpleasant it makes us adults feel.

But research in the field of attachment sheds important light on this dynamic. Children use their caregivers as a secure base from which to explore their inner and outer worlds with ever-increasing degrees of confidence and proper risk taking.[20] They move from desiring milk from their mother's breast to desiring the toy on the other side of the room, from playing guitar to attaining a driver's license, from talking to the dark-haired girl in English class to joining the Marines. This desire never ends, but if we have not learned as children how to live into it, we will have to, as adults, become like children to learn about it properly for the first time—as Jesus himself indicates.

A great deal of parenting energy is devoted to channeling and shaping a child's desire in such a way that the child learns at least two important realities about the world. First, he learns that his desire is important. His parents attune not only to what he wants but *that* he wants, and they support the child's experience of asking for things. In this way, a child is formed into someone whose inner emotional state expressed in longing finds a receptive audience, strengthening his capacity to live transparently in the world. The child hears from his parents that they are glad to receive his desire as part of their joyful welcome of him, over and over, into the world.[21]

But second, and equally important, the child learns that his desires may not always be met—he may not get what he wants when and how he wants it. This necessary "no" in the face of the child's ever-expanding desire is as important as any "yes." At the same time, proper mentalizing (the awareness that one has a mind, that it enables navigation of the world, and that this is true for others as well, allowing us to imagine what is transpiring in another person's mind) on the part of the parent enables the child to sense that his desire itself is welcomed, even if the object of his desire is outside the boundary of what is good for him at the time.[22]

Let me assure you, this is not easy for a parent (or teacher, coach, employer, spouse, or friend) to pull off. At any given moment in which I set a limit for my child, I cannot predict that her reaction will be what I want it to be: swift compliance. Often there is, as any parent knows, resistance on the part of the child that I don't like, which requires even more work on my part. In essence, my child is now limiting what I want, which is for her to stop bothering me with what she wants! It is in this moment that desire is tested and matured—both hers and mine. As the parent, I must find a way to, as best I can, say "no" to the object of my daughter's desire while saying "yes" to her desire itself. This is eerily similar to what was happening in the Garden of Eden in that long-ago time. Our first parents clearly had trouble living within the limits. But more on that later.

In these moments in which "no" is properly limiting "yes," our interpersonal neurobiological experience of desire is being refined and deepened. These early exchanges in the development of secure attachment form us into people who will eventually know that desire in and of itself is to be honored and named. And we learn this not only as an abstract fact but also as an embodied reality. When this happens, we enter into a way of being with each other that is consistent with how our interpersonal neurobiological systems are intended to work.

Along this path something deeper and weightier arrives, emerging into our consciousness one neural network at a time. Amid all the targets of our longing that we've named, at some point we awaken to our desire to be known. The biblical narrative bears witness to the reality of this unquenchable desire, from the slave Hagar, who tells the Lord, "You are the God who sees me" (Genesis 16:13), to the prophet Jeremiah, of whom God says, "Before I formed you in the womb I knew you" (Jeremiah 1:5), to the apostle Paul, who states that believers "know God—or rather are known by God" (Galatians 4:9). We long to be seen, heard, and felt by one whom we sense desires to see us, hear us, and feel what we feel.

Every baby comes into the world looking for someone who is looking for him or her. To have a conscious, embodied awareness of being known by God is a necessary feature of the life of loving God, and our awareness of being known by God is measured by the degree to which we are known by each other. This type of hunger abides with us forever, echoing the author of Ecclesiastes when he writes that God has placed eternity in our hearts (Ecclesiastes 3:11). When regarding the notion of eternity, we are not merely aware of time and its passage, nor do we simply long to live forever. Rather, we long to be known forever, ever more deeply and joyfully, for the purposes that we will explore in this book. In the center of our souls, "eternity" is not just measured in time; it is measured in depth—a depth that feels infinite. And in this case, it is the depth of our desire to be known that is infinite.

No longing is deeper. As Jeremiah 1:5 suggests, the process of being known is a fundamental feature of what it means to be human long before we reach physical form, let alone consciousness. But it is something we are born to grow into, and it is a process that requires our interaction with and pursuit by others. We are formed by being known by others, which enables us to know. Moreover, regardless of our level of awareness of it, we long to be so consummately known that we carry the reality of it with us in our interpersonal neurobiological experience wherever we go and in whatever endeavor we find ourselves. We long for that state of confident expectancy with every footfall that lands on life's pavement.

Granted, most of the time we have little to no idea that this is going on in our minds. During much of our life we are consciously aware only of what we are immediately sensing—what we want but don't have. We don't at some random age suddenly say, "Oh my gosh, I so want to be known by God and others." Instead we travel a subtler path, one that begins, hopefully, in the context of secure attachment to our parents. Each of us experiences our own particular awakening to this desire—or not, depending on the security of our emotional attachment. If we are unaware of it, deny it, actively resist it, or misdirect it, our lives tend to be more afflicted.

I want to be known by my parents and siblings, then by my friends and teachers and coaches, then by the one in whom I have a romantic interest or by my spiritual guides. The desire to be known in these contexts emerges for the most part as tacit, nonconscious interpersonal neurobiological events. But it is fair to say that in every one of these relational instances, the fire of God's Spirit is burning in a way that reflects what the biblical story contends is, ultimately, our desire for God and our desire to be desired by him—albeit without shame as part of the conversation.

Embedded in the process of being known is our awareness that the one by whom we are known desires to know us. As such, a critical element of our desire is that of being desired. We long to be infinitely desired, wanted by the other yet—and crucially—without being consumed by the other. Without being exploited. Without being ignored or imprisoned. This begins at birth and winds its way through all of our relationships at every level of intimacy. It is desire that enables us to differentiate from our parents and siblings and that draws us to connect with other differentiated beings. No matter how superficial or deep, this seminal drive for connection is preeminent. Wisdom suggests that in fact the more deeply connected to God we are, the more able each of us is to realize our unique individuality. That we seem to have a fathomless depth of wanting suggests that our longing indeed will be fulfilled only in a relationship of comparable, infinite depth.

DESIRE AND THE MIND

In the world of interpersonal neurobiology (or IPNB), we speak of emotion as the neurobiochemical and interpersonal energy around which the brain organizes itself.[23] Using the metaphor of an automobile, it is the gasoline in the tank (or, for you hybrid owners, the electric charge in the battery). This does not mean it is the most important activity of the mind, but there is nothing we do that does not in some way require the regulation of emotion.[24] Hence, when we speak of "desire," we are not reducing it to "feelings," but emotion will be an integral part of whatever it is. We use words to symbolize collective clusters of human experience. This is how we use the word "desire," but we are not able to identify or measure it as a singular homogenous "thing" in the material world. I don't have a localized set of "desire" neurons in my brain, despite the fact that parts of the brain are activated during experiences of pleasure or arousal or anticipation.[25]

When we experience all of the sensations, images, feelings, thoughts, and behavioral impulses that we equate with the notion of desire, there is a primary emotional element to our experience that provides the basis for what we're talking about. However, it would be more helpful to speak of desire as our experience of this entire collective convergence of what we sense, image, feel, think, and are primed to do behaviorally that amounts to "what we want."

"What we want," then, is a complex constellation of experiences, sensations, and impulses, all of which we are continually trying to make sense. This process of "making sense of what we sense" is fundamental to how we humans, unique among living creatures, develop into storytellers. As we have seen from attachment research, the stories we tell are contingent on the type of attachment we form with our primary caregivers.[26] It is here, then, in the attachment laboratories of our families that we learn to tell our story of desire. Not only that we desire but that we are a delight because we do. Our ability to name what we want in our developmental years enables us to seamlessly enter into praying the Psalms in all of their naked honesty, leaving no stone of desire unturned, whether it be for God's rescue, his blessing, or his smiting of our enemies. We Christians believe in a God who can take it (at least I want to believe that), and I live into that reality by naming what I want, even if I'm not going to get it.

Fine and good, you may be thinking. This thing called desire may be real. It may even be interesting. But what does it have to do with healing, let alone with redemption and the renewal of all things? Isn't desire what led to Aaron's (and so many others') trouble in the first place? Wasn't that Eve and Adam's problem, their desire? Best that we simply know what and where our desires are so that we can keep an eye on them. So that we can keep them from getting out of hand and leading us down paths we don't want to travel. What does desire have to do with solving the hard problems of the world? What does it have to do with mental illness, spiritual malignancy, climate change, sexual dilution or abuse, racism, immigration convulsions, or fear of economic collapse? If desire doesn't speak to those realities, why are we speaking about it at all? Further consideration of our topic may seem like wasted time. The real world, the one that matters, the one with real problems, is waiting for real answers. It is not waiting for one more distraction in the direction of desire.

Perhaps. But it turns out that our brains and our relationships won't stand for that conclusion. As we will see, everything we imagine we must do to practice for heaven by creating beauty in the ash heaps of our world, be they marriages or toxic waste dumps, begins with desire. In this world of brokenness, that which is broken was not always so; it is merely the outgrowth of defiled desire. And for the world to be redeemed, God does not destroy desire; rather, he resurrects and renews it while using it to renew everything else, beginning with us.

In *The Soul of Shame* I explored the nature of shame and its place in our stories. In the wake of that project two things came immanently into view. First was the overwhelming profusion of shame as a dominant feature that evil uses to shape our lives, my own not the least. The echoes of others' resonance with that contention has and continues to be deafening. But second, and unexpectedly, is that the very reality of shame—the pitch-black darkness of the vault in which we often feel trapped and suffocated—makes possible the blinding brightness of the light that fills a crack in the vault's door.[27] Evil did not see that light coming in the early stages of its planned attempt to overthrow God that morning in Eden. It hijacked our desire—not least our primal desire for beauty, goodness, and joy (the traits of God that, among others, evoke our worship of him)—and exploited it in its attempt to devour the creation. But God renews our desire while using it to renew everything else, beginning with us. God's utter, joyful desire is for us to be with him and he with us such that we might together create beauty in the world. God's desire calls to ours and breathes life into the lungs of the world. Here we are confronted with a deep paradox: it is desire that evil exploited, inserting shame in its place, yet desire is the very substance of our created being to which God is calling. He is calling out our desire in order to redeem it and make it the leading edge of the renewal of all things.

Because our yearning is the fuel shame depends on to ignite and keep burning, followers of Jesus can far too prematurely dismiss desire as a source of danger. We think we must avoid desire at all cost in order to keep away from the pitfalls of sin and the shame that accompanies it. Paradoxically, it is in naming our desire for beauty that we align ourselves with the most primal call of God, which is being broadcast from the heights of heaven and is planted in the core of our souls. No wonder Jesus' first words as recorded in the Gospel of John are "What do you want?" (John 1:38). God knows we are people of desire and longs for us to name our longings so that we can get on with the business of living together in his kingdom of beauty, goodness, and joy.

So when I asked Aaron, sitting in my office, what he wanted, my question at first caused confusion. He thought he was there to discuss his problems, which was not untrue. But for Aaron to realize healing and recommissioning into the fullness of life, he would eventually need to name what he wanted. As is true for so many others whose stories I have been privileged to hear, Aaron was unaware of his longings at their source of earliest emergence. Given how much of his narrative was flooded with the pain and shame of his current circumstances, it was not easy for him to turn his attention to the first two decades of his life, let alone consider that they had much to offer that would relieve his agony and point the way to a regenerated life. Given that reality, we began where he was able to go.

As we took the first tentative steps in exploring his affair, he spoke of how that relationship awakened desire in him in ways he never knew existed. He described the deep sense of feeling seen, felt, and understood. He could not recall a time in his life when he had so effortlessly been in the presence of someone who seemed simply to find pleasure in being with him, who delighted in him. He recalled how she created space for him to name, in the absence of judgment, those things in his life that were overwhelming and those things about himself that he hated the most.

When, I asked him, had anyone else been this eagerly interested in him while seeming to place so little demand on him? His reflection on this question led eventually to a moment he later described as a revelation.

It turned out that as a child Aaron had on many occasions longed to be seen and felt and heard. But the dynamics of his family prevented him from becoming aware of this, let alone expressing it. Instead, he simply and nonconsciously buried that longing under the work of survival. This was not obvious to him in the early stages of our work together; only as he began to risk being curious about his story did he begin to notice *that* he wanted, and only then did he begin to approach *what* he wanted.

He told of growing up in a family that was chaotic despite overtones of religious piety and weekly church attendance. His father's unpredictable outbursts (directed especially toward Aaron's siblings) had him running for cover to his room whenever the specter of his father's anger emerged. Being the middle of five children, Aaron was able to fade into the woodwork of his family despite the frequent shrapnel flying around the house. This penchant for camouflage protected him from his father's temper and his mother's enabling behavior. Aaron did his best to avoid standing out—except in his schoolwork, where he excelled.

His ability to work hard and be rewarded with good grades and attention from teachers led Aaron to develop a narrative in which the necessary sensation of acceptance—of being desired—was neurally spliced together with his working hard to achieve it. The notion that someone could possibly desire him apart from his hard work simply was not part of his mind's neurobiological or relational landscape. When he had a deeply meaningful spiritual awakening in college, his encounter with Jesus, albeit real, was not separate from his implicitly remembered narrative. Despite what Aaron's left brain heard about God's love for him, his right brain had not facilitated an actual, embodied experience of what love "meant" in real time and space. Yes, he felt the love of God, but the neural payload of all the years prior was not about to vanish quietly overnight. His anticipation of fear and shame should his weakness or imperfection be exposed was far more entrenched in his mind than he knew.

You may be reading this and asking, "Okay, so what's the problem? I still don't see how that set him up to have an affair." Let's delve a little deeper.

Doubtless, we parents hope our children will exhibit the character traits of resilience, kindness, courage, and depth far into adulthood and after we're gone. And Aaron had plenty of all of that. Being a good soldier was not a problem for him. The problem was the degree to which his soldiering covered the deeper waters of longing he didn't know he had. Neither of his parents was able to mentalize him (imagine what he was thinking and respond accordingly) in a way that provided an opportunity for him to ask the questions or speak the thoughts peppering his young mind: *What if all I believe about God isn't true? How do we know the resurrection is real? What am I supposed to do about sex? (And if it's so great, why does everyone seem so uncomfortable talking about it?) Who and what are females anyway? I hate how uncomfortable I feel around people I don't know well. What does it really mean to grow up, and why do I seem so afraid of it?*

Aaron was longing to be seen and heard in ways his parents simply did not recognize. They were not horrible people, and they loved their son. But not even Mary the mother of Jesus could see everything for what it was while parenting her boy (see Mark 3:20-24). If she had trouble with this, we all will—we can count on it. In fact, there's an endless list of people who sit in my office and recount to me that they grew up in a loving Christian home. And for many this is code for, "Life sucked, but I can't really say that out loud. I would just be complaining about something I have no right to complain about."

Aaron was just such a person. His desire was like a wellspring that had been capped off to keep it from overrunning and flooding the area at which it emerged. But water is a funny thing. Only with great force can it be held in place. And when it rises fast and deep, even the most brilliantly engineered structures cannot stop its movement. Eventually it finds its way to the surface, sweeping everything in its path to the ocean, caring not a whit who or what it takes with it. This is what happened to Aaron.

DESIRE AND DISINTEGRATION

At the same time, the human race is as impulsive and consumptive as it has ever been. The automaticity with which we indulge ourselves in "what we want" is deeply embedded, both interpersonally and neuro-biologically. Our ability to delay gratification and demonstrate restraint is severely underdeveloped in a world where we are routinely primed and prompted to "do what I want, when I want, how I want." AT&T knows this and is more than happy to encourage and exploit this posture.[28] It's a big reason I have a job as a psychiatrist.

But we are, it turns out, out of conscious touch with our deepest longings. Of course, we say we desire good relationships, well-paying jobs, comfortable homes, and opportunities to enjoy life in the "pursuit of happiness." Those are the things we are willing to admit in public. But privately, our desire for more goods, more ease and convenience, more sex and pleasure—whatever we can addictively turn to that we believe will relieve us from the stress of modern life—has us pinned to the ground. Those desires reveal their darker side when they morph into predatory behavior, greed, consumption, and contempt, all of which not only ruin our personal lives but poison our public lives as well. How we act on these fleeting longings often leads people to my office, as was the case for Aaron.

Evil does its best work in the middle of good work being done, and Aaron's story was no exception. For truly, it is a thin line that separates our longing for beauty and goodness from our exploitation of them. Aaron had been influential in the best of ways as he followed his heart's desire to exercise his gifts as a preacher, teacher, and caretaker of his parishioners' spiritual formation. Unfortunately, those longings became tangled in ones he didn't even know he had, yearnings that originated in the first two decades of his life. For humans to flourish, we must awaken to the fundamental nature and purpose of desire and the critical role it plays in the problems we face in everyday life—problems that range from inner conflicts to cultural conflagrations, problems like the ones Aaron was facing. In fact, our "problems"—not least our greatest relational sufferings—are directly related to misdirected and unmet desire.

My own personal story highlights how, when it comes to desire, our mind's pendulum can swing between denial and diffusion. On the one hand, we can bury our desire under denial without even knowing we are doing it (as was often my case); on the other hand, we can impulsively act on desire whenever and however we want, to the point that it reaches a state of diffusion—so diluted that it ceases to have power for creativity. As such, I have to admit that the idea of wading into the topic of desire at first made me nervous and at times still does. My parents loved God and loved me, but that love was intertwined with their own unfinished emotional business. They were in many respects deeply devout people, but they had their own woundedness and had not fully come to terms with it. They instilled in me a love of God and neighbor reflected in a conviction to intervene on behalf of those who were treated unjustly. They taught me to be kind, disciplined, and persevering. There is very little good in my character that is not rooted in my life with my parents. But that is not the whole story.

My father, a kind, affectionate, and just man, could also be stern with his sons and our mother. No one would ever accuse him of being an angry man, but that was to some degree because we worked hard not to incite him. One of his standard responses whenever there was a conflict between us that generated even a hint of tearfulness was, "You stop your crying, or I'll give you something to cry about." (I sometimes wonder if this was the single standard-issue instructional tool parents at that time were given when they were sent home from the hospital with their child.) I remember once opening the hatch on the cover of his pickup truck bed too quickly, not realizing how close he was to it. The hatch struck him in the face, bloodying his mouth. What I noticed was how surprised—and relieved—I was at his restrained, "It's okay. I'm all right" response. Again, it was not common for him to offer a harsh outburst. But it happened frequently and forcefully enough that the absence of it was what caught my attention, revealing to me, even at the age of fifteen, the "bracing for impact" undercurrent running subtly under the surface of my relationship with him.

My mother, a person devoted to prayer and the study of the Scriptures, whose life was transformed by her conversion to follow Jesus, was also anxious about a great many things. She grew up functionally as an orphan and suffered untold relational traumas, and she often seemed on the verge of the next potential loss, her relationship with God not the least. She didn't say that, of course. But I felt her worry about what God would think about any number of things should we make a mistake in judgment.

I recall as a boy of about ten years old playing football with my friends in our front yard on a warm summer Wednesday evening. Wednesdays were the nights our church held a midweek meeting, when about fifteen people would gather for prayer and Bible study led by our pastor. I was the only person—ever—under the age of forty who attended these gatherings, and I was there every time my parents were. On this particular night, only my mother was planning to attend (a fact that the attuned reader realizes is important). She came out of our house and in front of my friends asked, "Are you going to prayer meeting with me tonight?"

I replied, cautiously, "Do I have to?"

To which she responded, "Where do you think Jesus would want you to be?"

What I wanted but did not have the courage to say was, "I think he wants me here playing football with my friends." Or, had I been even more courageous (or foolhardy), something akin to, "I'm not sure. Let me go ask your husband who apparently thinks it's okay to stay home from prayer meeting tonight too."

These are not stories of catastrophic deprivation or violence. My home was never a physically or emotionally dangerous place, as far as I was consciously aware. It was very much a place where I felt safe. But neither was it a place where I could be completely emotionally open, although I didn't know it at the time. I was not aware then how much energy I was burning making sure I didn't make my father angry or my mother anxious. As a result, the notion of what I wanted at any given time was always somewhat tenuous as an emotionally processed experience. It turns out that my desire was frequently viewed through a lens helping me ensure that whatever it was I was asking for was permissible to request. Consequently, if I was not certain in advance that my desire was valid, I simply didn't ask. This didn't mean I was never asked what I wanted or that I never asked for it myself; I did, and my parents were deeply generous. So the problem was not that I did not have desires or that I was unaware of them. Rather, the problem was my fear of naming my desire lest I make someone angry or anxious and my inability to tolerate the discomfort I would then feel. And that led me to practice becoming unaware of my desire in the deepest places.

These details of my story shine a spotlight on the significance of the relational process of attachment to human flourishing. The development of secure attachment is enabled by a child's experience of feeling seen, soothed, safe, and secure.[29] We first must, literally, be seen across the entire breadth our emotional condition. When we are in distress, we need to be comforted, to be soothed. When we are soothed, we develop a sense of safety, of confidence in our bodies and in our environment, both physically and relationally.

As we will see later, however, we need to be made safe not only from outside forces but also from self-inflicted harm, both physical and emotional. This is where limits and boundaries become significant parts of our development and the shaping of our character (not least our desires): with our caretakers (and later ourselves) offering the word "no." Hence, our desire needs to be validated in the context of proper boundaries, much like how the pruning of a tree channels its growth in a direction that produces fruit in the most bountiful way and also strengthens the life of the tree itself—all of which reflects the state of affairs in Eden at the conclusion of Genesis 2.

These three needs—to be seen, soothed, and safe—make way for the fourth: to be secure (collectively referred to here as the four s's).[30] Security is about being able, in the face of feeling seen, soothed, and safe, to move away from our relational base and step out to take the risk of new adventure, whether that's across the crib, across the room, or across the country. It means we are willing to try new things and make mistakes, even difficult ones, because we know we have a place to return to where we will once again be seen, soothed, and safe. It is significant to realize that the four s's, although they develop in early childhood, are necessary for growth and integration throughout our lives. Our need to be seen, soothed, safe, and secure never stops. The only question is who is providing those experiences for us.

In my growing up years there were many ways in which I was seen, soothed, safe, and secure. But there were also many occasions when neither of my parents, despite their general posture of generosity and kindness, were curious about what I was thinking or feeling or sought to understand my behavior before acting on their own impulses of fear or anxiety. Rather, they simply operated as if I would respond to what they wanted me to do and be. But when what I wanted ran counter to their desires, or when I was angry with them, I was faced with contending with my father's sternness or my mother's anxiety. Hence, there were many times when I was not seen, soothed, or safe, and, without knowing it, I was kept from developing the security that would support healthy risk taking. This affected decisions about my future, sex and relationships with women, and especially my sense of my relationship with God.

As we will see as we continue in this book, and as Aaron and so many others have discovered, to be seen, soothed, safe, and secure are necessary states of mind in our discovery of desire and in the setting of limits that channel desire into patterns of beauty and goodness. But the unhealed tracts of our soul's landscape, those that still wait to experience one or more of the four s's, distract us from or blind us to our longing. Our desire can become muted under the fear of relational affliction or misdirected in our attempt to cope with the pain of trauma. We do not nullify desire; we merely regulate it. We may try to redirect its course or seek to contain it, but we cannot extinguish it. For God has made us with desire for connection that ultimately leads to the co-creation of objects of goodness and beauty with him and others with whom we have difference, be it great or small.

This is as powerful and inevitable as gravity or the pull of the tides. We cannot overcome it. But in our pain that leads to avoiding desire, or in our haste to cope with unmet desire through an infinite array of addictions, we ultimately find ourselves in places of great desolation—and then in my office.

BEAUTY

Desire Made Manifest

"**WHAT IS THE NEXT BEAUTIFUL THING YOU WANT TO CREATE?**" Carmen and Graham wondered what this question had to do with anything when I put it to them early in the course of their marriage therapy. Between the trauma they (especially Carmen) had experienced in their church, Graham's unwanted but ongoing practice of viewing pornography, and the emotional wounds they both had sustained in their families of origin, the notion of creativity in their relationship was a nonstarter. They were hurt, angry, and pessimistic about their future as a couple. I was inviting them to consider that working on their marriage was nothing short of creating an object of beauty. A work of art. Creating even as God has created—living fully into his image.

They looked at me like I had two heads. A work of art? They were here for marital therapy—what did beauty have to do with an imploding marriage? Yes, perhaps when all was said and done, when all the redemption had been accomplished, all the hard work to forgive the infidelity (in its most obvious and subtle forms), condemnation, boredom, and resentment had been completed—perhaps then they might consider their marriage as something beautiful, something God had created out of what looked like a train wreck. But only after all the slogging.

It is virtually impossible for us to imagine our pathos and affliction in the moment as beauty in the making. And believe me, evil has every intention of preventing us from seeing it that way. Who among us, when contemplating the mistreatment we've suffered in church or the barrenness and brutality of a home fraught with addiction, can imagine beauty emerging from the very places where trauma hides? But Jesus has plans for exactly that—plans we find impossible to imagine on our own but that are more possible to comprehend as we permit ourselves to be seen by others in our vulnerability. Plans for new creation.

For Graham and Carmen to imagine such a reality would require them to enter a different dimension than they had known before. This entrance would expand their imaginations partially through the acquisition of new information (a function primarily of the brain's left hemisphere) but mostly through right hemisphere encounters over time with me, each other, and members of a confessional community. These encounters would enable Graham and Carmen to know in their very bodies that "working on their marriage" was nothing short of joining the Holy Trinity in the dance of the new creation, of "[clothing themselves] with the Lord Jesus Christ" (Romans 13:14). And that meant beginning the practice of putting themselves in the path of oncoming beauty. We will explore this idea in its fullness in chapters seven through nine, but for this couple, suffering under the weight of their lives, it would eventually grow into a work of art that initially defied credulity.

The beauty of Berlioz's *Symphonie Fantastique* depends on each section of the orchestra being well-developed, or well-differentiated. Moreover, all the parts need to listen for the other parts; they need to be linked together. Otherwise the orchestra behaves chaotically or rigidly— all the musicians play anything they want or they all play the exact same notes all the time, neither of which is worth listening to. Just as with an orchestra, the mind is maximally able to flourish when its various functional domains are (1) differentiated and (2) linked. In the language of IPNB, this increasing movement toward flourishing is what we refer to as the process of integration.[1] Integration is like a river that flows between two banks, one bank being chaos and the other rigidity. Living in a state of integration keeps us in the river and away from the extremes of the other two options. When our minds are more integrated, they are more open to the possibility of creating beauty.

Moreover, the orchestra above needs a conductor, and for humans, anatomically that conductor is the middle prefrontal cortex, the location in the brain where much of the work of integration takes place. But our middle prefrontal cortex does not develop on its own. It needs the relational interaction of secure attachment—in essence, interaction with other brains—in order for it to eventually function more independently when other brains are not around.

When we are in distress, the notion of creating anything, let alone something of great beauty, is not at the forefront of our minds—we are instead focused on reducing our distress as quickly as possible. When our brainstem and amygdala are running the show in their attempt to protect us (when we have left the river of integration and found ourselves aground on the bank of either rigidity or chaos), it is virtually impossible to engage our middle prefrontal cortex to turn our attention to beauty. Carmen and Graham found themselves disintegrated both as individuals and as a married couple, with their middle prefrontal cortices offline. As a result, they were unable to regulate the distress they were feeling in their bodies or the stories they were telling themselves about what the other was thinking and feeling.

They needed an outside regulatory source that could provide a steadying presence, a way to move back into the river of integration. In the same way a child's developing middle prefrontal cortex requires the presence of an adult's well-regulated middle prefrontal cortex, so we all, even as adults, at times need the presence of others when we are overwhelmed by our chaotic or rigid mental states.

Hence, educating Graham and Carmen about the mechanics of their minds' functioning enabled them to, literally, use my mind (and later, to an even greater extent, the collective mind of the members of the confessional communities they each joined) to regulate their own. It also helped them begin to imagine that they were no longer simply trying to "fix their problems" but were in fact endeavoring to, in their marriage, create a masterpiece. They become increasingly familiar with the nine domains of integration of the mind[2] and rigorously applied their awareness of those domains in everyday life. They learned in the process about the nature of their minds,[3] what it meant for them to be integrated, and what it meant to love God with all of their minds so as to love each other and those around them more effectively. This took time, practice, and patience (much of which took place in their confessional groups), along with encountering beauty with more frequent intention, the notion of which we will explore later in this book.

Another important skill set Carmen and Graham began to develop was their awareness of what neuroscience researchers call "the window of tolerance." With his landmark work *The Polyvagal Theory*, Stephen Porges has provided a way of understanding how we use interpersonal relationships to coregulate our autonomic nervous system.[4] It turns out that this more primitive part of our central nervous system, one we have in common with reptiles and lower mammals, plays a crucial regulatory role that enables us to navigate the range of emotion we experience, especially that which is distressing.

We do so through a neurological hierarchy that begins with what is termed the "social engagement system," a network of neurons spread throughout the brain that is present but immature at birth and must be developed through interpersonal interactions. This use of the "external brain" of someone else is the most effective way over time for us to regulate our distressing or overwhelming emotions.[5]

One function of the social engagement system is to help an infant develop flexible, adaptive responses to emotional distress. In collaboration with others, the child establishes and widens his window of tolerance—the range of emotional tone within which the child can effectively flourish, even in the face of distressing circumstances.[6] Over time, the process of developing secure attachment and deepening integration leads to a widening of the window of tolerance and an expanded capacity to tolerate and regulate distress.

However, in circumstances of trauma and neglect, our social engagement system can become overwhelmed, moving us outside the boundary of our window of tolerance. Our brains follow a regulatory algorithm in which we tend initially to enter a state of hyperarousal (in which we can be anxious, irritable, restless, hostile, distractible, panicked, emotionally flooded, sleepless, and hypervigilant), and then, should that not prove helpful, a state of hypoarousal (which can make us feel depressed, fatigued, listless, anhedonic, anergic, helpless, and hopeless). These are the two default systems of autonomic regulation;[7] at times we find ourselves fluctuating back and forth between them, depending on our circumstances.

The first state (hyperarousal) is governed by our sympathetic nervous system, or our fight-or-flight mechanism. We do sometimes literally flee or fight when confronted with physical danger, but much of what we humans sense as threatening comes in the form of intolerable emotional states. When Graham revealed that he had again been viewing pornography, this evoked in Carmen a primal sense of fear. In reaction, she "fled" by withdrawing emotional connection, limiting how much she spoke with Graham, and, of course, refusing to have sex with him. At other times she simply lost her temper at the slightest things—"fighting," as it were—as a means of regulating her fear and hurt.

When the sympathetic system itself is overwhelmed (when, for instance, we are so overwhelmed that we can neither flee nor fight), we default to our parasympathetic nervous system, which tends to shut down our functioning (hypoarousal). It should be noted that neither defaulting to or activating the sympathetic or parasympathic system is an indication that the brain is malfunctioning. In fact, the brain moves in their direction as a means to protect and help us. Should I be faced with a dangerous situation and run away from it due to my sympathetic system's involvement, I can then reach safety and be better regulated. Likewise, shutting down at times keeps me from being so overwhelmed by my emotions that I cannot function at all. Although existing in neither of these systems is the preferred way to live for extended periods of time, it is important that we note that when we find ourselves in one or the other of these states, it is not primarily because there is something wrong with the brain; no, it is doing exactly what it was made to do. The problem has much more to do with my traumatic relationship with the world and other people.

Integration strengthens our social engagement system, while disintegrating events such as trauma and toxic shame move us to more primitive neurological systems and less mature ways of relating to others. When facing Carmen's rage or withdrawal after she learned of his unwanted sexual behavior, Graham, stricken by shame, often withdrew into silence and immobility. His thinking would become muddled, he would be unproductive at work for days, and he would be disabled from moving toward Carmen in the way she needed, despite her protestations should he attempt to do so.

When Carmen and Graham's social engagement systems were overrun and they found themselves outside the boundaries of their windows of tolerance, they were in no position to imagine their marriage as a work of creativity. We often find ourselves similarly positioned. When we are outside our window of tolerance, we often default to a pit of shame, feeling powerless to climb out and enter a curious state of mind. We are severely limited in accessing our right hemisphere's capacity to imagine beauty, goodness, or joy because our brain is functionally on high alert to anything it suspects may be threatening, despite our desperate longing for intimacy. For Graham and Carmen, the fact that they were in my office was at least an indication that they were making a bid for intimacy with each other. However, it was their very desire for connection that was activating neural networks associated with hurt and shame, and these were currently taking center stage in their conscious awareness. This overwhelmed their right-brain anticipatory networks, informing them that the future was not safe and not a place of emerging beauty but rather a relational ambush that would leave them eternally trapped in a whirlpool of emotional distress.

No wonder they thought it odd, confusing, and even unsympathetic that I would ask them what they wanted to create. When we are in the throes of trauma, we are not ready to be creators and curators of beauty, whether interpersonally or neurobiologically. But it turns out that the way we answer that question is fundamentally linked to what it means to be human—it is just as primal as our desire to be known. And if we want our relationships and the systems they are associated with to flourish, it is necessary to consider such primal things.

As we will soon see, the group encounters we provide in our practice— what we term "confessional communities"—are designed to enhance integration of the mind's nine domains of functional activity, not least at the level of the middle prefrontal cortex. This leads to the development of earned secure attachment, primarily through providing the opportunity for participants to be seen, soothed, safe, and secure, and bolsters the social engagement system while enabling participants to widen their windows of tolerance, which prevents them from moving into states of hyper- or hypoarousal. These processes hinge on participation in a setting where the deep desire to be known is met. Throughout the remainder of this book we will continue to refer to these features of IPNB and discuss the mechanics of the work involved, which will help us further "make sense of what we sense."

We explored in chapter one that our deepest desire as humans is to be known—to be seen, soothed, made to feel safe, and then launched into the world from a place of security, always able to return to that community when we sense the need for the resources made possible by secure attachment. We long to be desired without being consumed or exploited. We hunger and thirst for connection that anticipates nothing short of deep and lasting joy. However, this desire to be known is just the beginning— necessary and primary but also a preparation for something more.

Being loved as God loves us readies us to make, as God has made us and the world around us. As image bearers of the triune God, we reflect his image not only in our character, in the capacities of our minds, and in our constitutional interdependence; we also reflect his image in our desire to create and to do this within relationships as well. Moreover, in our acts of creativity, we long deeply for our creations to be objects of beauty, artifacts that unquestionably draw our whole selves in, that captivate us and hold us. In other words, we are created to be known in order that we might further steward and create beauty—which in turn cycles back to deepen the relational process of being known.

Much has been written about beauty, not least from a philosophical point of view. For instance, Roger Scruton offers an extraordinary short book on the topic that I would recommend for all interested readers.[8] (I think the book itself a work of art.) It isn't my intention to argue what beauty is. But one way to consider it is that which draws our attention with wonder and welcome and that ultimately leads us to worship—not worship of the object itself but worship of God in gratitude, humility, and joy. During an occasion of wonder we are often surprised and overwhelmed—so overwhelmed, in fact, that the revelation must take place at a pace we can tolerate. I recall once when coming upon the south rim of the Grand Canyon near sunset that the beauty was so staggering that it almost felt too painful to look at. More to the point, I was not capable of containing what I saw; I felt myself too flimsy, too fragile.

Beauty welcomes us in the sense that it is invitational, vulnerable, and unhurried. It tells us we are wanted in its presence. As we will see soon enough, beauty in art welcomes our broken parts as well as those with which we are more comfortable. Beauty leads us to worship by enabling us to live in the real world, the world of trauma and shame that is so pervasive, and then to see through it. We see and feel this as Thomas did when, invited by Jesus to touch his side and the nail prints in his hands and feet, Thomas's response was, "My Lord and my God!" (John 20:28).

Irish poet John O'Donohue rightly spoke of how badly our world needs beauty as well as our deep hunger and thirst for it to survive. There is a great mystery in which our encounter with beauty evokes within us a sense of coming home, as it were—a sense that we are encountering something we recognize but that we have never seen before.[9]

Twentieth-century Catholic theologian Hans Urs von Balthasar sheds piercing light on the indispensable and axiomatic role of beauty, both as a primal attribute of God's nature and a necessity for human flourishing. In *The Glory of the Lord*, the first installment of his towering theological trilogy, he addresses beauty as one of the three fundamental transcendentals—truth and goodness being the other two—the concepts upon which Western philosophers and theologians have believed the essence of human nature rests.[10] Much of Western philosophy, beginning with the work of the ancient Greeks, describes the significance of these three realities, but in recent centuries we have tended to tacitly (though not always) do so in a particular hierarchical order: truth first, then goodness, then beauty.

This is the assumption Descartes voiced when he famously uttered, "I think; therefore, I am." We modernists believe that "to think" is the foundation upon which the house constituting what it means to be human is built. And by thinking, we can accurately and rationally perceive what is good. And once we know what is good, we can—again, rationally—decide what is beautiful.

Of course, philosophers don't think quite this simplistically. But I'm not far off, and I'm hoping you get the point, which is that in the West, we believe that thinking is ultimately more important than what we experience with our physical senses, let alone what we know to be ethically good. And we have applied this no less in our life in the church.

Balthasar turns all of that on its head. He proposes that how we actually live requires a reversal of the order in which we approach the three transcendentals, so that beauty is first, followed by goodness, which is followed by truth. Why? He contends that before we "think" as humans, we must first encounter things with our senses—and indeed, this is how the brain works. First we sense, then we make sense of what we sense. Moreover, Balthasar suggests that beauty is what attracts us to goodness in the first place, and being immersed in the beautiful and the good necessarily enables us to comprehend what is true.[11]

We Christians believe the Bible to be the unique, trustworthy written Word of God and the authority for our lives. But before anything was written, it was embodied. Before the writer of John's Gospel penned, "The Word became flesh and made his dwelling among us," he first had to actually encounter the Word dwelling with him in the flesh. Before he could report, "We have seen [beheld, gazed upon] his glory, the glory of the one and only Son, who came from the Father, full of grace and truth" (John 1:14), he first had to see, behold, and gaze upon that glory. Thinking and writing about the Word followed an embodied encounter with the Word, which enabled the writer to "know" that the "Son, who came from the Father," was "full of grace and truth." The beauty of the Word was what first captivated the author, long before he "understood" who he was dealing with or what he was getting himself into.

This is not a short course on theology or philosophy; I am not a trained theologian or philosopher. Nor is it an excursion into abstraction. But grappling with the way we Westerners understand our world turns out to be a big deal, for it is founded on a primarily left-hemispheric orientation. We begin with right thinking, which leads to understanding what is good, which tells us what is beautiful. Hence, when we consider what it means to be followers of Jesus, to be Christians, we often begin with what we think. Do I cognitively assent to the "right" set of thoughts, beliefs, doctrines, and so on?

The trouble is that this way of forming mature followers of Jesus doesn't account for how the brain works. When we develop symptoms of any kind—say the kind Carmen and Graham or Aaron from chapter one were facing—admonishing them to "think" can have only a limited effect. And this is where Balthasar is so helpful. He suggests that it is beauty that beckons us, that captivates us, that draws us in.[12] And indeed, what Graham, Carmen, and Aaron all needed from me when they first entered treatment was to see me seeing the sadness and fear on their faces, hearing the anguish in their voices, and feeling the affliction in their hearts—and still imagining for them the beauty in their future they could not yet see. What they needed from me was not, first, right theology; they needed me to be their embodied imaginer of beauty, if you will, while their brains tried to catch up.

This does not make beauty more important than goodness or truth, but it is what we first encounter about the world through our senses. And it is what we have been made to create in an almost infinite array. But some of us (not all, mind you) would be hard-pressed to know this from what we experience in our faith communities. Over the last four to five hundred years, we have so pushed beauty in its proper form to the margin that goodness is no longer attractive, at which point truth no longer matters.[13]

As we will see later, humans are primed in general to look for trouble so that we can help fix it. This is especially true of clinicians. In my training as a psychiatrist I had plenty of courses that taught me what was wrong with people; I had not one lecture, let alone a course, on what a healthy mind actually entailed. We are not primarily primed to look for beauty (sin and evil work to ensure that). But that, in fact, is exactly what we are created to do. Evil knows that the day we discover that Jesus is the ultimate embodiment of beauty, it will be in trouble. This is not a journey into abstraction; this is a journey of deep, embodied awareness of the world as it really is. And as we will see in the second half of this book, this makes all the difference in our lives.

Makoto Fujimura, in his book *Culture Care*, identifies the significance of human generativity, or our ability to make new things for the benefit of others.[14] He highlights how we have been made to be generative even as our triune God's nature is that of generativity. And in Jesus, God has inaugurated a new age, an age in which he is making all things new. This is presaged in Jesus' life and comes to full expression in his resurrection. From that time on, God has been and is in the business of renewing all things. For those who follow Jesus, then, the idea that God's mercies are new every morning is of great significance—we need his mercy if each new day holds forth the hope that we will be making new things, not least the relationships we occupy, no matter how deep or shallow, lengthy or brief, whole or traumatized.

Moreover, these relational acts of creativity are intended to be imagined in the same way Michelangelo imagined the *Pietà*. As many other artists bear witness, Michelangelo did not believe his artwork was a hobby. It was not something he did to earn a living. It was the height of his response to being given the gift of life. It was his response to his God.[15] And if we would turn our attention to even the smallest of moments in our lives as he turned his attention to imagining a ceiling or ascending staircase, everything about our world would change. Who would we become if we could see the moments we occupy as opportunities to create beauty, not least on our relational canvases?

What does any of this have to do with Graham and Carmen? Or, for that matter, with men's penchant for the exploitation and mistreatment of women? With our racism? With our political polarization or the way we respond to a gradually warming earth? Despite all the knowledge we modernists have accumulated, we don't seem to have improved much of our behavior. It is here that it will be helpful for us to pause and consider how what we are learning about the function of the mind is deeply related to the notion of beauty and creativity. In so doing we will discover that there are directions in which we can point Graham and Carmen that will enable them to imagine their marriage not so much in terms of what is wrong with it but more in terms of the possibility for creative renewal.

But—and this is crucial—this manner of living requires a firing of our imaginations in a way we are not used to. It demands that we work to envisage our story not as one in which God points out our sin merely in order to forgive us so that, should we agree to this arrangement, we will go to heaven when we die. Nor does he identify our wounds and shame in order to heal them simply so that we will feel better about ourselves. Rather, he is transforming us—creating us anew—to recommission us to do the work of new creation along with him. In this sense, God sees us not as problems to be solved or broken objects to be repaired but as beauty on the way to being formed. Sin, then, is what keeps us in a posture of resisting God's desire for creating beauty in, with, and through us. His desire is for us to join him in creating and adding to the beauty we are becoming, which transforms the world around us into much the same. But shame, mediated by our traumas both large and small, has a way of shearing off our capacity to imagine this. As such we often remain mired in telling our stories mostly through the lens of sin and pathology.

How, then, do we begin to imagine our desire to be known as a means to create and become the beauty that God is anticipating? It just so happens that when we turn to the stories of early development—of children and of God's creation—our minds are awakened to what he has been up to from before the foundation of the world. We turn first to the creative life of children; in the next chapter, we extend our curiosity to the creative life of God.

IN THE BEGINNING

If you are around children long enough, sooner or later you will have the experience of a little one bringing you something they have made. Who hasn't known the joy of the three-year-old who runs to you, holding the sheet of crayon-covered paper, her eyes bright, her voice high-pitched with excitement? As she extends her hand and offers her rendering of—well, you really have no idea what it is—she exclaims, "I made this for you!"

Several things are emerging simultaneously in a moment like this. First, play is one of the most prominent developmental expressions of childhood. It is rightly said that play is for children what work is for adults. (There is more to say about how work often doesn't feel like play, but that's another story.) For children, play often involves the act of making things, of creating as they have been made to create. We do not have to teach our children to want to make things. They were born for this. The impulse to put things together—to paint, draw, scribble, or form things out of play dough—is as common and natural for children as breathing. What they make is often of the material world, and they find ways of putting things together that to us adults seem to have nothing to do with each other. Not only do they bring things together that don't always add up; they also give meaning to things that equally, in an adult world, don't "make sense." A toy truck is suddenly flying, converted into an airplane. A tub of mud is a cake. A tricycle becomes a Toyota. Naturally, we know that the trike isn't a car, and we're not about to ingest the mud, but we allow for it because we know they are children, and we did the very same thing. Their imaginations are expanding in ways that enable them to joyfully create, not worrying whether their creations "make sense" in a literal way.

This imaginative process begins to weave various, sometimes seemingly unrelated parts of the world together. They create imaginary friends. They create dialogues between their dolls. They run trucks in and around newly imagined construction sites. They fight battles between good and evil using whatever wooden firearm they can find in the woods. They write scripts for plays in which they conscript you to act.

Hence, the first thing we notice about our Crayola-wielding artist is that she has made something. And her making something is fundamental to what it means to be a child; it is a developmental activity that is common to children. We adults, drowning as we are in anxieties, often cease to imagine this creating as essential in the life to which God still calls us. For children, the energy of playing-by-making is eventually transferred into learning that takes place in educational environments. But as educators, we often forget that the primary purpose of "learning" is not simply to inculcate information for its own sake into our students, but rather to facilitate their opportunity to practice making new things and thereby reflect God's image. We make new things by learning words, figuring out how to do math, expressing ideas, and discovering how to write. Along the way we hopefully accrue wisdom that enables us to discern what, how, when, where, and with whom we will make the next new, beautiful thing God invites us to join him in creating. And although we segregate "art class" into its own domain, the reality is that everything we learn is part of our training in becoming artists in any number of domains of life. All of this begins with those first games we play and drawings we offer to our parents when we're very young.

Second, these acts of creativity are embodied. In some way, shape, or form, they are fashioned through the physicality of children's interaction with the world. They (hopefully) have not yet learned to spend unlimited hours on their smartphones and are instead engaging with the world they can see and touch and taste, not merely the one emerging in their minds in the form of abstraction, although that is important too. Even those elements that are constructs of their subjectivity (their imaginary friends) are eventually paired with something from the material world (they often talk, out loud, with them) as a way for them to become meaningful.

Third, the things children make are usually made with the expectation that others will enjoy them. It matters to the three-year-old that you delight in the abstract creation she has offered to you. This expectation presages the notion that what she has created is something you enjoy because it is beautiful, not just because it is she who has made it or it is you to whom she offers it. As Alice Ramos reminds us, quoting Thomas Aquinas, "No one takes pains to make an image or representation except for the sake of the beautiful."[16] Even at a young age, a child's yearning is to make something that, when you see it, will delight you at the very sight of it. Granted, she might consider it to be beautiful in a different way than we adults think of beauty. Should you ask her whether it is beautiful, and then further require her to provide a philosophical account of what beauty is, she will look at you strangely. But the point is that early in our development we humans are already living responsively as people who are made to make things—and we deeply want those created artifacts to be objects of beauty.

Fourth, what she has made is a conduit, a broker for relationship. A three-year-old who brings you one of her creations or invites you to participate in her play is demonstrating that the two of you already share some sense of being comfortably known. She trusts you. You matter to her, and she believes she matters to you. In this way, you are known to each other at some dimension of significance. It is this very reality of being known that provides the grounding for her to bring you her artifact in the first place—and then witness how that act of creativity engenders greater connection between the two of you, deepening your co-created sense of being known.

This propensity—creating embodied artifacts of beauty as a means of more deeply connected relationships, which themselves are living, breathing objects of beauty—begins in childhood and is derailed only by those circumstances in which emotional or relational ruptures are left unrepaired. From the beginning, life was intended to give us the opportunity to "have dominion over . . . the earth" (Genesis 1:28 KJV). With every endeavor we undertake as God's stewards—regardless of how brief and insignificant the moment appears to be—we are being invited by the Trinity to create beauty, anticipating that the beauty we create will itself bring connection, healing, commissioning, and further beauty to the world.

But fifth, the beauty we long to create is in fact an extension and expression of who we long to become. In the same way that artists' expressions are extensions of themselves, so also we long to relationally express much the same. We want to create beauty as a means of expressing what we desire to be and to make possible our being enjoyed as such by others. When we view Rembrandt's *Return of the Prodigal Son*, its beauty in and of itself notwithstanding, we feel the longing to relationally embody the essence of what we sense when encountering it. We are reminded of C. S. Lewis's words when he said, "We do not want merely to see beauty, though, God knows, even that is bounty enough. We want something else which can hardly be put into words—to be united with the beauty we see, to pass into it, to receive it into ourselves, to bathe in it, to become part of it."[17]

It is not hard to imagine beauty in terms of the material universe. Who would argue with the notion that Michelangelo's *Pietà* is beautiful? We constitute beauty in a virtually infinite array of artistic expressions that we can easily identify as products of the material world. But relationships? In what possible universe would we imagine that every interpersonal interaction, no matter how small or great, is an opportunity to create an artifact of beauty? The three-year-old's work may not be a Rembrandt or Michelangelo, but she is already demonstrating, developmentally, what we all want to do on the way to becoming embodied beauty, most particularly in our relational interactions.

Artists remind us of what children naturally engage in, whether Georges Rouault or Agnes Martin, Mary Oliver or Malcolm Guite, Gustav Holst or Amy Beach, Rodin or Anne Whitney. We do not have to be professional artists to appreciate the work of these masters. But we must be willing to put in the effort to spend time with great art—not only to appreciate and benefit from it directly but also to allow it to foster within us a deeper capacity to be aware of opportunities to create beauty, not least in our relationships. The work of great artists not only reminds us of things we do not pay attention to; it also invites our minds to imagine the beauty we long to become—the beauty Carmen and Graham sought but could not sense in the midst of their trauma and shame.

THE BEAUTY OF CO-CREATION

Children make things because there is someone else with whom to share them. It is the very presence of others that draws out their creative impulses to their fullness. Of course, as Georges Rouault expressed, artistic expression is also a means of spiritual wrestling, and contemplation and solitude are crucial aspects of it. Should no one see his work, Rouault said, "Of course I would go on; I would have need of that spiritual dialogue."[18] Even so, children create because they anticipate someone being there to receive it. Even if the three-year-old is the one with the crayons, it's the anticipation of her mother's and father's delight that fuels the movement of her little hands on the paper. Creating beauty, then, is a collaborative act, as is the fundamental work of the integration of the mind.

This collaboration that begins in early development extends throughout our lives. For it is the intent of God that this work of creativity take place in, be fueled by, and be supported by deeply connected community—it is built into the mechanics of interpersonal neurobiology. Of course, God deals with us as individuals, as he has throughout the biblical narrative.

But who we are as individuals and the stories we tell about ourselves are always shaped and developed collaboratively. This is one of the primary ways the attachment process facilitates who we are becoming. Who I am is always being formed as a function of my interaction with other people. The statements "Male and female created he them; and blessed them, and called their name Adam, in the day when they were created" (Genesis 5:2 KJV) and "It is not good for the man to be alone" (Genesis 2:18) are not merely flat accounts of the facts brought to us by the writer of Genesis. They are anthropological declarations of how we become human.

J. S. Bach is generally regarded by many as the father of classical music. His work is highly esteemed, taught, and performed around the world. But for a long time his music was buried under history. Not until Felix Mendelssohn revived it nearly a hundred years after Bach's death did the world meet him again for the first time.[19] And not until the early twentieth century did people rediscover his cello suites through the work of Pablo Casals, when the world was transfixed and transformed by them. Similarly, Vincent van Gogh's works are renowned today, but for years much of the English-speaking world was unaware of them until British art critic Roger Fry's essay drew attention to them—and since then, attention has not waned.[20]

So even the creative work of one person depends on others to make it what it is. But each of us is commissioned by God to create in multiple domains of life. Who I become as a man, friend, husband, father, psychiatrist, and so on depends on the presence and engagement of others. No one "self-identifies" in the way we tacitly suspect we do. No one heals in isolation. No one creates in isolation.

Finally, I want to draw our attention to how our desire to create beauty facilitates the integration of our brains and the renewal of our minds. From our attention to our bodies to our memory and storytelling, from our states of mind to our deep awareness of our interpersonal connectedness in the world, our encounter with and formation of beauty provide the opportunity for us to become "perfect [complete, whole], therefore, as your heavenly Father is perfect [complete/whole]" (Matthew 5:48). In this way we co-labor with God (1 Corinthians 3:9), working out our salvation with fear and trembling (Philippians 2:12), as in the labor of a potter working with the clay on his wheel to form an object of beauty. For us to become complete—to complete God's work of our being made in his image—we must enter into this most grounded facet of who God is: an artist who makes because he first loves what he is about to create.

If you're finding it challenging to connect the dots or apprehend the significance of what I am saying, you're in good company. As Iain McGilchrist points out, our society is hell-bent on paying attention to the world primarily through the functional mode of the left hemisphere of the brain, on "understanding" it in order to manipulate it.[21] This means we end up not attuning to beauty—actively disregarding it, in fact, albeit often nonconsciously—and consumed with engaging our world as a problem to be solved or a pathology to be diagnosed. Shame and fear truncate our awareness of beauty, not least as it pertains to our own lives.

I have had my own difficult journey being able to see beauty in places that have not been obvious. I have not always found it easy to imagine beauty as something that I am or that I am becoming, and because I do not imagine that, I have more difficulty in seeing the beauty hidden in plain sight right before my eyes—not least in those places of shame and trauma that are within and without me. I end up burning great energy managing my shame, energy that is then not available for me to be an agent for creating goodness and beauty right where I am living.

It is this beauty that we long to create and become that evil finds anathema. Evil seeks to devour beauty at every turn, and it does so by wielding the traumatic experience of shame as its primary weapon. One of the most obvious results of its work in the world is the way in which our imaginations are wounded, stunted, and anesthetized. We will see shortly how this is embodied in the activity of the brain, but suffice to say it is our fear of repeating the experience of shame and trauma from our past that leads to the atrophy of our imaginations.

Somewhere in Carmen and Graham's past, God's intention for them to create and become beauty, both as individuals and together as a one-flesh union, was sheared off and immersed in a cistern of shame. It was not simply that they were being ruined by shame (and they were); shame was embedded in their embodied stories, stories that would require being transformed by a different story that could effectively open their imaginations in ways no amount of logical information could ever do. And so, as we first explored the longing for beauty we began to experience in early childhood, we now turn to the biblical narrative, the story of how God imagines the beauty he longs for us to become while co-creating it with us at the same time.

BEAUTY

Becoming What We Create

FOR SOME OF US, familiarity with the Bible has led to its becoming dull or even invisible. The creation narratives of Genesis 1 and 2 can be like that. But when we allow our imaginations to be drawn into new places, those stories of God creating not only take on new meaning themselves; they also foster a perception of new creation emerging within us. We begin to see how what we have just explored—the nature of creativity in children and its movement toward relationship and beauty—has its deep source in the opening pages of the Bible. Furthermore, we see how Genesis 1 and 2 are reflected in what we are learning in the science of interpersonal neurobiology. And, what's more, we will start to see how all of this makes a difference for Aaron, Graham, Carmen, and others.

OUT OF CHAOS . . .

Genesis 1 opens with an acknowledgment that the world—life—is chaotic: "The earth was formless and empty" (Genesis 1:2). This is not much different from what it is like for most newborns to enter the world (or perhaps for us to leave our home for the office or school). There's not much to enjoy about the journey from the warm comfort of the amniotic bath through the vice-gripping vaginal canal into a cold world in which the brain, only incompletely neurally connected, must begin to go to work at "life," a job for which there is no description. Who wouldn't feel anxious if they were forced to travel like that every day to a job for which they had been given no clear instructions?

In Genesis, over the deep void sweeps the Spirit of God. And he begins to act. That action is one in which he is attuned to what is happening and appears by the account of his actions to have an intention, a vision of what he is doing. Hopefully, too, the newborn enters a world in which those who receive her are actively looking for her, actively seeking to care for her and facilitate her coming fully into the world and into herself. As God has an intention for creation, so also in the first moments of life the newborn's brain begins to sense the intention of those there to receive her. An intention, ideally, for the emergence of secure attachment. Although her social engagement system is underdeveloped and brand new,[1] it already begins to sense the gazes and voices of the adults in the room who are looking and speaking with joy into the baby's eyes and ears—desiring, in the best of cases, to let her know they are so very glad she is in the world.

This welcoming of the child into the world is not confined to the day she is born. It begins then, but it will be an ongoing journey of being welcomed into innumerable communities, hopefully over the course of her lifetime. She is being formed, as it were, as a potter would form a vase on the wheel, as a painter forms color and texture on the canvas, or as a composer forms the theme of the symphony. In this way, human development reflects how God functionally creates the world over time.[2] We also see how the processes of interpersonal neurobiology are a reflection of anthropology, of the story being told in the text of Genesis 1 of what it means to be human. I am certainly not the first to suggest this, but what we see in the biblical creation story is an artist at work.[3]

Several things immediately suggest such artistry. For example, God follows a pattern, each day separating things and then placing them in rhythmic, cadenced relationship with each other.[4] He creates light and then separates it from darkness; he separates the water above from the water below; he separates the land from the sea, the birds of the air from the creatures of the deep, and eventually he creates humankind and separates us into male and female. He "boundaries," if you will, what he is making, keeping each boundaried part in seamless connection with the other. This is not unlike the boundary of the edge of the canvas, the rest in the middle of the measure of the sonatina, or the dashes in the poetry of Emily Dickinson.[5] Most of these "pairs" are then set in motion to live in relationship with the other, each acquiring its meaning, its own identity, by virtue of the presence of the other.

What we are witnessing is the emergence of a work of art, one in which the whole (the totality of six days of creation) reflects a collection of interlocking parts (each day's workmanship) that all work together and yet are all separate and differentiated from each other. Moreover, each day's artisanship is itself an interlocking, relational system—a system of differentiation and linkage (night and day, water above and below, land and sea, birds and fish, male and female). From the nonliving to the living to the most advanced sentient beings—humans—the world around us is a relational world. But recall that it has all been shaped by the Spirit of God, who brings the order of rhythm and cadence out of chaos.

Notice furthermore that the order is not rigid; it allows for flexibility within itself. The evening does not "stop" abruptly only to have the morning begin suddenly, as if God were turning a light switch off and on. So also the relationship between the "dry ground" and the "seas": within the larger order of their distinction, the same wave never hits the beach twice, not even during hurricane season. And in each instance (light/dark, dry ground/seas), the border areas are indistinct—where exactly does the land end and the sea begin? When exactly does the evening end and the morning begin?—while at the same time their essences remain separate from each other. Not unlike the colors of Fujimura's paintings, which are distinct and at the same time not rigidly separate from each other at their borders.

This is the type of order that, ideally, we hope to see in our family life. Each member of the family is unique, distinct. At the same time, a great deal of work is involved over the course of years determining where my life and what "belongs to me" ends and where that of my wife or child and "what belongs to him or her" begins. (This process can at times be quite clear, at other times quite confusing, and I am chief among sinners when it comes to wanting to be in charge of my children's stories, even now that they are adults. Why can't they see that my vision for their lives is the vision they should have?)

This form of relational artistry is an example of life in the river of integration, life that is lived between the banks of chaos and rigidity. Life has boundaries and limits while providing a wide place for exploration and making mistakes, all while a masterpiece of differentiated, interlocking relationships is created. Like any valuable artistic expression, it makes the community in which it is on display or performed that much more beautiful, as any of our homes are made more beautiful because of the art placed there. Ideally, Graham and Carmen's marriage was not worth saving solely for them. Marriage, as one of God's forms of artistic expression of himself and his relationship to us, is not just for the married couple. It is a gift, in many respects, for the community in which the marriage breathes and from which it draws breath, the community to whom the marriage bears witness of God's love for us. It is God's artistry put on display in the world for everyone to see and be able to say, "Oh! This is what God looks like! This is who God is and how he loves and works and forgives and creates!"

To imagine our lives as expressions of God's artistry is not easy. Evil pushes against that effort with all the weight of the earth, and both Graham and Carmen could feel that weight in their chests. However, relational artistry flourishes most readily in the context of a community whose members are willing to reveal their hopes and horrors with vulnerability and without fear. For when our longings, griefs, and brokenness are welcomed by others with empathy and limits, they can be reborn, reimagined, and re-formed into the beauty and goodness God ordained before the dawn of creation. To repeat, the work of peering into the future to see beauty when all you can see before you is the detritus of your life is hard indeed. Which is why we so desperately need others in the room who can help us do it. Bach needed Mendelssohn. Van Gogh needed Fry. We need those whose empathy becomes the base from which we begin to imagine a story other than the one we believe we are living.[6]

They are that cloud of witnesses who enable us to create as God first
created, all of us interlocking parts that dance together in the ballet God
envisions for his creation to become.

Returning to Genesis 1, this manner of linking differentiated systems
(each day's creation), each of which is itself a system of differentiated
parts linked together (night and day, sea and land, and so on), reflects a
pattern we eventually see in the description of the mind from the IPNB
perspective. We see God's artistry moving from the creation of the world
to the emergence of the human mind, all mirroring the relationship of
the Holy Trinity, a relational God who is differentiated into three persons
yet eternally linked in beauty, the nature and form of which, should we
be exposed to it, would likely overwhelm us, as I was by the view of the
Grand Canyon from the south rim.

The creation story includes the repeated refrain, "God saw that it
[whatever he had made] was good." There are three aspects of these edi-
torial comments that are noteworthy for our purposes. First, God *saw*
that what he had made was good. We do not read that God "said" or "declared" that it was good (although we no doubt could easily assume his
doing so). Rather, what we read is intended to enlarge our imaginations
in ways perhaps not immediately obvious.

The writer invites us to imagine God observing what he has made
with intention, curiosity, and pleasure. The text doesn't say so explicitly,
but this is clearly more than an account of the facts. This is literature at
its best. This is a compelling story, and the writer is a master at doing
what the best art does: he shows; he doesn't tell. Great art, like Genesis
1–3, does not explicate itself along the way. A painting, a movie, a symphony score does not explain itself. The conductor doesn't stop in the
middle of the second movement of Beethoven's Fifth Piano Concerto
and say, "This is what this is about," any more than Makoto Fujimura
does midway through completing one of his paintings, any more than
Flannery O'Connor would have in the middle of one of her short stories.
This would be to do what we often do in life when we attempt to use the
logical, rational functions of the brain's left hemisphere to shoehorn

information into the right brain, assuming that knowledge of this logical form will somehow transform the heart whose terminal psychosomatic neural networks are found primarily in the right hemisphere.

The author of Genesis assumes that the reader or the listener is an active participant in what is happening. We are invited to participate just as we would if we were attending the symphony—and we are witnessing a master conductor putting his craft on display, both the writer and the God of whom he is telling a story. Because Genesis does not just tell us something about what God has done; it also shows us what kind of God he is. The God of the Bible, as it turns out, is a God who looks at and sees his creation. And in so doing, he sees that it is good. It is not, then, just that what he has made is good in and of itself (although we presume that to be true) but that the goodness is discovered *as* and *because* God is looking at it—looking *for* it. Its goodness emerges as a function of being seen by God.

With this description of who God is (along with what he is doing), we also get the first hints of what it means for us as his sons and daughters to be made in his image. From these phrases we learn that an object's goodness (and also its beauty, as we will soon see) emerges not merely of its own accord, not just because it happens to be good in and of itself (which indeed it is because God has made it), but also as a result of the experience of being seen by God. Our goodness, our beauty, is not something that exists on its isolated own. Rather it emerges as we are seen by others who call it forth. This is not unlike our identity being called forth as a function of secure attachment in relationship with another, Jesus not the least. In the same way, our goodness and beauty are brought into being precisely because we are seen by and drawn to and into Christ, who himself is in God (Colossians 3:1-4).

So also we, being made in his image, are agents whose vision is endowed to bring forth goodness and beauty as we look for it. These qualities emerge in our friends and enemies, our spouses and children, our employees and employers as we look for them on purpose—but also as we look for them in everything we do vocationally. From making tools to raising vegetables, from painting canvases to painting houses, from carving wood to carving out time to be with God or our children, what goodness—what beauty—is waiting to emerge as a function of our looking at and seeing it? However, we cannot see this beauty if we ourselves have not experienced goodness and beauty being seen in us by another brain. As in Genesis when God sees what he has made, in John 9:1 we read that "as [Jesus] went along, he saw a man blind from birth." What Jesus saw was goodness and beauty waiting to be revealed in the very presence of the chaos or rigidity the blind man's life represented. This is the same chaos and rigidity many of us carry around in our lives, camouflaged or buried as it is—or is not—by shame and our response to it. The same chaos and rigidity that Aaron, Graham, and Carmen were embodying.

Second, we read that *what* God saw was good. The Hebrew (*tov*) and Greek (*kalos*) words for "good" intend not only to convey that something is functionally useful (as in, a knife is good for cutting) or morally good (as opposed to "bad"); they also suggest that something is aesthetically beautiful. Hence, when God sees that something is "good," he also sees that it is beautiful. When we read in Genesis 2:18 that "it is not good for the man to be alone," we could legitimately read, "It is not beautiful for the man to be alone." The word *kalos* is found in familiar Gospel passages that could be translated, for example, as, "I am the beautiful shepherd" or, "Every tree that does not bear beautiful fruit is cut down and thrown into the fire."[7]

Beauty is what we sense when we apprehend that which is genuinely good, that which is living into its divinely appointed purpose. Good food, music, or surgical work can each be described as beautiful when we behold the presentation of the dishes and taste the fullness of their flavor, or hear the movement from tension to resolution in the concerto, or view the precision and near-invisibility of the suture lines. Moreover, our minds are nonconsciously detecting the intention of the chef, composer, or surgeon to bring delight or healing to the one who is the object of their actions. And when our delight is perceived sensually—literally, via our embodied modalities of sensation—goodness becomes interchangeable with beauty in that beauty is what we "sense" of something that is truly good.

What we sense involves our embodied selves, even if it is not physically available to us, such as a beautiful idea or mathematical equation. Long before the idea becomes the blueprint that becomes Fallingwater, it emerges in the activity of the neural networks of the mind of Frank Lloyd Wright as he engages with his world. It is an "idea," yes, but it is never separate from the activity of the mind. What's important is whether we are attuned to the emanation of beauty, not only in the physical world around us but within and between us in our relational interactions.

Third, we can imagine "and God saw that it was good" to be a celebratory comment. There is joy in God's observation of what he has done. With each new thing he is bringing into relationship with all other things, joy flows from God in the same way that joy is what we experience as a newborn enters each new developmental stage, progressing to infant, toddler, young child, and beyond. It is also the joy we feel when we create something beautiful that others also enjoy and find meaningful. One might even imagine that the process of creativity is perhaps fun for God. It is an act replete with joy. With each stage of creation, one can imagine him pausing, standing back, and saying, "Man, I love that! I think we're really getting somewhere—this is going to be great!"

Hence, beauty is something that emerges as God is creating with intention and joy. It is something we, too, can recognize (depending on our state of mind, as we think of that state in the context of IPNB) whenever we encounter something in an embodied manner. For indeed, as John O'Donohue points out, "Beauty is so quietly woven through our ordinary days that we hardly notice it."[8] We perceive it in a flower but also in the cultivation of the garden in which the flower grows. We awaken to it in the healing of a broken bone. In listening to Vivaldi or Switchfoot. In preparing a meal for someone after they've given birth. In repairing a relational rupture by giving someone the experience of being seen, soothed, safe, and secure. In thanking the person who has just bagged our groceries. We speak of a beautiful film or hockey game (yes, you read that right—all the power, speed, and grace on the ice adds up to nothing but sheer beauty. The fights notwithstanding). We experience beauty in writing poetry or working with watercolor or constructing the code that will run the computer that will help track the details of the new microfinance endeavor. In fact, anything we move with intention to do is freighted with the potential to create even as God has intended for us to do as a direct function of being made in his image. And all of it is done to some degree by bringing order out of chaos. The work before us is to strengthen our awareness of the reality that this is what we are at all times on the precipice of doing. We are called to be like our trinitarian God and create beauty as he has and so become more fully formed into the image of Jesus.

All of this I write with Graham and Carmen's marriage in mind (or any system, for that matter, in which we are involved and invested, whether it's a company, school, or church). Evil was on their heels at every turn, working to keep them from sensing the beauty, the work of art that God was intending to form in and with their marriage, its pathos notwithstanding. It was their pain that had brought them into my office—my studio, if you will. And, to be sure, one does not begin to compose or perform difficult musical pieces without a great deal of practice. It requires perseverance in the presence of supportive instructors who will continue to encourage us in the face of mistakes and roadblocks. We need a patient, engaged, limit-setting, kind, enduring community that will be to us as God is: one who, in the words of C. S. Lewis quoting George MacDonald, is "easy to please, but hard to satisfy."[9] A God who, in the communion of the Trinity, is ever in relationship and thereby never despairing. It was God's community of three persons that would enable God to take the risk of creating us in the first place, given what he could see would become of us.

You may still be finding it challenging to imagine your own life in the way I am describing. Your story of loneliness, of sexual abuse, of addiction, of having to be the one in your family who always kept the peace while, as David Wilcox laments, "trying to get a medal, trying to get some shrapnel in my head,"[10] of being the perfect one, of being the outcast, of being whatever role shame and trauma has had you playing in order to regulate your affect, to keep yourself from screaming at the darkness that shrouds you like so much volcanic ash. But as we continue together, I believe you will begin to awaken to new creation in your life in the same way Graham, Carmen, and others have. The way they have awakened to beauty that emerged as they entered into community that provided a holding space in which their disintegrating marriage was contained, refashioned, and recommissioned.

REFLECTING THE MIRROR

The creation narrative in Genesis 1 reaches a climax in verses 26 and 27 when we read how God reflects before he makes humankind. One could fill a library with impressions of the significance of this reflection: "Let us make mankind in our image." That God was thinking about making us before he made us is a wonder. One senses the difference between this and the apparently straightforward, creative emergence of all that has preceded it. Had he followed his typical pattern ("And God said, 'Let there be . . .' And it was so"), one would expect the text to read, "And God said, 'Let there be mankind,' and there was mankind." But he didn't—and doesn't. God considers us, just as he considered the prophet Jeremiah before he formed him (see Jeremiah 1:5). God made us because he loves us, not the other way around. Even now as you read these words, the question is not do you know this as a fact but rather do you feel it in your bones? Because if you don't, if it is not embodied in what you sense, image, and perceive on a moment-to-moment basis, it is not yet fully real for you. It has not taken up residence as robustly as God intends. God longs for us to be aware that he longs for us, that he was thinking about us forever before we even became a zygote, let alone a newborn or adult.

Moreover, God did not love us into being as uniform creatures. We are not paramecia that reproduce asexually through binary fission. If God had wanted several billion people to inhabit the earth, I suppose he could have made us all at one time. We all would look pretty much the same, like a colony of sea sponges, with little or no variability in genetics or genitalia. We would not have fights with each other in the kitchen or at the Somme or bring forth *Les Miserables* or van Gogh's *Irises*. But in making us male and female, God created us with great difference. Yes, we have much in common; in fact, men and women have more in common than they don't. But where we are different, we are infinitely different. Deeply connected yet deeply differentiated. Not unlike the trinitarian God in whose image we are made.

In this way, differentiated and linked—integrated—we mirror his image in all of our interpersonal neurobiological expression. Not merely in that we are bipeds or can reflect on what we are thinking. No, rather, we poignantly and powerfully live as God's image bearers when we move to be known in order to create and cultivate beauty and goodness in the world. When we move to consider and then make, even as God has done. And if so much of what he has made is good, then its beauty necessarily is just as present. We humans have been created to bear God's image in order to reflect it by extending his endeavor to create goodness and beauty as we become those very things.

DOWN IN THE MUD

And then things get personal. And painful.

As we proceed through Genesis 2, the writer introduces us to accounts of deeply intimate, physical, and perhaps even uncomfortable creative acts. In verse 7 we read that God forms man out of the dust of the earth—out of mud, as a potter shapes the vase—and then, just as we would perform mouth-to-mouth resuscitation, God breathes his breath into the man's nostrils in order for man to become a living being. Dirt and breath. Differentiated elements that when brought together form an integrated human being. God does not do this from a distance, from across the room or the galaxy, but proximally. And he doesn't stop there. In verse 18, seeing that it was not good for the man to be alone, God started making things out of the earth, but he found them all inadequate for the vision of creativity he had in mind. And here is where we see the first hints that the creation of beauty might cost us something.

God could easily have made the woman out of the earth, just as he did the man. But instead he went the surgical route. The writer indicates that Adam was effectively given general anesthesia for the procedure—"God caused a deep sleep to fall upon the man" (Genesis 2:21 ESV)—which I appreciate. Anyone who has ever had surgery knows this is a very good thing. But you also know that after the procedure the wound is sore for days or even weeks. And it leaves a scar. Again, the writer doesn't stop to provide a commentary on this; we are simply invited to become aware of what is happening. Our paying attention to and being curious about the story, and exercising our imagination to extend beyond its limits, is itself part of the work of new creation the Spirit is conducting when we read the Scriptures. In the same way that the writer is artistically constructing a story about an artistic endeavor on God's part, we also are expected to be curious about how our reading of the text creates its own artistic possibility, its own opportunity for our lives to become more beautiful as we ingest, digest, and metabolize the text, being formed into the image of Jesus.

But just as with Adam, this process is not a painless one. It often involves God intimately, surgically transforming or removing parts of us via uncomfortable processes that require our vulnerability (anyone who has lain on an operating table knows what this is like) as part of his creating new life of beauty in others, just as God fashioned woman out of man. You see, in all that God is doing to form us, he is doing it not only for us. He is using us as a means to form new life in others.

And the end result of all of this surgical intervention? Poetry and song:

"This is now bone of my bones
    and flesh of my flesh;
she shall be called 'woman,'
    for she was taken out of man." (Genesis 2:23)

After God brings the woman to the man, Adam bursts into a flame of creativity, once again mirroring the God who has made him. Adam presumably sees the woman (as God saw in Genesis chapter 1) and responds with a resounding, "Finally! She's here!" This is poetry and song, an integrated, right-and-left, collaborative hemispheric expression, not left-hemispherically dominated, bland prose providing a rational account of the facts. This is celebration in the presence of a wound. Joy resulting from an act of creativity that involved Adam paying a price to which he did not consent. But this is often how beauty emerges, how new creation is wrought, how we are born again. There is always some form of painful experience that accompanies it, but in the biblical narrative, God is never at a distance from that which we suffer. Rather, he is an intimate participant in our suffering on the way to making things new.

From this artistic expression it is but a short journey to where the writer takes us in Genesis 2:25: "Adam and his wife were both naked, and they felt no shame." The first couple, as it were, stood on the precipice of a new world, destined to create together as the Holy Trinity had created. Their state reflected at least three elements that would make the creation of beauty possible and allow them to grow into who they were destined to be. Again, our writer simply shows. He doesn't tell.

First (as we saw in Genesis 1), they are differentiated. They are drawn to each other and in many ways are similar, but where they are different, they are deeply so. For beauty to emerge, for creativity to flourish, we must work together with elements that are quite different from one another. I often tell people that when I married my wife, I really wanted to marry her. But as it turns out, in many respects, I didn't really want to marry *her*. Rather, I wanted to marry myself—I just wanted that person, among other things, to look as beautiful as she looked. I wanted someone who thought like I did, who wanted the same things I did, who never worried about any of the things I never worried about (and did worry about the things I worried about), who thought the same things were funny that I did (especially everything I said). I think you get the picture. I wanted to create a new life, to make a new home with . . . myself! "Adam and his wife . . . " Differentiated beings, just as God is differentiated in his trinitarian nature.

This differentiation is powerfully demonstrated in multiple genres of art. It is found in the different sections of an orchestra or in the various

mineral forms that make up Makoto Fujimura's *nihonga*. Although similar
in their general characteristics (as instruments or minerals), they are
well-differentiated in their particularities. It is differences such as these
that enable artists to create beauty in ways that would be impossible with
comprehensive sameness. Of course, Carmen and Graham could see only
their differences, and those were woven into their stories as battle lines
of hurt, anger, and condemnation. Each of them could see only that the
other was the enemy, not someone different who provided the opportunity to create a new work of art, the nature of which they could not
imagine without the presence and help of a third party, who happened
to be me in their case. As has been true from the beginning, the trinitarian God is present as a third party, first separating and then bringing
together different elements (as in Genesis 1 and 2) to bring forth beauty
in a way that none of those elements on their own would be able to do.

Second, they were naked. The writer is expressing the Hebrew notion
of nakedness not just as a physical state but as a state of vulnerability.[11]
We humans, in our natural state, are the most vulnerable creatures on the
planet. We need protection; we need covering—we are creatures who
need. But the biblical view of vulnerability is not just about risk; it is also
about our common nakedness being a stage for collaborative, creative
possibility. This creativity emerges only when our needs make it possible
for another to meet them in such a way that what we create together is
more beautiful and complex than the sum of our individual selves or
what we could produce on our own. We are naked, susceptible to harm,
but our vulnerability is the very state that enables the greatest potential
for creating something new. It is not primarily about the danger of being
hurt—although that reality is present—but about fully emerging into the
image of God as creators, as he also is a Creator.

It is the couple's nakedness—their vulnerability—that enables them
to have sex and bear children. And it is in the bearing of children that the
notion of becoming "one flesh" is fully realized. But this does not happen
unless the couple exposes the most fragile facets of their interpersonal
neurobiological makeup to one another, those parts—their sexual

anatomy—that carry the bulk of the potential for creating something (children) while simultaneously representing the source of some of the greatest pain we inflict and endure as humans. This difference, then, is a two-edged sword in that it holds the potential for the creation of great beauty while being the source of some of our greatest suffering.

Here, too, we see the nakedness and vulnerability of God. It is easy for us to imagine that God has created us without having any skin in the game. Our culture tacitly characterizes him as a singular being (if he even exists), creating the world and us from a distance and then keeping himself at that distance ever after. We do not imagine him being vulnerable. We do not easily perceive that a three-person Father-Son-Spirit community intimately fashions us by breathing his breath into our nostrils after forming us out of mud and then comes to us in Jesus, naked at birth. We do not imagine that he takes on our suffering and death in Jesus naked and crucified and then indwells our very bodies through the presence of the Spirit. For God to create us, it was going to cost him something from the beginning. In Jesus, he has always been vulnerable. He has not simply run out of options when his vulnerability has him sweating blood even before the Roman hammers and spikes draw it out of his body. It is God's differentiation and nakedness that make possible the beauty that we are and are becoming. Beauty emerges in the context in which we, like our God, are willing to be naked, entering into the risky endeavor of new creation.

But we must be clear. At the end of Genesis 2, the need of the man and the woman for each other as a function of their vulnerability is a reality of beauty and goodness. In Genesis 3, after what we Christians would call the rebellion, the awareness of vulnerability and need is laced—sometimes subtly, sometimes explicitly—with shame. Given our underdeveloped, sin-trending natures, we are reluctant to imagine that our needs could be met by someone who is different from us. Different in the way our shame has shaped us to use that word. We might imagine someone meeting our need who gets us, who understands us. Someone who meets our criteria for safety or desirability. And usually that person is one with whom we have something, even a great deal, in common—someone who is like us, or at least like us enough. We do not naturally imagine someone meeting our need who is different from us, so different in fact that we might even call them our enemy. What African American expects a White person, or a Jew a Muslim, an Irish Catholic an Irish Protestant, or a female a male to act on her behalf (or vice-versa) when our most vulnerable selves are in play?

Later, this is what Jesus is getting at in his story of the Good Samaritan (see Luke 10:30-37). The man who has been robbed is vulnerable, but in that land, so is the Samaritan. Still, he opens himself and his agency of means. And this is the story of the Bible as it tells us about God and his people. He desires to make something with us—and for all of us to do likewise in our vulnerability. The point is that at the conclusion of Genesis 2, Adam and his wife are naked, and that is a necessary feature of what it means for us to create and become beauty.

The third hallmark the writer of Genesis emphasizes is the absence of shame. God's intention for us to bear his image as co-creators is truncated by the great payload of shame we find ourselves managing. In doing so, we burn so much energy that we are rendered unable to create in the ways envisioned by God. No wonder Graham and Carmen were finding it hard to imagine their marriage as a garden in which to cultivate new life. Cloaked in the story lines of condemnation of themselves and each other, most of what they were working at was overseeing and managing the interpersonal neurobiological activity of their shame.

Even though this is where God found them, it is not where he intended to leave them, just as he had no intention of leaving Adam and Eve where they were either. In order for Graham and Carmen—or for any of us—to overcome our shame and create beauty in the dance of our trinitarian God, we must first come to terms with what has brought us to where we are.

4

TRAUMA *and* SHAME

A People of Grief

Tara desperately longed to be relieved of her despair. And don't think I didn't want to relieve her of it. I felt her anguish in the center of my own chest, and I wasn't the one who had endured it. When Tara was fifteen, her youth group leader had repeatedly taken advantage of her sexually. Only when she was in college, when her depression became too much to contain, was she able with the help of an effective psychotherapist to reveal her experience. This led to an investigation in which it was discovered that the youth leader had abused several other young women in addition to Tara, which culminated in his dismissal.

To the church's credit, its leaders engaged in a concerted effort to take responsibility for what had happened on their watch, providing support for the healing of the women who were victims of this crime. That was fifteen years ago. Unfortunately, that same youth pastor somehow managed to remain active in professional ministry for some time after he left Tara's church. This is the world we live in.

In her midtwenties Tara married Seth, a young man who was thoughtful and kind, working hard to follow Jesus, and able to receive her story of trauma with great compassion. Early in their dating relationship, Seth had revealed to Tara that he had occasionally viewed pornography before they met, but he had worked faithfully to address this issue and no longer did. They had both worked to recover from wounds in their sexual lives and, in fact, this was part of what drew them together. By the time I met Tara, the couple had three children and were active participants in a small group in their church fellowship.

What brought Tara to my office was her discovery that her husband was again viewing pornography and had on two occasions solicited sex. Around the same time, a friend informed her that her former youth pastor, now working in another part of the country as a senior church administrator, had once again been accused of sexual misconduct.

I had no words.

● ● ●

We are people of grief.

In the presence of our desire to be known in order to co-create and become beauty with God and others, we often encounter instead a depth of grief and brokenness that can make the hope of new creation seem like a cruel joke. It doesn't require a psychiatrist to tell us that grief is the painful emotion we experience in the face of losing something or someone to which we have meaningful attachment. It is no surprise, given the significance of our attachment and social engagement systems, that it will be painful to lose something that provides us with a sense of being seen, soothed, safe, or secure. But knowing this fact does not make the reality of our loss any easier.

For all our desire, what we often experience is grief resulting from unmet longing. We grieve the loss of things we have had and sometimes the loss of things before we have even had them. My father died when I was seventeen. I wasn't aware then that I would sense my loss of him repeatedly over the years when he was not present for graduations, my wedding, or the births of my children. We want our lives to be a wondrous symphony, but when we turn to face our own music, what confronts us too often is something quite different. For all our hope in the glory of the resurrection, life continues to offer plenty of occasions to persuade us that the whole story of new creation is a figment of the imagination of some first-century itinerant preacher. The meek shall inherit the earth? All Tara was inheriting was an unbearably crushing weight of existence, all seemingly a direct result of her involvement in the very faith community in which she had come to believe that God was love and would deliver her from her enemies. Some deliverance.

Evil's intention for our space and time is very different than the creation of beauty, and it is difficult to resist its attempts to get a foothold. Evil intends not only to cut us off from God and each other; it intends to annihilate beauty and tempts us to do the same in our response to shame and fear.

Everywhere we turn the world appears to be enduring pathos without end. Sometimes it's associated with our own traumatic experiences and sometimes not. We know this not just because others "out there" are encountering pain or foisting it upon us; we carry it in the center of our own souls, and it courses through our own bodies. It's in our irritability with our friends and our fights with our children and parents. It's in the deaths from cancer and the coronavirus and the losses of jobs and relationships. It's in bullying on the playground and bullying in the workplace, in our abuse of our racial and class privilege and abuse of our environment. Anxiety. Depression. Addiction. Disordered eating. Hoarding. Bigotry. Greed. Political contempt. Violence. Emotional, sexual, and physical abuse. These are the effects of evil—but we are complicit in them, for we are actors in the play in which all of this happens. Evil couldn't do it without us. I would like to think that only "other people" were involved in such matters, but I know better. Perhaps this is why the Old Testament prophets Isaiah, Jeremiah, and Ezekiel are so full of words of warning and judgment while offering, by sheer number, far fewer words of comfort and hope. Perhaps they were forever having to speak to what they witnessed, and most of what they witnessed was the same as what we see, in the same proportion.

Despite our deepest longing to be known on the way to creating beauty, our attention, often ultimately via the neurobiological force of shame, is drawn to some form of beauty's opposite. Instead of attuning through the function of my right hemisphere to the present moment and being open to creating with God whatever may be in front of me, I find that my imagination, furiously locked as it is into the analysis and judgment of the left hemisphere, lives temporally in the anxiety of the future or the regret of the past. Or I am submerged in the ocean of infinite options the world offers to distract me from myself and my real life, all kindly presented to me by my web browser. My addictions are the result. I do not create in this life; I cope.

Yes, coping can be necessary for a time, but it is not life in its fullest. It is not the agency of creativity. In fact, it often devolves into denial of grief. And who would blame us? Grief is no picnic, and we're not stupid. But we can be naive. When we do not share our grief in a community committed to our flourishing, we disrupt our ability to extend ourselves as agents of creativity. The loss of an attachment, unsurprisingly, can create in us a fear of forming new attachments. Who wants to go through that kind of loss again? Genuine, healthy grieving is a necessary part of the experience of loss. But when grief is not addressed openly and vulnerably, it can keep us from entering new relationships—stuck in isolation, cut off from others. This resistance prevents us from being known explicitly in our grief, and by extension it keeps us from creating the next new object of beauty God has prepared for us to join him in making. As we will soon see, our grief is the very source of much that God is making in his new creation.

When we bury our grief instead of offering it to one another, the result is like a bacterial infection. Once the antigen is hidden, it multiplies, developing into the symptoms that lead people to my office, symptoms we tend to believe indicate a problem to be solved, a mental disorder or form of psychopathology to be diagnosed and treated—which in and of itself is a reasonable response. But rarely do we interpret these symptoms as heralds of a wounded, disfigured, misdirected, and ultimately unmet desire, let alone see them as the opening movement of life's next great composition.

We are people of grief. If we ponder these words, we eventually gain access to the parts of our stories that remind us they are true. Most of us know what it means to lose someone we love, whether through death or a broken relationship. Some of those losses come to us expectedly, albeit still painfully. My mother died at age eighty-six after a full life, but when her death came, the loss was still sharp. I felt the reality of the words of my friend Steve: "It's just not the way it's supposed to be."

But some of us lose things unexpectedly, blindsided by events or decisions out of our control. Some have lost children and lived the excruciating words of King Théoden from *The Lord of the Rings* (as interpreted by Peter Jackson): "No parent should have to bury their child."[1] Others have been involuntarily cut off from relationships we hoped would grow and blossom, finding ourselves crippled by the shame of wondering what we did to cause the loss. Still others of us have been the ones who had to set limits in relationships we desperately wanted to nourish. How many of us have longed to be seen, soothed, made to feel safe and secure with parents or with friends who proved unable to deliver? After innumerable trips to the dry well, we simply had to stop lowering the bucket.

Some of us have lost marriages in the wake of ruptures that, no matter how hard we labored, we couldn't repair. We often feel powerless in our grief, to the point that it interferes with our ability to function. Sometimes we feel loss even in the context of a relationship we maintain. I have worked with many people who feel suffocated, trapped, or invisible in their marriage. Being committed to following Jesus, they do not take comfort in the prospect of divorce and have no intention of leaving their spouse (I am not speaking here of unions that are abusive in any respect). But their grief is ongoing despite all they have done to rouse their spouse's interest in making necessary changes. There is no answer one can theologically package and wrap up as a simple offering that will resolve suffering. In each of these cases, the individuals feel not only the loss within the relationship but also the loss of parts of themselves that feel dry and withered in an emotionally barren landscape.

As a teenager Tara lost relationships, but she also lost—had taken away from her—a healthy sense of herself. She became mired in confusion, feeling desirable in the eyes and arms of her youth pastor but in reality being exploited and then tossed away with nothing left but humiliation and isolation. How was she possibly to imagine that she was an artifact of beauty, let alone that she was destined to create it?

As Tara's ordeal reveals, much of our grief is the direct result of traumatic events. But our losses need not be as obvious or as brutal as hers to lead to genuine and ongoing grief, as we will continue to explore in these pages. In the language of interpersonal neurobiology, the word we use to depict Tara's experience—or that of anyone who veers off the path of creation to that of coping—is "disintegration." Beauty is a function of integration; disintegration describes systems that are coming apart at the seams. Where we have seen that the new creation is about the convocation of different elements, disintegration is the separation of things from one another.

As we explored in chapter one, a flourishing mind in all of its embodied and relational nature is integrated. Disintegration, then, describes what happens in and among our minds in the context of either poor differentiation or poor linkage of any of the nine functional domains, be that through insecure attachment processes or in the wake of traumatic events. We move away from living in the context of FACES: of being flexible, adaptive, coherent, energized, and stable. Rather, we move out of the river of integration and toward either extreme state of chaos or rigidity. For Tara, this meant a shattering of her capacity to attune her attention as she most desired, for it had been hijacked by the reactivation of dormant memory networks of terror and shame. Concentrating on the task before her became increasingly difficult because images of her husband with another woman kept intruding into her conscious awareness. She became unwilling to attune to her own body, for to do so led to intense nausea that overcame her, something she was working hard to ignore due to its overwhelming discomfort.

Tara's conscious mind became filled with reactivated memories of the abuse she sustained in high school, which intruded into her daily routine. Why, she asked herself, was this happening again? Would she never escape the trauma and shame of her past? Was her marriage to Seth merely a setup God was using to humiliate and torment her? How could she have been so foolish? Perhaps the answer was simple—that indeed she was foolish. . . . All of this shaped the narrative domain of her mind, with the various states this narrative represented following in due course.

She found herself increasingly cut off from others, imagining that once people discovered the truth about her marriage, they would perceive her to be the fool that she was. There was little room in the interpersonal domain of her mind for others to come to her with intention, mercy, and joy. There was only condemnation. She could visualize her future only as one of abject sadness and despair, trapped and isolated as she was in the whirlpool of her mind's temporal domain, kept company only by her shame. Getting out of bed required Herculean effort, and she had to expend a great deal of energy just to get her children's lunches packed and help them with their homework. This is what disintegration looks like.

But we would be mistaken if we thought disintegration referred only to situations like Tara's. Many of us suffer these states in the privacy of our minds, hidden from the view of anyone who, if they knew, would surely shame us for being where we are. We are particularly susceptible to this in the church, for in our deep longing to create goodness and beauty in our worshiping communities, they become the very places where being exposed feels so risky. Our intention is to live into something other than what we are all walking around with, but we fear that the grieving and broken parts of us, should they be revealed, would lead only to further humiliation and isolation.

Disintegration is found in each of our stories, and so is the trauma that underlies it.

GRIEF AND TRAUMA

Grief is associated with loss—the loss of things both large and small. It often involves something we would consider minor. I may discover that the grocery store no longer carries my favorite cereal, and this carries with it a certain sadness, a grief, if you will. (By the way, although I am not a conspiracy theorist, I believe my particular grocery store has secretly found a way to systematically discontinue carrying all of my favorite things. But I'm not taking this personally. That would mean I was inching toward paranoia, and you just can't afford for your psychiatrist to be paranoid.) However, when considering grief, we usually think of more substantive privations such as death or loss of a job or marriage.

Still, grief is not merely about loss in and of itself. It is not simply that I have lost something. Nor is it only about what I lose. I "lose" plenty of things by misplacement or forgetfulness that I don't care much about. I would offer you a list of those things, but I can't recall what they are, which is the point. Rather, the emotional state of grief occupies the space where several interpersonal neurobiological phenomena converge. It is, to be certain, about what we lose but even more so about how we sustain our losses, as well as the withdrawal of the possibility of anticipated beauty and goodness that our desire for the object or experience represented in the first place—always with a view toward how that creation of beauty would have enhanced our deep connection to and joyful experience of others and ourselves. Hence, it is about the place the object occupies in our lives—and the hope it represents for the emergence of beauty—as well as the way that we lose it.

I have a small collection of fountain pens, and each one occupies a particular place of joy and beauty for me. Once I lost one of them, and I found myself surprised at the strength of my emotional reaction. I mean, come on. It's a pen, for crying out loud. It's not my child. But that pen occupied a personal place for me. To begin with, it was a beautiful artifact in and of itself. It was the instrument I used to write in my personal journal, the one with which I have written some of the most intimate words I have ever thought or expressed. It was an instrument with which I created what was, for me, an experience of great beauty and meaning. How on earth could I have been so careless to have misplaced it? The loss, then, was that I lost it (the event), how I lost it (my carelessness, sparking a sense of shame), and what I lost (something of beauty and personal significance). I was sad for a number of days. And that's just a pen.

Here we catch a glimpse of trauma. You will think, "That's not trauma. That's a pen." And to a certain extent you would be correct. Trauma and grief (or suffering) are not the same thing. But to assume that the loss of my fountain pen is a minor event that should in no way evoke the depth of sadness it did is exactly what evil would have us believe. (My goodness, Curt, people are dying from Covid-19. Why would you be upset about this?) It is the minimization of grief, the dismissal of afflicting emotional states via insecure attachment processes, that eventually makes us more vulnerable to trauma.[2] The reason traumatic events like Tara's occur in the first place is that collectively the smaller emotional ruptures within and between us, even about a pen, go unnoticed and unnamed and then have the opportunity to move underground and fester. 9/11 didn't happen in a vacuum. Tara's sexual abuse didn't appear ex nihilo. Her perpetrator's story, unknown to me, was undoubtedly filled with early microtraumas that went unnoticed and unnamed. Her youth pastor's behavior was inexcusably evil, but we don't become monsters for no reason.

We are people of desire and people of grief. How we live in response to this juxtaposition makes up the largest portion of what is meaningful in our lives. Our grief is often (though not always) a response to trauma, and although trauma has been explored helpfully and effectively elsewhere[3] and may be something you are quite familiar with—either as one who has endured it or as a clinician who walks with patients wounded by it—it will be helpful to briefly overview it in order for us to see how it ultimately, in the story that God is telling and in light of the mechanics of interpersonal neurobiology, leads us to a new creation of beauty.

Trauma is never a good thing. Rather, as in the story of the nation of Judah at the time of Jeremiah, God is literally in the middle of all places and events, not least those that are the most appalling, debilitating, and anguishing; he is never away from us but always willing and working (Philippians 2:13) to use even our most painful experiences to create beauty in the context of vulnerable community, the likes of which we are otherwise unable to imagine.

Trauma results from an event, series of events, or set of circumstances perceived by an individual as physically or emotionally overwhelming, which has lasting adverse effects on functioning and mental, physical, social, emotional, or spiritual well-being—effects one also perceives himself or herself to be powerless to change.[4] In this sense trauma refers more to one's perception and response to an event than the event itself. The loss of one of my favorite writing instruments felt "traumatic" at the time (perhaps not unlike a badly scraped knee may feel "traumatic" to a three-year-old). But it in no way kept me from functioning, despite the sadness of no longer having it with me. This is not to imply that events are neutral and our "trauma" is merely how we respond. No one would wonder if the presence of SARS-CoV-2 in our midst was traumatic. Technically, however, it is our responses we pay attention to, since how we respond will dictate what type of help we need.

Trauma has been classified in multiple ways. For our purposes here, we will focus on two categories, each highlighting different dimensions of trauma. First, let us consider Trauma A and Trauma B. Trauma A refers to the absence of the physical, emotional, or psychological support people need to flourish.[5] This could be the absence of vitamin C in a child's diet or living in a cold and distant emotional environment in your home growing up. It could emerge because of physical or emotional negligence resulting from a lack of connection or joy in the home. This leads to the underdevelopment of necessary brain networks such as the social engagement system as well as poor bonding with other people.

In circumstances like these, the brain's neural networks do not integrate well at the level of the middle prefrontal cortex and its connection to the brainstem or limbic circuitry. We are left unable to regulate our emotional states, even those considered to fall within the normal range of life experience—those to which most people would respond with resilience despite finding them unpleasant and even capable of inducing suffering. Upon reflection, Tara was able to identify that to some degree her weak attachment relationship with her father helped create the emotional vulnerability her youth pastor took advantage of. There was a deep crevasse within her soul representing what her father had not been able to provide for her emotionally. This in no way made her father—or her—responsible for her youth pastor's behavior, but it did increase her vulnerability to predatory behavior. This is how subtle these forms of trauma can be.

Trauma B refers to events or circumstances in which things happen to us that should not happen.[6] This would include things we usually would consider to be traumatic: war; rape; natural disaster; or physical, sexual, or emotional abuse. Whereas Trauma A results in our brain being poorly equipped to begin with, Trauma B overwhelms the brain with what it cannot tolerate. This is what happened to Tara in her abuse. It is also what happens to people who have endured Trauma A–like experiences who then are overwhelmed by events that healthy individuals would respond to with greater resilience.

In addition to the classification of Trauma A and B, trauma is also classified as Type 1 and Type 2. Type 1 trauma refers to single incidents that are unexpected, often blindsiding and overwhelming a person. Examples of these would be a serious automobile accident, a severe or life-threatening illness, being a victim of or witnessing a violent act of assault, sustaining or witnessing a physically traumatic event, injury, or military combat incident. Type 2 trauma refers to more complex and diffuse experiences. It occurs over longer periods of time in the context of oft-repeated events and often involves people with whom the victim is relationally close; this creates an environment of vulnerability in which the victim feels coerced and powerless to escape or change their circumstances. Examples of this would be repeated experiences of sexual, physical, or emotional abuse.[7]

Different presentations of trauma require different kinds of interventions; you may have been the beneficiary of one or more of these forms of help. Our purpose here is not to explore that in detail (though by all means I encourage you to seek out someone for help should you find what you are reading to feel familiar); rather it is to highlight that trauma has the effect of disintegrating our lives, and common to the context of both categorizations (A or B, Type 1 or Type 2) is the role played by shame.

In *The Soul of Shame* I explored various elements of the interpersonal and neurobiological features of shame. Here I want to emphasize one feature in particular that is related to trauma. Shame isolates particular domains of functional and neural activity of the brain from others. This disconnection begins with neural communication disruption and mushrooms into the wars we wage in our family rooms and between people groups. As of this writing, the crisis of Covid-19 is forcing new forms of isolation on us that we have never experienced previously. In this way it has the potential to neurally mimic shame by restricting our access to the connections we usually take advantage of to help us regulate our emotional distress. Likewise, the racial injustice in our country has recently been harshly exposed, revealing the severity of our separation and isolation from each other. In both instances shame is given the opportunity to fill the space between isolated parties on its way to leveraging contempt and violence toward anyone we deem to be "other" than us.

In this sense, all experiences of shame in which any part of us remains in isolation is a form of trauma, if only on a microneurobiological and relational scale. When I first met Hudson, he was surprisingly anxious considering all his success in life, both materially and relationally. As part of the initial psychiatric evaluation, I naturally asked questions about what it was like growing up in his home. He easily replied, "I grew up in a loving Christian family," which, as I mentioned earlier, is sometimes code for, "Life sucked, but I can't really say that out loud."

My follow-up question was, "Who was in charge of discipline in your home?"

After a long pause, he responded, "My mom was. Because every time my dad got involved, things would get nasty."

It turns out that Hudson's older brother had wrestled with his own emotional difficulties, which often led to explosive confrontations between himself and Hudson's father—a deacon in their church—who would frequently become physically violent. This was a repeated event that often had Hudson trying to make peace and keep the kitchen from exploding.

Hudson carried an unmeasurable payload of sadness, grief, and anger that he had kept isolated from himself and everyone else. Governing all of this was shame, which convinced Hudson that if he revealed any of this to anyone, he would implode. Not that he considered this consciously; rather, his entire body carried his automated responses to potential conflict without his having to think at all. Because these memories and physically mediated reactions were kept inside, Hudson experienced microtraumas every time the implicit memories were reactivated, even though the events had occurred many years ago. These microtraumas weren't things that any of us, Hudson included, would ever recognize as such, but there they were nonetheless. No wonder he was anxious; his brain was being taxed beyond its capacity to manage all the neurophysiologically mediated shame that tried to reveal itself (with his anger and grief following in its wake) whenever Hudson found himself facing potential relational conflicts, be that in his marriage, with his children, or with friends or work colleagues.

These were experiences that had disintegrated—isolated—Hudson's emotions from his cognition, his conscious memories from his body, and his middle prefrontal cortex from his limbic circuitry and brainstem. What's more, they drove his mind beyond the boundary of his window of tolerance and outside of his brain's social engagement system, usually leaving him to survive by use of his sympathetic nervous system. Occasionally, especially when his shame was particularly present, his isolation led to the default mode of hypoarousal, leaving him feeling depressed and unable to imagine having agency to create or change the circumstances of his life.

RIGHT TO LEFT

Hudson's life shows how the micro- and macromoments of shame—mediated as they were by trauma in real time and space when he was younger (his father's brutality) and when he was an adult (in the form of his implicit memory)—lead to fixed states of emotional isolation. These were tantamount to disintegration, leaving Hudson unable to function within his emotional window of tolerance and leaving him outside of the river of integration, at times living in states of rigidity and at times in states of chaos.

One of the most significant ways this disintegrating process affected Hudson was to shift his primary posture of paying attention to the world with his brain's right hemisphere to paying attention with his left hemisphere. When we become overactive in our analyzing, assessing, and judging mode of engagement with the world, we tend to see the world at a distance and not to engage with it in the present moment.[8] When it comes to how we "understand" who we are as people and how we come to behave the way we do, our analyzing minds—seeing us from a distance and unengaged with us in intimately embodied and relational ways—easily identify the problems we have and judge them in need of being fixed. We are puzzles that need to be solved, not people who need to be loved. Subsequently, then, when living more exclusively out of our left hemisphere's posture of attunement, we inhibit our ability to receive the love of others because our left brain, in these circumstances, constricts our access to our right brain and its attachment circuits.

In any scientific endeavor, we categorize the objects we are studying in order to gather data to understand and then predict their future behavior, whether in a chemical experiment or a study of interplanetary movement. In the field of psychiatry, we study the processes of mental illness—of emotional and behavioral dis-ease, if you will. In medicine, we understand these as categories of pathology (from the Greek *pathos*, or "one who suffers"). We render a diagnosis and proceed to offer a treatment strategy that will bring healing. This way of seeing the world primarily through our analyzing left hemispheres is absolutely necessary for us to survive, let alone accomplish any constructive work. If I don't have left-brain function, I can't change my flat tire or build a spreadsheet. Nor can we collectively do the work necessary to combat the coronavirus.

The challenge here is not that our left brains are doing something wrong. Rather, they have become disproportionately overactive. Our tendency is to become so fixated on our lives as problems to solve that we are unable to imagine that our primary feature of bearing and reflecting God's image is that of creating. God's intention for the world is not first that it is a diagnosis to treat or a problem to solve. It is, rather, a studio in which the artists are expected to paint, the symphony hall in which we are intended to compose and perform, the garden in which we are intended to cultivate, grow, and reap a harvest. It is even a laboratory in which we are intended to be curious about the nature of viruses—but with the left hemisphere working in service of the right, not the other way around. In our urgency to solve problems and diagnose pathologies, we leave little space to even consider creativity. We are virtually unable to imagine that our pain and suffering are anything but pathological. We do not recognize that it is our brokenness that God intends to use to create something new.

In *The Master and His Emissary*, Iain McGilchrist elegantly paints a picture of where we currently find ourselves in the West.[9] He observes that in our insistent, fierce movement toward independence, we moderns have increasingly become people whose lives are dictated and dominated by the mode of attunement our left hemispheres provide for us. This is the mode of analysis from a distance, the mode in which we control and manipulate our environment rather than live in and with it, the mode of separation from each other rather than being with one another, the mode of judgment rather than curiosity. It is the dominant mode of engagement with the physical world and with people offered to us by the scientific method. And as Lesslie Newbigin suggests, reflecting on the work of Peter Berger, the prevailing plausibility structure of our world—the matrix of tacit, nonconscious assumptions we make with which we judge reality—is science.[10]

This means we are primed to continually consider our symptoms (not to mention other people) as problems to be fixed, living dominantly as we do out of our left hemispheres. (And remember: this is not about the right hemisphere's activity being good and the left's being bad; it is rather about the disproportionate degree to which the left hemisphere dominates our minds' activities.) This did not begin with modernity. It began at the beginning. As I suggest elsewhere,[11] evil used shame to hijack the left brain of the woman and the man, putting them at greater distance from each other so that they saw each other not only as different (as in male and female) but with enmity ("the woman you gave me . . . " [CEB]). They were no longer "with"; they were "against." They found themselves viewing each other as problems to be solved and the solution as a piece of fruit (something apart from them over which they had no authority) rather than as opportunities to create something new with God.

We now copy their behavior. It has become a socially normative response in many circumstances to see others as culturally repulsive, and this sense of repulsion is directly proportionate to the distance we have from them as real people. This is laid out plainly in the account of Genesis 3 between the woman and the man, extends into the next chapter of Scripture in which Cain murders Abel, and now is clearly evident in countless relational interactions, whether on the internet, between ethnicities, or in politics. In many respects this is a function of our inability to agree with God's "no"—our inability to show restraint. Just as the woman and man consumed the fruit, so we consume each other in our lack of restraint. But this impulsivity, this mindlessness, is directly related to the degree of isolation we experience with each other. And so we "take" (as the woman took the fruit) rather than "receive" (as the man and the woman were meant to receive what God had made for them, and as we receive both Communion and others into our hearts)—especially from those with whom we have great difference.

Indeed, "When the woman saw that the fruit of the tree was good for food and pleasing to the eye, and also desirable for gaining wisdom, she took some and ate it" (Genesis 3:6). Prior to the woman's conversation with the serpent, it would have made sense for the couple to see the fruit representing the good, the beautiful, and the true, the three transcendentals we have previously considered. They would have known goodness, beauty, and truth to originate outside themselves, existing beyond their domain of authority yet representing what they were to create and steward and also what they and their offspring were to become. The fruit could have been something for which to be grateful, not something they wanted to own. All the best they were to become was a byproduct of being known by God and each other while co-creating what they had been given to steward.

But shame has a way of disintegrating our neural networks and the story we tell about the world and our relationships along the way. Consequently, while in the middle of her encounter with the serpent and in an attempt to regulate her shame, the woman, instead of attuning her attention to what she had already been freely given to receive (Genesis 2:16), took the fruit from the tree of knowledge of good and evil. This "taking" was a maneuver representing our penchant for manipulating the world and each other. It is not only through this act but in the way it is enacted that we have inherited our tendency to move out of our brain's right hemisphere—which interacts with the world by being with it, being curious about it, and standing ready to imagine, see, and create beauty— and instead attune to the world through our left hemisphere, seeing the world and our relationships as things to be analyzed, judged, manipulated, and exploited for our own purposes.

It is in the isolated hyperactivity of the left brain that our shame is given so much room to play. The condemnation shame offers us lurks subtly and silently, occupying tremendous neural real estate. Attuning to the world through the lens of shame via the left hemisphere's analytic tendency keeps us in a low-level state of disintegration just beyond our conscious awareness but always ready to overwhelm us in even the most insignificant relational ruptures or faintest emotional distress. Our pain is always a mirrored, blurred reflection of our longing for deep connection on the path to creating beauty and goodness. But our capitulation to evil's hijacking of our left hemispheric mode of attunement to the world, both within and without us, leads not to beauty but rather to devouring it, just as evil would devour us and all of creation. This disintegration happens via the vector of shame in the context of traumatic events, no matter how large or small. Tara's trauma is plain to see, but many of us experience the trauma of shame as death from a thousand cuts, largely out of our conscious awareness. When this occurs, we are led not to consider creating beauty but to gluttonously consume it. And what follows is the corruption of the very dynamism of desire itself.

Consider sex. There is no more creative or powerful act in which humans engage over which we, simultaneously, have so little control— our zealous attempts to corral and tame it, to bend it to our ultimate will in our relentless quest for absolute (albeit illusory) self-determination notwithstanding. Although it is not the essence of our identity (despite our modern assumptions to the contrary), sex plays a preeminent role in what it means for humans to be embodied image bearers of God—we were made as male and female, created to create. Not only does sex physically and emotionally represent the equivalent of plutonium in human relationships; it is equally as fragile and requires explicit, contained environments in which to exist and flourish. It movingly, compellingly directs our imagination and attention to the beautiful, good, and true. And like the rest of creation, it is given to us as a gift. But also, like the fruit of the tree of knowledge of good and evil, it ultimately points us to something beyond itself, beyond ourselves. It is beautiful. It is good. It is true—and it is not ultimately something we are in charge of, hard as that is to believe.

But instead of receiving it and stewarding it as the gift it is within the space in which it was intended to flourish, we, like Eve, take it. We wield it as a thing to be used. The object of our sexual desire also becomes something we use. Eventually, we clutch it. We hoard it. We manipulate it. We devour it. In our nonconscious states of shame and isolation, we do whatever we can with it as a means to cope and to regulate our disintegrated states of mind that have emerged as a result of trauma, moving outside our windows of tolerance, swimming out of the river of integration toward the banks of chaos or rigidity. We isolate our right brain from our left, with the left tyrannically using sex as a means to cope. We do not have to be brutes or villains. We can simply use the privacy of our imaginations or our laptops, or leverage our positions of power, all the while slowly corrupting the creation and ourselves rather than joining God in new creation as we were destined to from the beginning.

Human sexuality, for which God has always had beauty and goodness in mind, has become a wasteland for the souls of many who have been abused and for those who have mistreated their own bodies as well. We are enduring a dramatic period of history in which countless incidents of sexual exploitation have been publicly exposed (not that our behavior is new but the degree of exposure is). An incomplete list would include #MeToo, the sexual abuse of women and children in the church, and human sex trafficking. Along with these, the pornography industry, which we aid and abet through our use of the internet, has exponentially added to the number of women, children, and men who have been brutally mistreated.

Each of these collections of personal stories of agonizing trauma and anguish represents ways in which perpetrators have repeated the acts of our first father and mother. How? At first glance, we see only trauma—carnage and pathology. But if we pause and gaze, we *see*—not unlike how we *see* when viewing a contemporary abstract painting like those of Mark Rothko—that there is far more going on here. Far more underneath. In every moment of relational and material ugliness we witness, we are actually observing the result of traumatized, shamed, and misdirected desire, desire to be known and to create beauty. And that misdirected desire leads not to the creation of beauty but to its defilement. With sexual distortion in all its forms, we do not see beauty; we see its antithesis.

This is what happens when the left hemisphere overruns the right in our need to "take" from the world outside us as a means to regulate the afflicting affect inside us. This is what Eve did when she "took." And Adam, by extension, also took by not refusing her offer of the fruit to him. Whether actively or passively, we contribute to the desolation rather than the creation of beauty. There is no excuse—ever—for sexual misbehavior, whether in thought or embodied action. But the driving emotional current beneath that behavior is desire. On the surface it can appear to be sheer physical appetite and lust. But running beneath is always the unquenchable, fathomless desire to be seen, soothed, safe, and secure. It is a longing for connection and beauty that has become so bent and calloused—so exploited itself—that we would be hard-pressed to believe any beauty or goodness existed within. How on earth can we imagine that sexual exploitation was once a longing for beauty? We are reminded of how Sméagol devolved into Gollum in *The Lord of the Rings*— first drawn to the One Ring, then eventually possessed by it. Desire and its objects are unable to match that which we were made for, and what we call "symptoms" begin to emerge. As we can see, our grief abounds.

However, in these places of desolation, we dare not assume that God's fundamental desire for beauty has somehow left the building, despite what we see on the surface. There is just too much of God's life in us. What we initially take in is Tara's tragedy and Hudson's early life of brutality. And this is not a mirage. But we are not seeing the most real thing either. For in the words of David Wilcox, even though "there is evil cast around us," even more so, "it's love that wrote the play"; despite it being true that at times we are surrounded by darkness, it is even more true that "in this darkness love can show the way."[12]

■ ■ ■

Imagine for a moment, if you will, Good Friday. We call it "good" only because of Easter. But what if resurrection had never happened? If that had been the case, there would be nothing good about that particular Friday. In fact, there would be nothing to remember because no story would have been told to draw our attention to such a horrific event.[13] There would be no artwork commemorating it. There would be no *Pietà*. There would be no *Crucifixion* by Georges Rouault. There would be nothing. Nothing for David Wilcox to sing.

As for the disciples? The women who followed Jesus and remained at the cross? Witnesses, merely, to a gruesome execution. Trauma. Torture. Death. Disintegration on a cosmic scale. I'm sure Joseph of Arimathea was not imagining that beauty was just around the corner, two days hence. There was nothing here portending beauty, heralding new creation. There was nothing to do but clean up the mess. He would bury the body and file the pathology report. What began with the hopeful beauty of feeding five thousand and healing dozens and loving outcasts and turning over tables ended like all other shattered dreams—just like Tara's, just like Hudson's and Carmen's and Graham's.

Without Easter, it turns out, there is no beauty anywhere that really lasts.

But we are an Easter people. And from the view of Easter, there is nothing more beautiful than a crucified Lord. It is now time to turn the page to see how beauty is coming to find you, calling to you in your grieving, traumatized, disintegrated life in order to transform the crucifixion of your soul into the beauty of resurrection. How that will happen might surprise you. But I can assure you, if Wilcox is right, love can show the way.

5

CONFESSIONAL COMMUNITIES

Telling Our Stories More Truly

"I'm furious," Ian said. He repeated, "I am just so furious."

His comments were directed toward Gabe, seated across the room from him during one of our group therapy sessions. Gabe looked at him quizzically. "I don't understand," he replied to Ian.

"Well, first of all, your mother's constant criticism of your father in front of you and your brothers . . . there's just no excuse for that. And then, when she would turn that on you! And to boot, your father would just take it and wouldn't defend you when she mistreated you. I mean, no wonder you don't want to go home for the holidays."

"But most of that is in the past," Gabe responded. "I just don't listen to her anymore. And no, I don't want to go home for Christmas. But I probably need to find a way to do that."

I turned to Ian. "What part of your story is being touched by Gabe's?"

"I don't know. I just know I'm really, really mad for Gabe. That's just not right, how his parents treated him. And," he continued, turning his attention once again to Gabe, "there's no way you should be going home for Christmas."

"Ian," I interrupted, "we'll get back to Gabe. And I appreciate what you're feeling as it has to do with him. But I'm also curious about you. What part of your story is trying to find its way into the room?"

Ian paused and thought for a moment. His fists were clenched and his arms crossed over his chest; he was fighting to keep his composure. Before the words came the tears.

"Why couldn't she have been kind? Whatever I did, it was never enough. It's still never enough. To this day I hear it in the phone calls. She loves to talk about my siblings' successes, as if my being a teacher just isn't glamourous enough for her. She only wants to talk about how hard my sister is working in med school or how much money my brother is making. She always sounds disappointed or uninterested in my life. But then, if I don't show interest when she talks about my brother and sister, she acts hurt. I mean, heck, I've been married for ten years to a great woman, I have three wonderful kids, and I'm a really good teacher. I'm just tired of walking around with this voice in my head reminding me that I'm not enough."

"Wow," Gabe said, unexpectedly. "I don't think I had any idea just how angry I am."

The entire group turned to him. "Ian, I knew I was hurt and have been for a long time. But I grew up in a house where no one was ever really allowed to be angry without paying a steep price. It's almost as if I wasn't aware how angry I am until you spoke the words."

Now in his late thirties, Gabe had initially come to see me to find relief for an undercurrent of anxiety he had been coping with since high school, one that had recently escalated into panic attacks. He was smart and had an uncanny knack for business. He had started and sold his first company within five years of completing college and was now about to sell his second. But no matter how gifted or effective he was in that realm of life, he was never able to escape the feeling that he was only a day away from being destitute.

He and I had worked together for six months before he joined this group process, this confessional community. We had often addressed his rocky relationship with his mother and how he felt cut off from her and his siblings ever since his father's untimely death when Gabe was sixteen. Anger had never been expressed in his home—except by his mother, and that was usually directed at either his father or Gabe. Somehow his siblings, all younger than he, were relieved of that burden.

Not surprisingly, Gabe had spent much of his young adult life avoiding two things: anger and women. Instead he buried both his rage and his desire for intimacy, channeling that energy into a creative genius for starting companies that flourished. But relationally, he remained isolated and lonely. He had initiated a number of relationships with women who appeared, from his report, to genuinely care for him. But the moment they indicated a desire for something more permanent in their relationship, or if they even hinted at being displeased with him for any reason, Gabe cut it off. His excuse was either that the relationship was taking too much energy from his work or that he simply could not imagine "being with someone who would criticize me all the time. I just don't need that."

Moreover, Gabe was underdeveloped in his entrepreneurial leadership in the way he responded to people who disagreed with him or did not perform up to his standards. He had a tendency to avoid confrontation, so he either bent over backward to accommodate those with whom he disagreed or he enabled his underperforming employees by permitting them to remain when he needed to correct them or let them go. Because there was enough cash flow for the business, it was simply easier to pay them than to work with them toward improvement or fire them. This was all part of his effort to avoid feeling the anger that was floating just below the surface of his conscious mind.

Despite his Midas touch with business, Gabe's relational skill set was limited, and this was playing no small part in his sensations of panic. His initial response to acute anxiety was to double down and work harder. But that led to sleeping less, which only deepened his sense of desperation. By the time he began to attend the group, we had treated his acute panic, but the source of it—the history of relational trauma and avoidance of afflicting emotions—remained.

No wonder Gabe felt uncomfortable with the words of St. Paul: "Be angry but do not sin; do not let the sun go down on your anger" (Ephesians 4:26

NRSV). Moreover, he was unaware of how, in burying his anger, he also buried his desire, ignorant as he was of Paul's words immediately following, inadvertently "mak[ing] room for the devil" (Ephesians 4:27 NRSV) and leaving less room for Jesus or any woman who would want him. And so wildly successful Gabe continued to avoid his anger, remaining in his protective fortress to languish.

That is, until Ian—without even knowing it—placed Gabe's anger in the crosshairs by talking about his own. Ian's words and presence in his own anger accessed Gabe's feelings, gave them language, and shed light on the first steps of a path Gabe could follow toward hope and healing. A path he had been unable to access before that moment, despite our having spoken of it many times in his individual psychotherapy. A path out of grief and trauma, out of fear and shame. One that would eventually enable him to tell his story more truly and would lead to greater creativity beyond his world of work and beyond his imagination.

■ ■ ■

When we're grieving or in the throes of trauma, we're often dull to our calling to bear and restore the image of God[1]—to create beauty in all domains of life. But it is in turning our imaginations in the direction of that calling—not just in the face of our grief but as a direct product of it—that God declares the gospel in and through us to the world and to each other. We are intended to be healed such that we become objects of beauty seen by the world, causing them to "glorify [our] Father in heaven" (Matthew 5:16).[2] But to turn our imaginations toward our calling to be God's image bearers in the presence of affliction, we often need help from the body of Jesus. As we saw earlier, Gabe needed Ian's words to awaken him to his own soul's condition, to help his mind become transformed, to support his sanctification. We each need our cloud of witnesses who enable us to practice together for the new heaven and earth, the new creation that is coming.

With this in mind, we now turn to the formation and cultivation of a confessional community, the primary interpersonal neurobiological vehicle to which we will refer here that provides the space for the work to be done—the beauty to be formed.[3] Each of the patients we have met so far (and others we will soon meet) joined one of these communities as a way to tell their stories more truly by explicitly naming their desires and griefs and doing the work of lament as a means of creating beauty out of the messes their lives had become.

This is an important part of the work of spiritual formation—taking place, in this instance, in what we otherwise could (and often do, for shorthand) call "group therapy." Indeed, the fundamental elements of rigorous group psychotherapy play an integral role in what takes place in the room (or, as I write this, in the virtual platform as well). But, in fact, what takes place in these spaces includes a great deal more than the typical group therapy encounter.

How we use language is important, and I want to highlight the way I use the term "community," rather than "group," in the work we do. These communities are not merely gatherings of humans limited to "doing psychotherapy," whatever we think that is—groups that are dealing with emotions, thoughts, and behaviors but not necessarily addressing life with God as we understand God in the context of the life, death, resurrection, and ascension of Jesus and the power of the Holy Spirit, as the biblical text informs us.

Rather, we form and maintain each group—each community—with the assumed presence and activity of the Holy Spirit in mind and with the explicit intention of incorporating stories, wisdom, and texts from the biblical narrative for the purpose of being formed into the image of Jesus (2 Corinthians 3:18; Romans 8:29) as agents of beauty and goodness in the multiple domains of life we occupy. In the language of faith we refer to this process as "sanctification"; in the language of IPNB we use the word "integration" to get as close as we can to describing the mechanics of that very mysterious transformation. It is with this mindset and understanding of context that we apply the principles of IPNB. Hence, these are not merely "groups" as commonly understood psychotherapeutically but rather communities of people whose mission is grounded in God's world as it really is, people being informed by God's Word in text (the Scriptures) and in the created, material world (IPNB).

Moreover, by referring to them as "confessional" communities, I am not implying that they are gatherings defined by the confession of sin (as that word is often used). I rather use the word "confessional" to describe how members tell the truth about their lives—about all aspects of them. They are learning to tell—confess—the truth by allowing their stories to be exposed to the biblical narrative revealed not just in our use of Scripture but in the "truth-telling," if you will, of other members of the group. Again, as we like to say, whenever the truth is fully spoken, we believe Jesus shows up.

It is in communities like these that we encounter the possibility of being deeply known and where we practice for heaven. It is in a body of like-minded people who are working hard to tell their stories as truly as they can that Jesus shows up, right in the middle of their narratives—rigid or chaotic though they may be—and utters, in the voices of others in the room, "Peace be with you!" (John 20:19). These communities provide a context in which we learn what it means for us to work out our salvation (Philippians 2:12) and what it means for us to put on Christ (Galatians 3:27) and to experience in an embodied fashion what it means for us to have died and now find our lives hidden with Christ in God (Colossians 3:3). If we don't have places to dwell in which these words can become embodied, they won't mean much of anything to us.

In Gabe's case, the community was not only able to help him discover an important part of his soul's makeup (his anger) and learn what to do about it; it also provided an embodied experience in which he was eventually able to imagine what it would be like for him to be angry in the presence of God—something he had never been able to do before. And it is quite difficult indeed to love God with all our being if we don't have access to important parts of it.

Necessarily, as is true of each person who enters one of these communities, I am inviting you to do work of the imagination. And I do mean work. Given the cultural dominance of a left-mode manner of attuning to the world, we do not have much experience practicing imagining, much less anticipating, that one of our primary callings in life is to create icons of beauty, be they software, relationships, pottery, organizations, or field hockey teams. Our imaginations are stultified enough (mine not the least) that in the pages and chapters to come we would be more likely to expect a straightforward, logical explanation of what a confessional community is and does, how to form and maintain it, and how to put it into practice forthwith. To put it more crassly, we lean toward being spoon-fed. Both Ian and Gabe, before joining the group, had their reservations about it. Each had built a significant degree of trust capital with me, but to do that with a group of total strangers, let alone imagine that this work would lead to greater beauty in their lives, required them investing even more capital in the bank of trust.

Just like them and many others who begin this journey, you may find that your mind has to work in ways to which you are unaccustomed. Those who are artists may more seamlessly make connections among the various features of our human condition that converge in the context of confessional communities (desire, grief, lament, beauty, and creativity, to name just a few). Regardless, I will be referring to a number of artistic expressions not only as examples of beauty but as a way to invite you to practice attuning to the world so that you see yourself as embodied beauty—beauty that simultaneously emerges as you create it.

Here I want to add a word about that very attunement that artists model for us and its relationship to prayer. In some respects, the conversations we have in our confessional communities are one continuous form of prayer, considering that prayer requires attunement to God regardless of the form it takes, be that supplication, praise, gratitude, or the silence of listening. To meditatively focus our attention on beauty, even in the places of our grief, draws our attention and attunes our hearts to the presence and activity of God.

Our confessional communities gather intentionally in Jesus' name. If it is true that Jesus is present wherever two or more are gathered, we can—and do—trust that the Holy Spirit is indeed present in the work of these gatherings. We are having conversations in the presence of God, and one of the exercises we encourage participants to carry out is imagining that God is active in the words we are speaking and hearing. As such, our conversations are a form of prayer and provide a framework for the members of the group to practice prayer in their lives when they are not together, not least by recalling the moments in which they have felt seen, soothed, safe, and secure—and when they have felt convicted and in need of practicing restraint. Practicing placing ourselves in the path of oncoming beauty awakens our imaginations to the presence and voice of God in the same way.

In the rest of this book I want to show how being part of a confessional community creates a space in which we gather to name our desires, lament our griefs and traumas—all acts of prayer—and out of them become outposts of beauty and new creation in the other domains of our lives. But I want to emphasize that "the group" is important only insofar as it provides a model—and it is simply that, a model—of how vulnerable community in any setting can establish the outposts I'm talking about. The point of what we are going to explore is not so much the communities themselves but rather the relational dynamism inherent in them that is required for us to become the people we were made to be and how this particular model facilitates that process. The nature of these groups is such that what happens in them does so in few other environments, for reasons that will become clear. My hope is that by the end of this book you will see how the elements surrounding what we do in these communities can be exported and replicated in any other domain or vocation, be it family, church, another spiritual community, school, business, sports, the arts, or any other endeavor.

Elsewhere I have suggested that being part of this kind of group is one way to understand what the writer of the New Testament letter to the Hebrews means by "a great cloud of witnesses" (Hebrews 12:1)—a cloud, an all-surrounding presence of those who literally bear witness to our lives in all their pathos and glory.[4] We need others to bear witness to our deepest longings, our greatest joys, our most painful shame, and all the rest in order to have any sense at all of ourselves. This process begins at birth—no newborn "decides who he is" apart from the presence of others to whom his little mind desperately looks to be seen and heard. His cries of distress are integrated only when received by others who see him, soothe him, and make him feel safe and secure.

You might wonder how these communities are different from any other, given the various ways we humans congregate socially. As they are intentionally arranged to address the most intimate desires and griefs of our lives, we might understandably furrow our brow and ask, "Isn't this what church is for?" Or, "I'm already in a small group Bible study." I'm not suggesting that what we're talking about here doesn't happen in those contexts, but the degree to which we long to be known—to name our desires openly and without shame, to lament our griefs, and to be encouraged to create—unfortunately does not happen as often as we wish it did in the places we might expect it to. Not in our families, not in our churches, and certainly not in our places of work.

We weren't created just so that God would have people join him in church or a Bible study. Rather, those gatherings, with their liturgies, teaching, worship, and sacraments (not least the Eucharist), are intended to impute to us the reality and be a powerful of reminder of the story in which we are living, a story in which, as redeemed daughters and sons of God, we have been recommissioned to go forth and co-create new life and beauty in every domain of the world we occupy.

However, for some of us, church—whether on the day we worship or in its other extensions—at times is not designed or equipped to provide the necessary structural or interactive ingredients out of which new creation emerges in the way we long for it to. Let me be quite clear. The confessional communities I am describing here are in no way a substitute for or additive to weekly engagement with the body of Christ gathered, as if that discipline required these confessional communities to fully do its job. Rather, the groups are intended to enrich our life in the body of faith and perhaps even offer a vision for what life is to be about in every community in which we dwell, the church not the least.

In fact, it is our consumeristic approach to the body of faith (as it is toward much of life) that provides the backdrop against which our work in these confessional communities stands out so starkly. For some of us, our worshiping community is limited in providing access to the deepest recesses of each other's lives where beauty is waiting to be revealed out of the remains of our brokenness. It is for this purpose that our confessional communities are being formed and are providing a context in which we can practice what it means to relationally flourish, extending that beauty into every vocational domain we occupy, be that farming, parenting, finance, civil engineering, teaching—you name it. We were made to fruitfully fill the earth and create beauty in every corner our lives reach.

■ ■ ■

What I am here calling "confessional communities" would be understood by mental health professionals as group therapy. As I mentioned above, I've called these groups "confessional communities" because, as much as this work takes place in a group, and a psychotherapeutic one at that, it's also more than that, given our attention to spiritual formation. But for many reading this, the term "group therapy" carries the assumption that we are mostly diagnosing and treating mental disorders of the participants—therapy for psychopathology. This is not an untrue way of understanding what we are doing, but as I have already said, we are about the business of naming the new and beautiful thing we want to make with God, not just naming our problem simply so that we can fix it.

I want to begin our exploration of confessional communities with a brief overview of the individual psychotherapeutic process, which many of you are already familiar with.[5] From there we will bridge to what is involved in becoming part of a confessional community, allowing the stories of several people to be our instructors. It is in the context of these communities that we not only heal but also practice being the "dwelling in which God lives" (Ephesians 2:22), both becoming and creating beauty along the way. To reiterate, I do not consider this to be the same as "church," but we will see how important elements of Christian spiritual formation take place in this context precisely because so much of our work reflects what the body of Christ is intended to do. Furthermore, these gatherings represent a way of engaging with each other, the underlying precepts of which can be applied to any system, be that a family, church, business, or school.

Some of you are familiar with psychotherapy, but for the uninitiated reader, I want to provide a cursory tutorial of some important interpersonal dynamics—of which we are usually quite unaware—that take place in most human interactions but that the psychotherapeutic process brings into sharper focus. You see, psychotherapy is not an endeavor in which we think or say or do things we don't do in any other relationship; it's just that in psychotherapy, we are made, finally, deeply aware of what those things actually are—we in essence tell our stories more truly, more faithfully to what is real but of which we have been mostly unaware. This is not unlike the way Jesus explains in more detail to his disciples the meaning of his parables. These stories are out there in the open for all who have ears to hear, allegories that hold "things hidden since the creation of the world" (Matthew 13:35), but more particular time and effort are required between the Master and his followers if they are going to suss out what he is revealing.

Asked, "How does psychotherapy work?" most people would say that a person with some form of psychiatric, emotional, or relational problem makes an appointment to meet with a mental health professional to talk about their difficulties in the therapist's office. Most people would not imagine that the patient would bring his spouse, friends, parents, pastor, elders, children, or work colleagues along to this appointment, and they would be correct again. The clinician helps the patient determine the essence of the problem, and perhaps with other specific forms of intervention or support,[6] they embark on a course of sessions (sometimes a few, sometimes many over several years) in which the therapist provides support and insight that enables the patient to heal and grow.

Of everything therapists offer their patients—insights, information about their life and the mind, particular interventions such as neuro-feedback or cognitive behavioral therapy, assignments to practice in the office or at home, or the empathy necessary to transport the whole enterprise—the most important feature they bring is themselves. It is the relationship of therapist and patient that establishes and continually strengthens an ever-more-secure attachment, first with the therapist and then with others in the patient's life, and is the foundation that enables change to happen. This therapeutic alliance has particular features that make it unique among human relationships. And those features enable the patient to discover things they otherwise would be much less likely to—things hidden from the foundation of the patient's life, so to speak. Healing, strengthening of resilience against shame, an expansion of their own curiosity, and openness to creativity ensue as they tell and permit their therapist increasing access to their story in response to the therapist's empathic curiosity. The patient experiences, in essence, what it means to be known and ultimately what it means to be loved.[7]

When therapy is effective, a patient can count on being able to identify concretely how their life is different, not merely in that they have acquired more information about themselves but by how the quality of their relationships are becoming (as we say in IPNB) more integrated.[8] Often a patient begins this endeavor assuming that psychotherapy is something she has to *do*, in the spirit of what I suggested in the last chapter—to fix her problem, to diagnose and treat her psychopathology. And once the problem is solved, she will no longer need, let alone want, to continue. In fact, some forms of psychotherapy are by design limited to, say, ten to fifteen sessions.[9] But interestingly, in many instances, once a patient begins to see the fruit of her labor, she finds that continued work augments and invigorates the gains she has made in an ever-deepening way. For those who are benefiting from psychotherapy, the rich really do get richer.

This, of course, is the best-case scenario. In actual practice, progression in the context of psychotherapy sometimes happens in fits and starts. Both parties sometimes wonder if what they are doing is of any use. Both will likely encounter the entire spectrum of the other's emotional range. As their relationship unfolds and their emotional connection deepens, there eventually, inevitably, will be ruptures, from minor to major, the repair of which will provide some of the most important growth that each of them will realize.[10] All in all, entering into a psychotherapy relationship often proves to be some of the most valuable—and hardest—work a person will ever do. This is akin to spiritual formation in that the work we do as therapists is intended to enable people to tell their stories more truly, and by "truly" I am not referring primarily to "an accurate rendition of the facts," although that certainly is part of what we are doing.

Telling a story more truly is about telling it faithfully, meaning we tell it by honoring all of its elements: what we sense, image, feel, think, and are primed and prompted to do with our bodies. This is not a mere recollection of data because what we recall (such as Hudson's account of having grown up in a loving Christian home) may be consistent with the "facts" as we have told ourselves but is incomplete at best, egregiously so at worst. Moreover, given that our stories are always told collaboratively, whether we know it or not, we do well to have as much assistance as possible in that undertaking.

Steve was one who needed that assistance. In his midfifties, Steve presented to me severely depressed. The primary event that led to his suffering was his seventeen-year-old son's death by suicide six months before his first visit with me. Steve was a scientist and was clear upon meeting me that he was not interested in psychotherapy and he wanted to hear nothing about God, especially not about Christianity. (His primary care physician, who knew I was a Christian, had referred Steve to me.) Steve was interested in being treated with medication alone. He had read much and even had suggestions for what I should consider prescribing.

I told Steve I would be happy to prescribe a medication, for indeed his condition qualified him for it. But given that he was a scientist, I wanted him to have the benefit of all the science available that would maximize his treatment. This would include not just the science behind the medication I would prescribe but the science of the mind itself. I was willing to give him a prescription but only with the stipulation that he be open to exploring additional aspects of what it meant for his mind to flourish, even in the face of such a horrific tragedy. He agreed to this, albeit reluctantly.

Steve's basic scientific curiosity soon got the better of him. As we explored the various domains of integration provided by the field of interpersonal neurobiology, he was intrigued to learn that "depression" was not some homogenous "thing" that "happens" to you; it is rather the result of a complex convergence of interpersonal and neurobiological processes that leaves the mind disintegrated as the person suffering from it seeks to cope unsuccessfully on his or her own. Most significantly, when we approached the narrative domain of integration of his mind,[11] Steve's stiff resistance to psychotherapy and even to questions of personal meaning and faith began to soften. For it was in the narrative domain that we explored the science of attachment and where I heard for the first time the truer, deeper version of what it was like for him to grow up in his home.

Steve's parents had been loving, kind Christians. For much of his first decade and a half of life, Steve had also felt a connection with God and believed in the person of Jesus. But when during middle and early high school he showed a keen interest in science, especially that of earth and human origins, his parents began to worry about the influence of the public school he attended and its commitment to teaching evolution. Unfortunately, they expressed their anxiety by stating their worry and dismay whenever Steve wanted to talk about the latest article he had read about geology or astronomy, not least because of the questions it raised for him about faith. Eventually they began to suggest he consider alternatives to science as a college major. The result was that when Steve left for college, he not only left his parents behind; he left his faith behind as well, never to look back on it. It was to science that he turned for its elegance, its beauty, and its promise to bring hope and healing to the world.

Except that science was not enough to keep Steve's son from hanging himself. And as it turned out, neither would the science of antidepressants be enough on its own to deliver Steve from his anguish. Not until he could see that his depression had much to do with his more ancient anger and grief wrapped up in the story of him and his parents—and the overwhelming guilt and shame he felt for having been emotionally distanced from his son—was he truly able to step onto the road to healing. But all of that required Steve to be willing to enter into the painful reality of his own story, one he had kept hidden from himself, his wife, and his children.

Over time Steve was able to see that his not wanting anything to do with God actually had little to do with God at all. It was far more about his ancient feelings of shame, which he still carried from his life as a teenager without realizing it. Steve was all about being smart and knowledgeable and at the ready with information. But he didn't know what it meant to be loved in the places where his heart most longed for it. And now his shame was compounded by perceived ineffectiveness as a father who was somehow unable to pull his son back from the brink. It was in psychotherapy that he was finally able to open his heart's door, if only a crack, to the possibility of God, of the love of Jesus, and that there might be hope on the other side of death. In his case, the death of his son.

I offer the above for those of you who may be unfamiliar with psychotherapy. But I do so for another reason as well. Individual psychotherapy has proved helpful for countless people, but even so, it has its limits. These limits are indications not that there is something dubious or problematic with the process; rather, it is like a good high school education: helpful, yes, but limited compared with a rigorous college education or vocational training. Moving from individual to group therapy, then, is like moving to a more highly developed and demanding form of the work one has already been doing.

Every person who truly benefits from individual psychotherapy eventually reaches a point where a number of things begin to transpire that make entering into a group process worth considering. First, from the moment psychotherapy commences, a patient will attempt to "outflank his therapist," that is, avoid certain topics that are simply too painful, despite knowing consciously that that is exactly what he is there to talk about. He will do this unconsciously, and his avoidance will involve topics both great and small. Of course, the therapist, being unable to read her patient's mind, may not be able to sense this, depending on how effectively the patient hides his story—again, nonconsciously. Hence, the therapist and her patient will share common blind spots. Being part of a group means there are simply more brains in the room; thus, it will be harder for the hidden parts of the patient to remain invisible. In Steve's case, his "outflanking" maneuvers were at times unconscious but at other times explicit. Especially early on he was hyperalert to any hint indicating that he needed more than medication to heal.

Second, when it comes to shame, we need as much help as we can get to hear the voices of others who love us and can tell us a different story than the one we tell ourselves. It's easy for me, in the privacy of my own mind, to be awash with my own self-condemning sensations, images, thoughts, and feelings of griefs and traumas I have experienced, all of which run on the rails of my brain's neural activity—the grey and white matter of the brain. The more actively I pay attention to those griefs when isolated in my own mind, the greater the strength of the connections between the neurons with which they correlate. Tara's mind and body were overwhelmed with activity reflective of her grief, much of it coming in some form of shame. It was helpful for her to hear my voice and to recall the voice of her previous therapist. But at the time she came to see me, my voice could not compete with the payload of shaming memory banging around in her head. A community provided more embodied energy of love and connection for her to receive as a way to wage war against her shame and to do so with an army of neural networks provided by the other members of the group.

Likewise, when Steve was able to acknowledge his shame and the power it had in his life, he quickly became aware of how deeply embedded it was in the stories of his own traumas. For him to push against it required the assistance of a community, which, after a long period of consideration, he finally consented to join.

A third characteristic of individual psychotherapy is that the patient rarely has any sense that they are being helpful for the therapist. That is not how the work is designed. Any good therapist will tell you that the work they do with patients opens the door to their own growth in innumerable ways—but they don't share most of these things with their patients. This highlights the power gradient of a psychotherapy relationship; it is more of a one-way street than most other relationships. However, a crucial part of healing, as we will see soon enough, involves the patient's opportunity to be helpful to others. When asked what action he would recommend if a person were to sense an impending emotional crisis, renowned psychiatrist Karl Menninger famously replied, "Lock up your house, go across the railroad tracks and find someone in need, and do something for him."[12] When we are broken, one of the most important elements involved in our healing is the opportunity to be of genuine help to others. It is in a community of common need that we are given the opportunity to do that necessary work.

Both Tara and Steve discovered over time that their own traumas, grief, and shame were changed as each of them experienced what it meant to be helpful to others in their respective communities. We will soon see how this takes place.

One need not have undergone individual psychotherapy to enter one of these communities; the group processes we are about to explore are designed to accommodate people with a diverse background of experience, from those who have had a great deal of psychotherapy to those who have had little or none. What matters most—and what mattered for Steve, Hudson, Tara, Graham, Carmen, and so many like them—is the desire to strengthen one's capacity to create beauty, especially in the places in life that feel most diminished. Furthermore, many of our relationships—not just psychotherapeutic ones—have common blind spots, power gradients, and a limit to how helpful one voice (as compared to many) can be in helping us overcome shame. The confessional community gives us a place to engage in real time and space those phenomena in order to achieve greater states of integration, and thereby be more perfect, more whole, even as our Father in heaven is also perfectly whole.

CONFESSIONAL COMMUNITIES

Each of the patients we have met thus far (and others we'll meet later) were invited to join a confessional community. These groups are usually made up of six to eight members and are facilitated by two clinicians. They meet weekly, each session lasting ninety minutes. The participants commit to maintaining confidentiality about all that is revealed in the room having to do with anyone else's story, and they have no contact with each other outside the group's meeting time. They can share with anyone outside the group the insights they are learning about themselves provided they mention nothing of the stories of others. By maintaining confidentiality in this way, group members together create a crucible of confidence (the root word from which "confidential" springs)—confidence to be vulnerable, and thereby creative, in ways most other social contexts do not provide.

Some of the groups are all-male or all-female and some are combined, women and men. The communities vary in their duration, some lasting a few months while others are ongoing; this influences the degree to which the therapists play more of a "teaching" role compared to a "facilitating" role. People require time to gain the confidence necessary to vulnerably reveal their stories, and other members in the group need time to assist them in telling those stories.

In the initial stages of a group's life, each member is given the opportunity to tell their own story as well as they are able. Over time, more and more of the story is revealed, both of their past and of their current life. Nothing is off limits. The longer people are in a group together, the more of their stories they can tell and the more truly they can tell them, as we'll see in coming chapters. I mentioned above that some of these groups are formed and proceed along an ongoing, indefinite timeline. Members of a group like this are actively involved for many months, some for years.

Many of them find in these communities an encounter rarely realized elsewhere in their lives, and the growth they experience only strengthens and encourages their commitment. This doesn't mean people never leave—they do—and, as is the case for any departure from any community, some leave well and others leave poorly, which of course leaves (no pun intended) the remaining members to respond to their departure, something that itself provides the opportunity for greater growth in integration.

Here I'll pause to address one feature in particular of most of our communities: it's a notable form of what physicists would call "potential energy"—in this case, the neurobiochemical and interpersonal potential energy bound up within and between each person that, through interaction with others, is released to create moments of healing and beauty. I mentioned earlier that some of our communities are mixed-sex groups. This is, of course, intentional, and for a number of reasons. First, it is reflective of real life, and in the way we often fear and avoid so much of real life, we avoid few things like we avoid sex—in the way that we don't avoid discussing it in our communities. Second, each member has the opportunity to be present with others from whom they are as fundamentally different as humans can be. If we are going to create in vulnerable, differentiated community as reflected in the biblical narrative, men and women must be in the room together.

Third, it provides the opportunity for each member to address longings and griefs that are related to people in their lives of both sexes. Father and mother. Sister and brother. Husband and wife. Power and weakness. Abuser and protector. And more that we could list. It creates the space for each participant to name what they want and how their trauma and shame are related, not just in the abstract but in the company of the real blood and bone of others who are not like them, others who can be the source of repairing ruptures that took place long ago—or that take place in the community itself. And when those ruptures are repaired, either vicariously or directly, each member is liberated to know joy and the courage and confidence of taking the risk of the new creation of beauty.

Fourth—and for many this is the most emotionally provocative point—anytime men and women occupy the same space, sex is in the room. And by sex, I am not offering a crass reference to "having sex." What I mean is that our sexuality is part of any interaction we have, as it has been a fundamental element in the development of our identity as humans from conception. Our sexuality is the physical representation of our most vulnerable and most powerfully creative selves, and we take it with us wherever we go. Hence we bring it into group therapy, to be sure. But it's also in the boardroom. In the classroom. In the church sanctuary. In our office where we work. When we're at lunch with a colleague. Sex is everywhere.

But shame and its outgrowth of lust—our impulse to take, to clutch, hoard, and consume—are what lead us, through the dominance of our left hemisphere, to see the other as an object we may use as we see fit. Not surprisingly, then, sex in the room scares us. For certainly, the prospect of that happening—lusting after someone—is not what we want. We worry that we will be aroused by someone who is not our spouse and will then have thoughts of wanting to have sex with that person. And so, to regulate this, we understandably set limits. Limits that include not being in situations where we could share things vulnerably with someone of the opposite sex, such that that vulnerability would lead to the very arousal we don't want. Why would anyone intentionally set up a scenario (like a mixed-sex confessional community) where everyone could be set up for bad things to happen?

These are all reasonable concerns. To be clear, sexual boundaries, like the boundary of God's "no" in Eden, are necessary if we are to faithfully, joyfully, fully reflect God's image to the world and each other. Just as a cell requires a wall in order for its internal organelles to do their work, we also require these boundaries. Our problem is that far too often we assume that the arousal sex generates is mostly or only about sex, when in fact it is most often about our deep desire to be seen, soothed, safe, and secure. The boundaries we often set between sexes—as necessary as they are—can also be easy ways for us to avoid naming our more vulnerable desires as well as the shame that is often associated with them. And not naming our desires or our trauma and shame leads only to a more likely outcome of making choices that are disintegrating. Moreover, the energy we must burn to manage our shame and trauma is then not available to us to create the work prepared by God beforehand (Ephesians 2:10).

Aaron, from chapter one, was someone who sexually acted out his deep desire to be seen. But his primary problem was not about sex. We live in a world where so much is channeled through sex that we don't know where sex ends and everything else begins. In response to this, we create structures ensuring that our sexuality can never be hijacked inappropriately. We make sure men and women are separated in any number of ways. This is often necessary and helpful. But I am not here decrying the settings in which separation of the sexes is helpful. I am highlighting the fact that we often avoid addressing the elephant in the room only to have it show up in the office, or in the sanctuary, or in the bar, or in our addiction to arousal and pornography. In our confessional communities, we address our tendencies to misdirect our sexuality directly with those of the opposite sex, those very ones who represent, by their very presence, "the other" for whom we are doing the hard work not to clutch or consume but by whom we long to be seen, soothed, safe, and secure and with whom we long to create a world of goodness and beauty. It is in the confessional community that women and men are given the opportunity, in the context of a well-boundaried system, to do just that.

What's more, this work that women and men do together also provides the opportunity to unmask the lie culture tells us: that sex is the center of the universe and that without it in some idealized fantasy, we will remain in our prison cells of shame. It is in the context of a vulnerable community with the opposite sex that each member has the opportunity to learn—to sense, image, feel, think, and be aware in his or her very body—that to be seen, soothed, safe, and secure in this context, at the end of the day and over many, many days, is far more beautiful than our culture's vision of sex. The revelation of the weight of glory to which men and women bear witness in these settings puts sex in its proper place. A place of dignity, not one of exploitation. It is here, then, where people once found sex to be scary that they now find it to be sacred.

Along the way, we clinicians shepherd the process, trusting that to the degree members are willing to tell the truth about their lives they will be transformed as they are renewed in the presence of Jesus and the activity of the Holy Spirit, presence and activity that are leveraged directly in the embodied presence and activity of the other members of the community. For we believe that when we are attuned to the reality that we live and move and have our being in God, whenever the truth is spoken, Jesus shows up looking for us looking for him—even if we don't know it's him we're looking for.

Part of our shepherding includes offering insights and reflections about each patient, the relational dynamics between patients, and patterns in the group as a whole as they come to know each other and themselves. There are more didactic moments as well, when one of the clinicians may pause the conversation in order to offer instruction, weaving together what is happening in the room with an important tenet of IPNB or the biblical narrative. A great deal of the work of the therapists is to ask many, many questions. Moreover, we presume that every single moment of every single session is a moment in which spiritual formation is taking place, with people moving toward or away from states of integration, where the intention is that they become ever more established as individuals and as a community as outposts of goodness and beauty in the world.

It is in these communities that the work distilled in the text of Psalm 27:4 emerges, and it is to this work that we now turn.

6

IMAGINE THAT

Looking at What We Don't Yet See

One thing I ask from the LORD,
this only do I seek:
that I may dwell in the house of the LORD
all the days of my life,
to gaze on the beauty of the LORD
and to seek him in his temple.

PSALM 27:4

"SIX MONTHS AGO—NO, EVEN TWO WEEKS AGO—I couldn't have imagined it. But last week changed everything. Katrina, when you told us what you did, I was inspired . . . and disturbed. The bottom line is, I have decided to leave my firm and do what I have always wanted to do but never could do because of my fear and my shame."

Ryan spoke with a tremor in his voice, his legs restless as he sat forward in his chair.

Two weeks earlier, Katrina had described the actions she had taken at her job, actions that were the culmination of her practicing for several months what it meant to, as she put it, "have you all in my mind." Because of the depth of the intimacy shared in these confessional communities, most people begin to experience what they describe as "taking others [from the group] with me wherever I go, especially into hard emotional places." This idea of picturing others' physical presence, their voices, and even their words becomes increasingly accessible as group members construct deeply connected community by vulnerably sharing their desires and griefs over time. And this new, practiced way of imagining changes people's stories forever.

This was the case for Katrina, who several months earlier had revealed that her boss was bullying her, in part through her demands on her time and in part through her general lack of consideration that Katrina might have a life outside of work. This had lasted for most of her employment at this company, where she worked as a marketing executive. But she loved almost every other aspect of her position and was loath to leave. Essentially, she was too straitjacketed by her fear and shame to set more firm boundaries with her boss, let alone leave the company. But as week after week she shared of her travail, the community's expressed empathy, anger, and feelings of protection for Katrina began to transform her emotional experience of her story. The members on many occasions spoke of what they wanted for her and how much they wanted to go with her into her boss's office to stand with her while she told her boss that the bullying behavior had to stop.

Over time, with practice, Katrina found herself increasingly able to imagine being in her boss's office, telling her she would no longer tolerate her behavior and that it must stop—all while visualizing the other seven members of her community standing in the office surrounding her. My colleague and I on a number of occasions had her role-play this experience so that she could practice what she would actually sense in her body and feel emotionally, then we assisted her in deescalating her fight-or-flight reactions, keeping her within her window of tolerance. In this way she was able to imagine her story having a different outcome, complete with being able to feel comfortable and confident in her body as she did so. Ultimately Katrina did go to her boss—and then to her HR department, all of which led to her boss being fired and Katrina's promotion. But this would not have happened without the support of her confessional community, which enabled her to practice imagining, one small moment at a time, a different future, a future of beauty and goodness that heretofore had been out of reach.

But the beauty of Katrina's story was only beginning. When she relayed what she had done, her words left Ryan unsettled. She unsettled him with her courage to step into a new future that felt hard and risky, with her success in reimagining her life. Ryan's own story of shame was awakened when Katrina told hers. It was a story he had kept hidden until Katrina's story opened the door and provided him the courage to speak.

To co-labor with Christ (1 Corinthians 3:9) to bring new creation, new elements of beauty and goodness, into being requires an expansion of our imaginations—one that entails great effort. Effort that for Katrina (and then for Ryan, as we will soon see) depended first on those who were part of her group. For indeed, imagining a different future often requires that others first imagine it on our behalf. This was Katrina's experience, and it is that of all of us whose minds are being transformed. Before we live into a different future, we must imagine it, and for us to imagine our future as God does, we will need his help in particular, for no human is going to imagine the future as God does. That help, in fact, has come. As N. T. Wright suggests, in Jesus, God's future came forward into our present moment, enabling us to imagine what God's future— and ours—can be.[1]

Certainly many of us long to imagine our lives being different than they are. Realizing those imagined changes is easier for some than for others. For victims of emotional trauma, their traumatic experience doesn't just shatter their memory of the past; it atrophies their ability to imagine a future that is anything but harrowing. And so they don't. At least not without the embodied assistance of a cloud of witnesses whose words and presence support them in that process.

Human flourishing, then, is about our being able to imagine in embodied form the new creation, the new works of art, that God is creating in, through, and with us. Being joyfully known enables our imagination to expand because it has for so long been truncated by the interpersonal and neurobiological features of shame, fear, and disintegrating behavior— our sin. Being known in the context of the gospel of Jesus changes all of this, not just because we receive new information, as important as that is, but because we are received into the presence and work of the Holy Spirit within the body of Christ. In what we are exploring here, that body is the confessional community to which Katrina belonged and to whom she was opening her story so that it could be changed into one of beauty and goodness.

Even so, evil has every intention of subverting and devouring any and all goodness and beauty, and our complicity with it as it runs right through the center of each of us leads not only to our problems but to our apprehending our condition in the manner we do: we are problems to solve rather than artistic endeavors waiting to be sung, sculpted, painted, and written. Hence, we need help that enables our imaginations to extend beyond where our shame and fear keep them imprisoned. Along with and in the context of a confessional community, we look to the biblical text and to encounters with beauty in our world to point the way to this new creation we long to see emerge. With this in mind, the rest of this book will appeal to one text in particular and to several works of art that will help us imagine who and what we are becoming.

Beginning with this chapter and extending over the three that follow, we will focus on Psalm 27:4, which will serve as a wellspring text, guiding our imaginations as we journey together on the path along which love is leading us. Proper exegesis of any biblical text requires that we pay attention to the context of the passage, in this case, the psalm in its entirety (and if we were even more careful, we would consider its place in the Psalter as a whole). Psalm 27 is a plea for help, acknowledging throughout that God is the source of the assistance the writer longs for. Of particular note is that, relative to most of the body of the poem, verse 4 may seem at first glance a bit out of place. It turns out, however, that the fourth verse is a distillation of the essence of what the psalm is pointing to, a fulcrum around which the entire psalm rotates and is held in balance, reflecting the state of one's life who fully trusts in and is cared for by God.[2] As we will soon see, the beauty of God and his people are at the center of all of it.

Alongside the biblical text, I will also begin to reference particular works of artistic expression that both speak to and model for us what God has made us to do and become in all of our collective joy—an endeavor that begins with the creative dance of the Trinity and is inherent in our primary attachment relationships. We will invite and allow the beauty of the biblical poetry held within Psalm 27:4 to reveal things about the relational dynamism that God and we share. We will also look to this text to provide the story within which the mechanics of IPNB are given their proper teleology, thus granting them God's generative authority. My intention throughout is that the psalm and the beauty of these great works of art become woven together such that they model for us—and form us into—what God desires for us to see and to become. It is this weaving itself—not just the "content" or "meaning" of the psalm or the art on its own—that becomes a crucial component of our mind's activity, enabling us to imagine and realize the beauty we are creating and becoming.

This brings us to another item that is important for us to address before we proceed in exploring the psalm directly. I have mentioned that a significant transition from an overly dominant left-hemispheric posture of attunement to one that is more properly shared between the right and the left (which eventually allows the right brain to do what it is meant to do) is necessary for any of the people we have met so far in this book—along with you and me—to realize the healing and recommissioning of our lives. It also requires that we expand our window of tolerance while simultaneously integrating the middle prefrontal cortex of our brain more robustly. This transformation requires a degree and type of work many of us are unfamiliar with, to our detriment, not least in terms of the depth and rigor of our spiritual formation. In fact, this is work Jesus appears to demand as necessary if we are to become people of "great faith," as he demonstrates in his interaction with the Syrophoenician woman (Matthew 15:21-28). Certainly he meets people where they are, as he did with her, as he has with Katrina, Ryan, and others in this book. But he nonetheless makes no apology for requiring people, once he is in their orbit, to follow him into his. This is what great art does. It finds us where we are, and, unbending to our whims, it lovingly, as did Jesus, unflinchingly—as does Jesus—remains near us but never without expecting us to eventually take some action of risk, just as Jesus expected Peter to step out of the boat to join him in a wind-whipped sea (Matthew 14:22-33).

Earlier I noted that our imaginations must be stretched, at times painfully so, if beauty and goodness are what we are going to see, create, and become. Life in the context of a confessional community does that very thing. But we do so endeavoring to

> stand at the crossroads and look;
>> ask for the ancient paths,
> ask where the good way is, and walk in it,
>> and . . . find rest for your souls. (Jeremiah 6:16)

In our confessional communities we are all standing at the crossroads of our lives, as we are doing in every domain of living at all times. Every moment is a crossroads of choosing to move toward or away from integration, toward or away from Jesus and each other, toward or away from goodness and beauty. Hence, we must ask for the ancient paths. We must look to how those who have gone before us created beauty and goodness as they encountered the God of the Bible. This was no easier for them than it is for us. This process of imagining a future of new creation in the midst of trauma and shame requires that we attend to moments in the past where wisdom was hard at work in the middle of trauma and shame, creating beauty in those times, places, and lives that have preceded us.

One of the most difficult things we have to do is wrest our attention from the painful memories of the past or dread of the future and turn it to something else. For example, Carmen and Graham found it virtually impossible to imagine a future of beauty in their marriage, given how deeply embedded they were in their shame-laden memory of their relationship. But as they moved through the process that we will ourselves soon explore, they were able to imagine beauty where before they could see only carnage, and they could do it while still lamenting what was painful about their life together. They began to make sense of what made no sense to them in their history of relational trauma, and it was the presence of a confessional community embodying Psalm 27:4 that enabled them to do this more robustly than they ever dreamed they could. But it required them to do what those who have walked "the ancient paths" have done before us.

Old Testament scholar Walter Brueggemann has said that the prophetic voices of the Old Testament—Moses, Samuel, David, Isaiah, Jeremiah, Hosea, and others—had to reimagine who this God was that was dealing with them, for he was nothing like any god they had heard of or encountered before. God had to meet them where they were and coax them—sometimes through affliction—to imagine something other than what they assumed to be the case about God and what he was up to in response to their circumstances of oppression: the oppression of Pharaoh, the subjugation by Canaanite tribes, the exploitation by the monarchs of Israel and Judah, and the forced exile and enslavement by the Babylonians.[3] Where the people of God saw only trauma, grief, and hopelessness, the prophets saw a realm no one else could.

Moreover, as Eugene Peterson emphasizes, the prophets offered much of what they were trying to "say" through poetry and even embodied dramatic presentation.[4] In other words, it is not too much to say that, at their core, they were artists. They were addressing the people of their day and the oppression they were enduring not primarily through the power of violence (e.g., David's refusal to kill Saul when he had the chance)—some stories of the Old Testament notwithstanding—or theological explication;

rather, they spoke and wrote poetically; they acted out (literally) what was taking place between themselves and God and between God and his people.[5] They engaged their audience relationally, just as our psalmist engages God relationally. Power and logic depend on keeping our subject at a distance so that we can analyze it in order to manipulate, as we have learned, in a dominantly left-brain way of attuning to the world. To engage our subject draws on the right side of the brain. But this required the people to stretch their imaginations, to expand their emotional capacity to hold what God was bringing their way.

Likewise, Jesus' disciples, and then the early church, had to do the same thing. They had to make sense of Jesus' life, crucifixion, resurrection, and ascension and the coming of the Holy Spirit at Pentecost in light of the Old Testament texts. But they also had to reimagine the texts themselves in light of those events. They had known only that God is one. Now what were they supposed to do with Jesus and the Holy Spirit in play? In the same way Moses and all the other prophets had had to contend with a God who was not playing by the rules of ancient Near Eastern religious cults, so also Jesus' disciples had to contend with him, for neither was he playing by the rules of the Jewish nation at the time of the incarnation—rules not unlike the "rules" of shame and disintegration that dictated the terms of Katrina's narrative, or Tara's, or those of the others we have met. The disciples had to contend with Jesus' parables, stories that required them to persevere in curiosity and continue to inquire of him when he made little to no sense. Not that his words were inchoate, but the stories did not fit the mental models of their right hemisphere's underdeveloped narrative domain of integration. His parables were not illogical; they simply were too much for them to bear. The stories—one form of Jesus' artistry—in essence pushed too far beyond the boundaries of their windows of tolerance. His actions did the same; much of what Jesus taught often came in response to what he did. He ate food without washing his hands—and *then* taught about how what defiles us is what comes out of us rather than what we put into our bodies (Mark 7:1-14). He gathered grain on the Sabbath—and *then* said the Sabbath was made for man and not the other way around (Mark 2:23-28).

The way Jesus did this, the way he expanded the imaginations of his followers, was not through logical, linear left-hemispheric teaching. His alerting them to the "facts" of his impending death and resurrection before his crucifixion provided no comfort or confidence for them. Moreover, at least in one instance, neither did it do much for them after the resurrection (see Luke 24:13-35). What made the difference was his embodied encounters with them, both before and after his death. And even though "he explained to them what was said in all the Scriptures concerning himself" (Luke 24:27), his followers' minds were still veiled until he broke bread. Having things "explained" to them—even by Jesus himself—was not enough. God does not expect to spoon-feed or shoehorn information from our left brains into our right by explaining the world or himself to us. Like any good artist, he does not merely tell. He shows. And he does so profoundly, if even mysteriously, as was often evidenced by his followers' initial encounters with him—and as evidenced for Aaron and Carmen and Graham when I asked them what new, beautiful thing they longed to create.

The process, then, of expanding our imaginations (i.e., greater integration of our minds, not least between our right and left hemispheres, and widening our window of tolerance) requires work not many of us have had much practice doing, not unlike the prophets and disciples in their contexts. But the active presence of the Spirit of God enables us to take steps of faith in the presence of a faithful community and in so doing transforms and renews the story in which we are living as our minds are renewed in the process, much as in Katrina's story above.

And just as the confessional community enabled Katrina's imagination to expand so that she could confront her bullying boss, so her story created space for Ryan's imagination to do the same. As Katrina shared the actions she had taken and described the two weeks that followed, Ryan's story broke open within him.

In the immediate years following college, while working for a nonprofit organization, Ryan had also spent time volunteering at an afterschool tutoring program for underserved families, where he developed a close relationship with several children from the same family. He spent the better part of five years becoming deeply connected to them and their parents. But when he left to attend graduate school, he felt a gnawing shame that somehow he was leaving them behind. He hoped to use his graduate degree in finance to begin a microloan program for small businesses that were trying to get their start in the poorer section of the large city where he lived, but when the job offers came and his debt was looking him square in the face, he took a well-paying entry level job at an investment bank. His hard work soon paid off, and he quickly advanced.

Every time Ryan received a promotion, he recalled his dream of starting a microloan bank—and thought of the family he had "left behind." What typically followed was a wave of shame so great that his only response was to turn his attention back to his promotion and the work at hand, in part as a way of protecting himself from these self-directed accusations. He feared that if he were to actually turn his focus to helping those in great financial need, he would invariably fail them when the going got tough.

That is, until Katrina shared her story, which led to Ryan sharing his. As the community listened to him, and as he braced for the condemning words that never came, he began to find the space in his mind to imagine doing what he had always wanted to do. He was protected from his shame by the community, much as they had protected Katrina from hers. They protected him by drawing his attention away from his shame and toward the deep desire God had placed in his heart, a desire that heretofore he had been too isolated in his own mind to receive. Before we knew it, Ryan had begun the process of starting his own firm. Eventually it became a financial outpost of goodness and beauty in one of the most vulnerable communities in his city.

This was all made possible because Ryan was able to reimagine his story in the absence of shame and fear—and in the presence of those who enabled him to be seen, soothed, safe, and secure, the very things we all need in order to practice for the new creation that is coming.

As we explore Psalm 27:4 in earnest, I want to invite you to expand your own imagination, just as Katrina and Ryan did. This invitation is being offered anytime you become particularly aware of emotional salience—puzzlement, confusion, or boredom; liberation, discomfort, or pain; or anything else in between. I assure you that once you are part of some form of confessional community, this, your cloud of witnesses, will remind you that you are not alone and that you are becoming beauty embodied with every incremental enlargement of your imagination, no matter how minute. You can be confident that the ancients have traveled the path you are on and even now are with you along the way.

■ ■ ■

One thing I ask from the LORD,
    this only do I seek . . . (Psalm 27:4)

One thing. Ask for one thing. Seek after one thing only. How hard can it be, as Kierkegaard admonished, to "will one thing"?[6]

"What was it about our interaction that you found helpful?" Sean asked Charlotte. "You said our conversation last week was really good—I'm wondering what was good about it."

"I don't know," she replied. "I can't remember."

Charlotte was the picture of sophistication while giving no air of thinking herself so. She was smart and articulate in a manner that exuded confidence without arrogance, and she was quick with her smile and with kindness—but no pushover, or so it seemed from her posture and the way she was seated in her chair.

It was Charlotte's third week in our confessional community. She had shared the facts of her story with the group the week before—how, over the course of her life up to and including the present, her parents, now in their eighties, had favored her sister over her, her sister who even as an older adult behaved at times at the emotional developmental level of a toddler. Over the course of many months in our group, which Sean was also part of, she would tell some version of this story through the lens of multiple vignettes, the same song sung in different verses representing the mistreatment she had experienced at the hands of her parents, her favored sister often being the star of the show.

To make matters more challenging, Charlotte was an accomplished and effective leader. She was the CEO of a company she had founded twenty years earlier with fifteen employees, eventually turning it into an agile and flourishing workplace that employed five hundred people and routinely received "best place to work" awards. As she often told the group, "I look around at my life and I don't have anything to complain about. This stuff with my parents and sister shouldn't upset me like it does" (her history of depression and recovery from alcoholism notwithstanding). But when Sean and others empathically attuned to her, she would respond with tears—and then quickly work to hold them back, albeit to no avail. That she was so capable in other domains of her life made being in this community, where mostly she felt the discomfort of vulnerability, deeply disorienting to her.

After telling her story and receiving compassion from the group, she would note how much better she felt, expressing deep gratitude to the other members for remaining extraordinarily present with her and validating her anger, sadness, and shame.

And then Sean asked his question. Although Charlotte easily recalled that she had experienced the group's compassion, she had a hard time putting into words what had actually taken place within her mind and body and between herself and the others who had given her such comfort. A form of this dialogue between Charlotte and other members played itself out over a stretch of many weeks, each time ending with Charlotte, after expressing her gratefulness for the group's care, exclaiming in exasperation, "Why can't I *get* this? It's as if each time we have this conversation I go home and forget that it happened. I *hate* that!"

Charlotte had great difficulty appropriating to herself in other settings the mercy she experienced in the group. Despite her effectiveness as a CEO and as a daughter, wife, mother, and friend, her "shame attendant" competed vigorously with her remembered experiences within the confessional community.[7] Regardless of how capable she actually was in her various roles, her internal dialogue was continually dominated by that same attendant, which narrated to her that whatever good she was doing in the world, she was in fact an imposter. Whenever significant conflict arose at the office or at home, she found herself re-experiencing what amounted to implicitly remembered reenactments of life in her family of origin.

Although sharing vignettes from her life story—singing different verses of the same song—led to her receiving comfort from the group, she interpreted her "need to keep doing this" as evidence that somehow, even in the journey toward healing, she wasn't doing it right. She should have been able to receive empathy from the group once and have that be enough. And there you have it: she wasn't enough, just like in her family. She saw how others in the group were growing in life-changing ways; why couldn't she? She was even courageous enough to report that at times she felt like quitting the group, not because she didn't experience good things there, but rather because she wasn't making progress fast enough. This after only a few weeks of being in the community.

However, her perseverance over many months enabled her to report that, in her business and in her relationship with her parents, her life had begun to resemble what she experienced in the community. The process was not easy for Charlotte. But she continued to come. She persevered, even when she could generate a hundred excuses for not returning. These are the excuses we all make to avoid vulnerable, intimate community, the price being the continued stifling of our creativity. But with perseverance, and despite the frustration of "not growing fast enough," change eventually made its way into the room—not just the room where we were meeting but every room Charlotte entered, including those where she found her parents and sister.

Charlotte willingly practiced over many months (a process we will explore in more depth in coming pages), and on one level it likely felt like she was "doing the same thing over and over again." But in fact she was facilitating the activation of a newly emerging neural network. She was generating neuroplastic modification that required a certain amount of time—the time it took for her to "get this." And to be certain, she was getting it. But not without perseverance.

ATTENTION TO PERSEVERANCE

Two millimeters per day.

That is the average growth rate of an injured neuron that is in the process of healing.[8] Neurogenesis and growth are possible, but it takes time. In fact, it takes longer than we would like. I am a modern man who lives in a world that has trained me to expect that I can acquire what I want immediately—so much so that Amazon now delivers my packages to my door before I even order them. Not so with the brain.

We have learned over the past twenty years that optimal neuroplastic change—the creation and growth of new neural pathways—can be enhanced by several variables.[9] One of those is frequently repeated, relatively brief activity to strengthen the signal of a neuronal firing pattern—in other words, to increasingly enhance our memory or the ease with which we repeat the same action. For instance, if you want to learn to play the piano (especially as an adult), it will be more effective if you practice for fifteen minutes a day, five days a week, rather than for ninety minutes once a week.

This frequent practice of small things is necessary and helpful to establish durable new network firing patterns. Practice, practice, practice, for we become ever more perfect versions of what we practice—for better or worse. For most of Charlotte's life, she practiced cutting herself off from her rage, sadness, and shame, and no wonder; who would want to pay attention to that? Who would want to pay attention to the pus of an abscess? (Although I do know people who find that subject rather captivating.) But in so doing she nonconsciously prevented her social engagement system from developing. Put more accurately, her parents prevented it, but not without her cooperation—cooperation that was necessary for her to survive. Utterly without her conscious awareness, her social engagement system, which was primed at birth to grow in response to attuned communication, never had the chance to do that in a robust way. Her social engagement system was not absent but under-developed. So when the group initially offered her empathy, she could receive it in the moment, but she did not have the established neural networks available to be able to hold on to it, to remember it.

Much like practicing the piano, Charlotte was learning to play a new piece of music. And she was practicing, ultimately, to play the music in a venue where there would be more pressure, not unlike the experience of performing in Carnegie Hall. Having the voices of the community members with her in her mind while she was present with her parents in person, she came to know a completely transformed way of being with her family of origin and in her leadership role in her company. Perseverance—practice—was a crucial element for her, as it was for the community.

The key to beginning that practice has to do with the manner in which we direct our attention. Our attention is the ignition key that turns on the engine of the mind.[10] Everything I do, consciously or not, begins with a shifting of my attention toward the desired target. Charlotte's attentional mechanism was immediately in play the moment I suggested she join a confessional community. I was careful and explicit in explaining that it would potentially be a transformative experience for her and would provide the setting in which she could confidently implement many of the things we had been working on in individual psychotherapy, things that seemed difficult for her to appropriate as fully as she wanted to in her family and at work. But instead of focusing her attention on what I had just said, she began to ask questions, revealing that she considered my proposal the equivalent of walking blindfolded into a busy intersection.

"Oh, I don't know if I could do that."

"I think that would be frightening."

"How long will I have to be in the group?"

"How many people are in the group?"

"Are there going to be men in the group or is it just women?"

"How do I know they won't tell anyone else about me?"

"What if I know someone in the group?"

The questions poured forth.

At first glance they seemed innocuous and reasonable enough, and I (patiently, I think) answered them all. But her questions were less significant to me in the information she sought than in what they revealed to us both about where Charlotte was directing her attention in response to my offering of a haven for growth. She did not orient her attention to where I pointed—an opportunity for becoming and creating beauty out of the very hardship of her life—but rather in her usual direction, a place some-where in the future where she imagined experiencing some ill-defined, shaming state of mind from which there was no escape. My invitation to Charlotte to move more deeply into the intimacy of being known, this time by several people at once, activated an ancient constellation of neural networks in her mind, a constellation she had practiced into being over years of repetition that spliced together and conflated intimacy with shame. For her to direct her attention to the vision I had described—being in a community that was creating goodness and beauty out of the detritus of people's lives—caused a minor rebellion in that part of her mind that was terrified of the very thing she desired more than anything: being known and loved deeply.

And so in addition to answering Charlotte's questions, I also noticed where she had directed her attention. I told her I was curious about what emotion she was experiencing and where in her body she sensed it just before she began her series of questions. I was inviting her to notice what she was paying attention to and how she was doing it—to become aware of her mental collage of sensations, images, feelings, and thoughts—and to be curious about what prompted her to pay attention to one state of mind and not the other.

With that observation, she paused. And then the tears welled. "I want so badly to want that kind of community. But I am so afraid."

And so it is that even considering becoming part of a confessional community reveals how we have practiced paying attention in our lives, along with the perseverance required to incline our attention in a dif-ferent way—over and over again—to that which we want to become.

Our brains' right and left hemispheres attune to the world differently, the right being more "here and with" what we are experiencing, the left being more "separate from" and analytic of what is happening. Charlotte's practice of receiving compassion from the group members while consciously attuning to that very experience as it was happening—practicing being aware that she was aware—was her effort to recognize and monitor her encounter primarily through her brain's right hemisphere. It involved being here and now with the group and with herself. The moment she turned her attention to analyzing "why can't I *get* this?"—and it took, literally, a microsecond for the transition to occur—she was effectively shifting to her left brain's analytic, judging, shaming form of attunement, seeing herself "over there," someone who has not done this well enough and as such is to be condemned.

This small shift—from observing and receiving to analyzing and condemning—is a microbehavior we enact dozens of times a day, one that gives rise to all manner of human travail, whether in our kitchens or between cultures. It virtually all begins here, in the short journey across the corpus callosum from the right to the left hemisphere. Consequently, to persevere in an integrating manner, we must pay attention to how we are paying attention to what we are sensing, imaging, feeling, and thinking and how we are behaving physically.

To persevere in paying attention to our lives in a way that brings integration (by attuning to our experience via the right brain), we move to SNAG the mind: stimulate neuronal activation and growth. We do this by focusing our mind's attention, over and over again, on that to which we want to be attuned.[11] This happens automatically in many domains of life without our being aware of it, especially when it comes to things we want and that come easily to us. But, as we have noted, those things that are the most durable and the most beautiful require hard work and take a long time to make. Playing a difficult piece on the piano requires practicing it over and over again with perseverance. In Charlotte's case, she had to practice attuning her attention to her remembered experience of receiving empathy from other community members—not recalling the experience as a fact that happened in time and space but recalling the actual sensations, images, feelings, thoughts, and movements of her body in response to being in the room.

Occasionally, after a group member offered Charlotte a word of empathy, I would pause the conversation and invite her to look at the person who had spoken to her and take in what she was hearing, to pay attention to what she was sensing, imaging, feeling, and thinking and to notice what she wanted to do with her body. I was inviting her to replay the event that had just happened as a way to reactivate the neural networks that represented the moment. I would then instruct her to replay this moment in her mind several times before she retired for the evening and several times over the course of the coming week. In this way, we harness the power of perseverance via the mechanics of neuroplasticity—while strengthening the experience of being known and loved at the same time.

We need to know up front that if we want beauty to emerge in our lives, it will require our willingness to stay the course, to play the long game. For not only are long periods of time required for the brain to change; it is equally true that we are not living in a neutral universe.

We are pushing against a resistance that St. Paul would describe as the cumulative effects of "the world, the flesh, and the devil" (Ephesians 2:2-3). At times our efforts to create beauty run into cultural riptides in the world that seem impossible to swim against, whether in our families or our schools or our places of employment. These cultural tidal movements are even (and often) made manifest in the behavior of people in the church itself. Chuck DeGroat poignantly outlines how narcissistic church leaders can create milieus of social malignancy that are made all the worse by virtue of their existence within a formalized faith-based organization.[12]

Moreover, we contend with our "flesh"—Paul's word that subsumes the paths of corruption we tend to follow in our brains and relationships,[13] despite our desire to think on "whatever is true, whatever is noble, whatever is right, whatever is pure, whatever is lovely, whatever is admirable . . . anything [that] is excellent or praiseworthy" (Philippians 4:8).

Believing in Jesus, in the way John's Gospel describes the notion of what it means to "believe," necessarily puts us on a new path. The hard part is that we take our old brains with us. And these brains remember more than we wish they did, in ways we wish they didn't, not least being via our bodies.[14] Between the implicitly and explicitly remembered elements of our lived existence, and despite our longing to think and act on things of beauty, we often find ourselves thinking on other things altogether. We all know what it's like to have to overcome the "flesh" of ourselves—the ancient, easily accessed sensations, images, feelings, thoughts, and behavioral impulses all converging in our narratives of insecure attachment that direct our desires toward states of disintegration.

Last, we must remember that evil has no intention of going quietly into the night, especially when it sees that efforts are afoot to mirror the kingdom of God by creating beauty from the trash heaps of our lives. As C. S. Lewis reminds us, it is common for us to take the devil either too seriously or not seriously enough.[15] Either option indicates that we are not awake, alert, or attuned to evil's attempts both inside and outside our heads to draw our attention to hoarding, clutching, and ultimately devouring beauty, not least ourselves and each other.

Hence, we "work out [our] salvation with fear and trembling" (Philippians 2:12), against the world, the flesh, and the devil, and also against the general inertia of our lives, a process that is just plain hard. At some point it will necessarily lead to suffering—suffering out of which perseverance will emerge (Romans 5:3-5). And it is Charlotte's perseverance in directing first her attention and then all that followed that reflects what we read in the opening lines of Psalm 27:4.

The psalmist offers these words to set the stage for everything that follows. For what does follow is nothing short of a vision for the establishment of an outpost of beauty, the city on the hill of which Jesus speaks in his sermon in Matthew 5, one that is illuminating and that flavors its surroundings with goodness. The psalmist is asking for just one thing, and that one thing is the only thing he will seek. Moreover, he is asking and seeking unabashedly, which reveals that he is someone who desires.

Someone who longs for something. And that something is the same thing we all long for.

The writer indicates that he intends to direct his attention to one thing only. This necessarily implies perseverance. It implies practice. It implies that if we follow his lead, we will continue to do this work in the face of stumbling, in the presence of ruptures and mistakes. We will persevere and practice even though we are tempted to focus our attention primarily on the grief, anger, sadness, and regret of the past, or on our fear and anxiety that our past will be reenacted in the future. Because when our attention is firmly ensconced in the past or the future, we remain outside the present moment, the only dimension of the temporal domain of integration in which we are able to find joy and create beauty, even in the presence of our suffering. The psalmist offers a commitment to focus on something different than what we commonly do.

This is not easy. For Charlotte, remaining in the group and staying put in her own discomfort while in the presence of others was at times excruciating. She was tempted to give up on the process altogether given how difficult it was for her to hold on to the empathy and courage her fellow pilgrims offered her, to keep them in the forefront of her mind, much as each of us is tempted to do the same. But as other people in the community drew her attention to their desire to be with her, not as her judges but as her friends—particularly in the very moments she felt ashamed—their very physical presence, with all their nonverbal cues of warmth and welcome, enabled her to stay.

The formation and recognition of beauty, then, requires perseverance and is a process that cannot be rushed, whether in a community or in the material world. It requires our willingness to patiently allow it to reveal itself to us, even when we might not initially grasp that we are in its presence. An oak tree cannot be compelled to grow to a height of eighty feet in a week any more than we can compel our right brain to become instantly comfortable with intimacy when it simultaneously accesses our fear or shame.

Strikingly, neither is beauty in a painting easily achieved or always even recognized. My relationship to the work of Mark Rothko is an example. Rothko was an American painter of the mid- to late twentieth century who is known, among other things, for his paintings of abstract expressionism. My initial encounter with his paintings marked the first time I had attended to this form of art, as I'd had little exposure and even less interest in it prior. Before, if I was going to view art, I wanted it to make sense, both in terms of what I saw and the "story" behind it (say, for instance, a portrait or sculpture of something plainly recognizable, such as Rembrandt's *The Night Watch* or Bernini's *Apollo and Daphne*). I wanted to be immediately taken by the art's beauty, and I didn't want to wonder, "What is that supposed to mean?"

Hence, to look at Rothko's paintings, many of which are large canvases with varying bands of color, meant to sit with them—to persevere with them—long enough to allow myself to "see" what is not at once revealed and to restrain my "thinking" brain from having to ask, "What does it mean?" I found myself, upon sitting quietly for thirty minutes viewing a Rothko painting in the National Gallery of Art, eventually—but only eventually—deeply moved by the "encounter" I was having with . . . color.

It is difficult to put into words, but I can say that my experience in persevering with Rothko's work first led, after about fifteen minutes, to my becoming aware of the layers of color present in the painting. There weren't, as it turned out, only three bands—two navy and one royal blue—as it first appeared. Rather, there were multiple hues and areas where the paint had run, and the borders between the bands of color were not nearly as sharp as they appeared at first glance. After about twenty minutes, I began to experience an emotional surge, which I can only describe as a sense that I was being "seen" by the painting—almost as if I were swimming in it, being enveloped by it.

Now, you might be wondering, "Is this guy sane? He thinks he was 'seen' by a painting?" I don't mean I believe the painting was "looking" at me, as if it were a sentient being. Rather, I experienced the same feeling I do when I feel seen with grace and compassion by another person. The point is that in order for any of this to happen, for my having any chance at all to encounter and be encountered by something in a way I would not have predicted, I had to persevere. I needed to remain seated in one place for an extended period of time. Not so that I could "work harder" to see what I had not seen before—using my analytic, left-brain function—but so that I could relax and permit whatever I sensed to come to me without my trying to "figure it out"—a more prominently right-brain function.[16]

You may also be wondering what on earth this has to do with our broken marriages, our unmended relationships with our parents or children, our racism, or our economics of efficiency. Apart from learning how to appreciate art, what does our willingness to persist in opening our right brains to beauty in the material world have to do with the new creation God is intending for our relationships?

I offer this story of my interaction with Rothko's work to introduce and highlight the practice of putting ourselves in the path of oncoming beauty, especially those works of art or natural wonder that require our willingness to remain long enough for our sensing brain to adjust and receive, long enough for us to "be found" by what we are encountering as much as we find it. This practice is exactly what we are about in our confessional communities. This is what enveloped Charlotte as she persevered. We are in the business of persevering, remaining attentive long enough, being open to the activity of the right hemisphere of the brain as much as the left, becoming maximally receptive to the stories of others as well as our own. They may be stories we do not immediately understand. We may be tempted to make sense of their stories using the lens of our own attachment patterns, ready to give our opinion about what we believe is going on in their narrative, only to find we haven't a clue what we're talking about, mostly because we are not so much reacting to their story as we are reacting to old emotional responses within ourselves that are more about our unfinished business than they are about theirs.

So when Charlotte's reactions emerged in the group—and they did, sometimes with intense, unpleasant features she didn't even know she was carrying—she occasionally wanted to run out of the room because she had so much difficulty tolerating her own state of mind. But she remained. She persevered. She worked hard, with the help of the others, to put words to her feelings. And the other members? They remained as well, making it plain to her over many sessions that they were not afraid of her rage or shame or sadness; they could take it, and they could take it for as long as she gave it. Okay, they didn't want her picking up the lamp on the end table and throwing it at them. But they were willing to peer behind the "obvious" color to see where the paint was running; they were willing to put up with the blurred borders of her feelings of confusion—because they knew that they needed time, time that was required for their own stories to be understood as well.

Perseverance is made possible because of the community we hold in our mind—this is what enables us to stay the course. I did not pay my first visit to Rothko's work on my own. I went with a friend who was just as willing to persevere as I was. This is yet another way the psalmist provides guidance. We must recall that the poetry of the psalter was not written primarily for individuals to read privately. Of course, private reading of the Bible is a good thing to do. But the Psalms were collected, as all of the canon of Scripture has been, with the intention of their being read in public, in a community of believers who affirm together the reality of what they are hearing or reading. It is the poet's intention that what he is saying for himself, he is saying with other people.

The brain can do a lot of hard work for a long period of time, as long as it doesn't have to do it by itself. Who among us doesn't have something in our life we have simply given up on—some wound we assume won't ever be healed, some ruptured relationship whose future we can picture only in images of the injured past, some addictive behavior we believe we can't overcome, some part of our character in which we are so embroiled that we no longer even consider that it can change? Our discouragement and even despair about such things are, more than anything else, deeply dependent on the degree to which our minds and hearts are living in isolation. Becoming deeply known, living interpersonally integrated lives, enables us to persevere in the face of all that tells us not to, to "will one thing" in order to see the beauty of the pure in heart emerge,[17] to see God in places and ways that heretofore we could not (Matthew 5:8).

Perseverance is not easy, but it is necessary. And anyone in a community on the way to creating beauty must be committed to it from the start.

DWELL

That I may dwell in the house of the LORD
all the days of my life.

PSALM 27:4

WE NOW TURN OUR ATTENTION TO what the psalmist's attention was also turned to, the "one thing only" that he would seek. He writes that his desire is to dwell. Specifically, to "dwell in the house of the LORD all the days of my life." What does it mean to dwell? What does it mean to dwell in the house of the Lord?

For Aaron, Tara, and Charlotte, for Hudson, Graham, and Carmen, for Katrina and Ryan to heal, they needed a place—a structure in which that healing and recommissioning could transpire, not unlike J. R. R. Tolkien's Houses of Healing in *The Return of the King*.[1]

Dwelling requires tending. Homes, gardens, neighborhoods all require routine, intentional maintenance. This does not happen on its own. Someone must be responsible to initiate this care. For us to flourish relationally, we need those who are initiating, leading, and attuning to others in the system. This begins in the family, which is the primary system on which all other social systems are modeled. We take our family to work, play, school, and church. And it is in each of these systems that we then nonconsciously replicate what we know via our implicit memory. We necessarily learn, then, how to dwell with ourselves by dwelling with others. To dwell with God is to dwell within his family—the trinitarian family of Father, Son, and Spirit—and necessarily to do so over a long period of time.

Given the above, the notion of dwelling, then, offers us at least two questions: (1) Where am I? and (2) With whom am I living? In the framework of IPNB, the first question addresses the "I" of the mind; the second addresses the "we" of the mind. First, where are you? If I were to ask you this in one of our confessional communities, I would in part be asking about your physically mediated response to the world. In the terms of IPNB, I would be asking about your embodied mind, given the crucial role the body plays in directing the attention of the mind. Moreover, when I asked Charlotte or any other patient, "Where are you?" I was inviting them to be curious about how their bodies were priming and further influencing the "location" of their minds.

"I'm not sure how to answer your question," Randall sighed. "Well, I may know how to answer it—I just don't have enough time and still give anyone else time to talk. Maybe not even for the next month."

He sounded tired, and not the kind of tired that was due to too little sleep the night before; rather, it was the tiredness of years of not being seen, soothed, safe, or secure. No small part of that was related to his life growing up in a single-parent home, his alcoholic father having left him and his two younger sisters when he was five. Some of it came from working as a public school administrator, where the hours required were more than the hours that existed in a day. Some of it came from having four children under the age of seven, one of whom had special needs. And a great deal of it came from being relationally isolated for most of his life. He had had so few people inquire as to his whereabouts that it took a great deal of getting used to when anyone in the group asked it of him. If no one is curious about your life, you won't necessarily be that curious about it yourself.

So Randall had to practice taking in that question and then considering how he would answer it. But once he got the hang of it, as he said, he became a veritable font of words and feelings, all tumbling out every which way. Eventually he was able to articulate on a regular basis that where he "was"—where he was dwelling—was in a story of scarcity rather than abundance, one in which he terminally worried that he could be fired if he did not work to perfection. And if that is where you are dwelling—anxious and alone—it isn't surprising that at some point you find your way into my office.

The question "Where are you?" is foundational to Christian anthropology, being God's first query to the man in Genesis 3. It is as integral to what it means to be human as a drive shaft is to the movement of an automobile. It is intended to be comprehensive in its scope, its desire being to draw forth what we are sensing, imaging, feeling, and thinking and the narrative that we are employing to make sense of it all. (For Randall, this was a narrative in which he lived in a world of scarcity, one in which the bottom could fall out at any minute.) It is a question of pursuit, a query intended to discover the whereabouts of our deepest desires and griefs, paving the way for discovery and new creation. And it is a question to which any effective parent, teacher, coach, boss, pastor, close friend, or psychotherapist regularly returns as a means of facilitating the ongoing vitality of secure attachment—and the creativity that emerges from it.

All that potential creativity notwithstanding, it can be nerve-racking to hear that question, especially if our interlocutor is serious. So serious, in fact, that we know we are not free to hide behind a quick, "I'm right here, and I'm good. How are you?"—those words tumbling out of our mouth as effortlessly and automatically as "Bless you!" in response to someone sneezing. No real thought. Just the autodiscourse we've learned since childhood. But when God asks Adam—and us—this question, and when we ask it in our confessional communities, neither God nor we are interested in autodiscourse; we're looking for the real, just as God was looking for the real when asking Adam where he was—where he was truly dwelling. Looking back on the story from our vantage point, we can reasonably presume that God was looking for Adam as he is looking for us and is curiously, lovingly, eagerly interested in us, albeit not without demands. He is the one by whom we are ultimately hoping to be found, to be seen, soothed, and made safe and secure. But I, like Adam, am skilled at hiding in the bushes and then, when asked directly, at deflecting God's question. Jesus was familiar with our penchant for this.

As I have mentioned previously, the Gospel of John often points us to the creation texts of Genesis,[2] and here again we turn to John 1:38, where we hear Jesus' question of John the Baptist's disciples who were following after him.

"What do you want?" he asks them.

This is an exploratory question, one in which Jesus is essentially inquiring of their whereabouts. What is your desire? What do you most long for? This is another facet of his pursuit of us, another way for him to ask, "Where are you?" echoing God's first question to humans as he was walking in the cool of the day, coming to find them.[3]

"Where are you staying?" they reply. We hear in John's disciples' answer, perhaps, the reply of men offering the deference due a highly regarded teacher. Or maybe they are trying to figure out for themselves if what John has told them—"Behold, the Lamb of God, who takes away the sin of the world!" (John 1:29 ESV)—is true, and they need to investigate his pedigree, check his references. In either case, one thing they do not do is answer the question he asked them. They deflect. Not unlike Adam, they too, for all we know, may be afraid to get too close, afraid that if the kingdom of God is coming, violence is surely on the way, as anyone with any sense knows is the manner of a conquering sovereign. Or, like us, maybe his question is too unexpected. Perhaps it catches them off guard—what rabbi would be asking *them* what *they* wanted? Wouldn't it make more sense for them to ask him what *he* wanted? Or, at least if they were like me, wouldn't they want to find out first what the right answer is to his question? I mean, even if you are asking what I want, I don't want to give you the wrong answer. Even more so, what if Jesus' query is simply too . . . real? Too serious, too penetrating, too intrusive, too intimately touching the parts of them that cannot tolerate that much beauty, not unlike my being unable to look for too long at the Grand Canyon. Hence, they allow his question to glance off of them, much as we find looking into bright sunlight too painful for eyes that have been too long in the dark—and so we look away.

Like God in the Genesis account, Jesus wants to know what the disciples want, wants to know where they are. But like them, we heap shame and condemnation on ourselves and others, building implicitly primed defensive behavior that resists receiving God's curiosity, attuning to it as we do primarily through our left hemispheres, keeping God at arm's length, worried about the same thing Adam was worried about. Because God had told Adam that the consequence for eating the fruit of the tree of knowledge of good and evil was death, one can easily imagine that Adam assumed God was coming to kill him—not kill in the sense we commonly think of but in the sense God meant when he said it: death as the excruciatingly painful alienation from him and from each other, suffused as it is with shame. This was the same alienation Aaron, Hudson, Tara, Graham, Carmen, and Charlotte were all experiencing at some level.

In our confessional communities, the questions "What do you want?" and "Where are you?" are asked frequently. They are questions of dwelling—questions that require the cultivating and tending of relationships over time so that they bear fruit. As you will see in the remainder of this chapter and in ensuing chapters, a great deal of what the members inquire of each other involves one or the other of these two questions. For those mental health professionals reading this, these queries will be unsurprising, for they constitute the warp and woof of the work you do, and they are familiar to everyone else as they are common to most people's everyday interactions. But in the context of confessional communities, they are directed in a manner that is anything but common. Their target is the center of our souls. They are not asking for our appetizer order or where we are in the house.

Taking this a step further, these questions are themselves the very substance of, the very act of, dwelling itself. To ask these questions is to move closer together, to be more deeply known and loved. They are bids for greater intimacy, questions that are fundamental building blocks with which members create beauty and goodness out of the community itself.

For there is far more going on in these communities than people doing what each needs to do to flourish as individuals. Eventually, the community as a whole begins to recognize that it is a living, breathing organism. And because of each member's willingness to dwell, it sustains each individual as a direct function of the beauty and goodness of the community as an entire body.

"What do you want?" and "Where are you?" are questions of desire. What patients do not initially recognize is that the asking of these questions is actually an expression of what each participant desires. We ask what a person wants because we long to know them as we long to be known. The one who is asked is invited to reflect on what he or she wants. Everyone eventually realizes that with each question and answer, beneath the information exchanged is the undercurrent of a bid for intimacy. The very asking of the question is a way for people to say, in essence, "I want to be closer to you. I want to love you more, and I want you to receive me even more deeply than you have already."

"Where are you?" and "What do you want?" are questions, then, that pertain to how an individual is dwelling, as a function of the mind's sensations, images, feelings, thoughts, and physical behaviors. But in interpersonal neurobiology the mind is understood as an embodied and relational process, so that we also dwell in the presence of and in relationship with others. I dwell. And I dwell *with*. This gets at the "we" part of the mind. The question posed by John's disciples, "Where are you staying?" could also be asked as, "With whom are you living?" The ancient Hebrews' response to this question was expressed in their longing to dwell "in the land of the living" (see Psalm 27:13). This speaks of the land (a "where?" question), but more importantly, it is the land "of the living," a "with whom?" question.

To dwell "in the land of the living" implied that one was living in this life, here and now on the earth with people are around, and not dwelling in Sheol (the land of the dead) or in the future eternal kingdom of Yahweh. It means to live where we are and not where we're not. When we are straitjacketed by our left brain's mode of attuning to the world, we tend to live in the past or the future rather than where we are actually physically located. To dwell in the land of the living means that we are alert to what is before us, encountering it for what it is, anticipating and looking to create beauty and goodness wherever the opportunity arises.

Each of the patients we have met thus far struggled to live in the present moment given how powerfully their implicit memory drew their attention to the regret of their past or the fear of their future. This kept each of them out of the present moment—the right-brain hemisphere's mode of attunement. By entering into a confessional community, they began to practice allowing themselves to be fully present to their desires and griefs in the presence of others—and thereby experienced the opportunity for lament and transformation of their brokenness. And we will soon see how dwelling in the land of the living is most powerfully manifested by doing so "in the house of the LORD all the days of my life" (Psalm 27:4).

Moreover, to dwell in the land of the living is to live long enough and at a pace and cadence that allows us to notice we are living with others in the first place. Part of the challenge we face culturally is that we live in places where we don't really dwell. Being in a place effectively enough that we can answer the questions "Where are you?" and "With whom are you living?" without hesitation is rare for us. Our state of isolation has been well-documented by research statistics on loneliness.[4] We frequently bypass others in ways that are lost on us and miss opportunities both to encounter and create beauty.

As I write these words, our world is caught in the vice grip of the Covid-19 pandemic. One of the side effects of this event has been (for some—not for everyone) a forced slowing of our pace, which enables us to recognize and embrace activity we otherwise never would. To slow our pace allows us to take in what is before us, to live in the present moment. This does not mean we have to live in the same location for our entire lives (although this can be helpful). The cultural and economic landscape may preclude that for some. However, our flourishing necessarily depends on our minds being afforded the time (and therefore the proper pace and cadence) to develop relationships in which we establish a community that enables us to create the works of beauty God has prepared for us to make. In this sense, we can't make the brain do what we want at a pace it cannot maintain any more than we can our lungs.

All of this implies that dwelling requires us to be in the presence of others substantially long enough that we can be seen by them and felt by them, and they by us. It implies that we remain. For the mind to flourish, it must spend time taking in beauty—like a Rothko painting—enough time that it can apprehend beauty for what it is. It takes less than three seconds for the neuroaffective effects of shame to register in the mind, changing the contours of our felt sensations and perceptions. It takes anywhere from thirty to ninety seconds for us to fully receive the emotional "load" of a compliment, of a bid for attachment, of a gift of goodness or beauty directed our way.

For goodness and beauty to arise, time for dwelling is necessary. There is no other way, and the psalmist assumes as much. There is no question that our community members can be tempted to bolt—sometimes in the middle of a session—due to the discomfort they are feeling. But their willingness to remain—to dwell—creates the bedrock on which their relationships are "in him . . . being built together to become a dwelling in which God lives by his Spirit" (Ephesians 2:22).

At the beginning of this chapter I alluded to J. R. R. Tolkien's *The Lord of the Rings*. Here I want to draw our attention to his work as an artistic example of what is entailed in the act of dwelling. I am asking you to imagine in a way you may not be accustomed to doing—which is what the members of the confessional communities must do in order to dwell therein.

Tolkien's epic story has monumental significance, not merely in terms of the storytelling itself but of what happens to the reader. As Anthony Lane reflects in his 2001 review of the books in *The New Yorker*, "It was, and remains, not a book that you happen to read, but a book that happens to you: a chunk bitten out of your life."[5] *The Lord of the Rings* and the book that precedes it, *The Hobbit*, are known to mobilize people's imaginations as well as, and maybe more than, any other work of fiction. But it also requires a significant effort on the part of the reader to enable that process to emerge. Tolkien does not spoon-feed the reader. The reader must be willing to work at the process. She must be willing to dwell with and in the books. One overarching element of beauty in the story is Tolkien's use of language and the lengths he went to describe in great detail different characters and physical landscapes.

One such character is Tom Bombadil. His story is enigmatic. He represents much of what I as a reader long for in life (joy, vitality, and agency) and yet, simultaneously, things that are difficult for me to accept (his actions and words frequently do not immediately make sense). In other words, he embodies what often feels like the longings and the confusions of my life. Moreover, I have to work to make sense of who Tom is and what his purpose is in the arc of the story. When reading *The Lord of the Rings*, I would sometimes find myself reading pages over and over again in order for the story to penetrate my understanding, in order to decipher what Tolkien was saying through his character. The point here is that in order to comprehend Tom Bombadil's character, you have to stay with the story. You have to dwell in it.

Some find this sort of thing, not least in Tolkien's works, to be tedious. I do not deny this. But this is what much of life is, the very stuff out of which some of our less attractive behavior ensues. As much as Graham and Carmen found the early years of their marriage to be life-giving, there came a time, as is the case with all marriages, when its tedium threatened to overrun their ability to flexibly adapt to it. It was then they found themselves drifting away from each other to find alternative means to be seen, soothed, safe, and secure. They were, in a manner of speaking, finding it difficult to dwell with each other. They were finding it challenging to "read the pages over and over again," to discern what each was sensing, imaging, feeling, and thinking and the narrative that made sense of it all. They were tired of reading the book of their marriage and just wanted to put it down and walk away, never to pick it up again.

In the age of the internet we are learning—in fact we are practicing—how not to pay attention. We are being trained to be unable to maintain attunement to a whole host of things whose flourishing depends on our paying attention for extended periods of time. And when we can't, we become anxious, bored, and irritated. Our mind's relationship with the intended, distracting features of our devices as mediated by their touch-screens is changing our brains and behavior in such a way that we are now distressed anytime we have to spend fifteen to thirty seconds without a stimulus from outside our own mind.[6] Hence, our constant checking for texts and emails.

To sit with Tolkien, Tolstoy, or Dickens requires what researchers call *deep reading*,[7] something that essentially employs many of the same neurobiological activities required for us to dwell in the presence of others when it is not immediately easy to do so. Deep reading requires willingness to tolerate ambiguity, to accept the distress that emerges in our bodies when we do not "get what's going on," be that in a novel or in the story of someone sitting across the room from us. We must practice synthesizing information along with our emotional responses to that information while being tempted to put the book down—to come back to it later or perhaps never at all—because of how difficult we find it to read. And what we read does not have to be lengthy to require emotional effort to engage it. Anyone who has read Flannery O'Connor's short stories knows what I mean.

The discipline of deep reading is necessary for us to allow the beauty of the written word to penetrate us. It is a way for us to put ourselves in the path of oncoming beauty—in this case, the artistry of exceptional literature—and to permit it to assist us in the transformation of our trauma and shame by revealing the parts of ourselves we have kept hidden in order to protect our hearts. This same discipline—the will-ingness to dwell with hard things—was what Graham and Carmen had to develop rather than throwing away the novel of their marriage. And in order to do that, they each had to learn to sit with what appeared to be the tedium of their individual narratives, fraught as they were with shame they had conveniently buried, but that was in actuality beauty waiting to be revealed in the presence of what they most feared about the relationship. No encounter with beauty guarantees a commensurate response of goodness and beauty, but if a life of beauty is what we seek, then an engagement with beauty in any form will support that effort. Effort is often required on our part to allow the beauty to work its way into our souls, moving as it must to persuade us to open the gates of our left hemisphere's bulwark of defenses, much as Carmen and Graham had to coax theirs to do the same.

Good literature, like all meaningful art, helps us access the beauty of what it means to dwell in the house of the Lord all the days of our lives. It wasn't *The Lord of the Rings* to which I pointed Graham and Carmen. Rather, it was the work of Flannery O'Connor, whose short stories require just as much effort and emotional investment as any life-changing read. As they both delved into her work, their own stories were revealed to them in ways that had been a mystery to them.

But not without their learning how to dwell. How to sit within their respective confessional communities, which were providing the framework and support they needed in order to increasingly discover how to tell their stories more truly.

Dwelling, then, is a fundamental element of participating in a confessional community. All of the people we have met entered their respective groups committing to dwell, only to discover that they had a limited understanding of what that actually implied. We remind our patients that there are usually three phases of the dwelling process in these communities. There is no strict period of time for which any of these phases lasts for each participant, and the boundaries between them are not sharp. But most people would report that the first phase begins with members believing they have joined the group to work on "issues" that exist outside the group (depression, anxiety, marriage, parenting, work, etc.). This is consistent with a way of seeing our lives primarily as diagnoses to be treated. In the first phase patients see the group as something separate from themselves that will enable them to address their "problems" more effectively.

As members of the community dwell for a longer period, they discover what it means for others to pursue them, to be curious about them (much the way Sean was about Charlotte), and for them to learn to do the same. This affords them the opportunity to become more curious about themselves and others regarding what each person senses, images, feels, and thinks and how each is prompted to behave—in order to be seen, soothed, safe, and secure. Increasingly, in this second phase of dwelling, members become consciously aware that they are part of the group and that they share common emotional experiences that enable them to be less alone. But still, at this stage of their development, they understand the primary work of the group to be a means to help them live in their life outside the group in a more integrated fashion. They are in this together but still primarily for the benefit of each person as individuals.

Eventually, members enter the third phase, in which they have dwelt effectively long enough that they begin to realize that this community is not some relationally artificial, synthetic experiment separate from real life. For instance, it began to dawn on Hudson that the community was as much his real life as his family or his work. In fact, he would eventually say that life didn't get any more real than what transpired in the community. Hudson was no longer "attending" the group as a means of helping his "real" life. He embraced that he was part of a group whose mission was to love each other in the community. This mission was not merely that of "practicing" or "pretending" to love each other in a contrived way in order to then "really" love others in the "real world."

In this phase Hudson discovered that he was not just working on his anger with his father or his wife; he was working on his anger with Karen, his embarrassment in response to a comment Dan made, and his feeling protective of Audrey. All were other members of the group, and as they all worked out their anger toward, disappointment with, or attraction to each other, they were necessarily addressing primal dimensions of their fundamental desires to be known and loved, as well as the traumas and griefs surrounding other parts of their lives. In each case, other community members were bearing witness to these interactions.

This cloud of witnesses is the land of the living in which Hudson is learning to dwell, in which he and the others are revealing their deepest desires to be known and loved—and all that that represents. It is a community that is forming those desires into beauty and goodness. For many, this community—this cloud of witnesses—becomes the template on which they model how they "work out [their] salvation with fear and trembling" (Philippians 2:12), be that in their family, school, business, or church.

Ironically, these three phases of development in the confessional community reflect how we posture ourselves in virtually any system we occupy, depending on the level of integration the system represents. For example, our functional involvement in a church fellowship often is a way to be nurtured such that we can live outside in the "real world." Or we find validation and connection with others in our worship communities as we share a common faith journey whose primary purpose is still that of helping us live outside the church walls. But as Jesus said, "By this everyone will know that you are my disciples, if you love one another" (John 13:35).

Loving one another. This requires that we dwell closely and long enough together that we don't just demonstrate how much we like or agree with each other. Rather, we turn each other's worlds upside down in our commitment to be known so deeply by each other that anyone who witnesses it will recognize the presence of Jesus immediately. For indeed, our deep and vulnerable interactions in that community make it a crucible in which we are being formed into the image of our King. This is essentially what happens in the third phase of the work of the confessional community.

However, we often remain limited in the deepening of our spiritual formation; in our worship or work communities we remain embedded in one of the first two phases of development rather than advancing to that which, in its most highly distilled form, is a means for us to grow in loving each other. Who would ever think that joining a police force would primarily be about growing in love for my fellow officers? My fellow line workers at a FedEx distribution center? My colleagues in education at the high school where I teach? This form of life is applicable to any system, any community we occupy, whether our home, school, church, or place of work. Beauty is waiting to be created in every square inch of creation.

We see, then, how crucial it is to dwell in the land of the living in order to be pursued by others who ask where we are and what we want. But our poet psalmist expands and expounds on what that means, elevating its essence to its ultimate manifestation. He states plainly that it is his heart's deepest desire to "dwell in the house of the Lord, all the days of my life."

My imagination wants to interpret his words symbolically. Surely he doesn't mean he literally wants to live in a tabernacle of worship around the clock? How would he play golf? Certainly he's not speaking of finding joy living in a tent. This must be a metaphor for something else. He must really be expressing that he wants the worship of God to be the center of his life, as if he wants what happens in "the house of the Lord"—the worship of Yahweh—to be the center of his dwelling, the gyroscope of his soul. He's not really talking about living in a church building so much as he is longing for what happens in the church to be the "place" where he lives.

That may not be an implausible understanding of the text. But I want to suggest that there is more, and it is the incarnation and all the fullness thereof that reveals what that "more" can be. Again, regarding our imaginations, from the grounding perspective of the biblical narrative I want to invite us to connect some historical dots. For the Hebrew, at the time of the writing of the psalm, "the house of the Lord" would likely have referred to the tabernacle, or "the tent of meeting," located at Shiloh for much of Israel's history before the construction of Solomon's temple in Jerusalem. At that point God's presence was understood to dwell in the Jerusalem temple until his departure recorded in Ezekiel 10. The Second Temple Period (586 BCE to 70 CE) saw the reconstruction of Solomon's temple, which was destroyed by the Babylonians in 586 BCE, culminating in the work of Herod the Great in 37 BCE. This was the structure Jesus entered saying, "Destroy this temple, and I will raise it again in three days" (John 2:19). Here Jesus is again, without apology, expanding people's imaginations.

After two thousand years of history, we get it. Jesus is saying *he* is the temple. But the fact that we so easily "get it" reflects how we actually don't get it. If we did, we would likely be as confused as the people who first heard him say it. In this statement, Jesus is directing people's attention away from a "what" (the house of the Lord as a tent or a temple) to a "who." In this way he is drawing their attunement to a right-brain encounter "with" someone in the present moment as opposed to a left-brain encounter with a nonliving structure whose rules of engagement are clear. I know where I'm supposed to go and what I'm supposed to do in the tent or the temple. There are clean lines and comprehensible, uncomplicated tasks. There is beauty that I can count on, beauty that will be the same when I come next year to bring my sacrifice. There won't be any of this nonsense of the temple actually speaking with me. Because if it does, then maybe it will begin to ask questions like, "Where are you?" and "What do you want?" And I would have to answer.

In essence, we see the progression from tabernacle to temple to Jesus. But it doesn't end there. During the last third of John's Gospel, Jesus begins to expand people's imaginations even further, coaxing their attention to include even more than their current understanding of him. He speaks of how he will dwell with each of them in the presence and power of the Holy Spirit, whose arrival he commands his followers to wait on. Remember, for some of you, this may all feel familiar—so familiar, in fact, that as you read this you feel nothing salient at all (which should be a warning sign in and of itself). But to those who were hearing it for the first time, it was likely making little to no sense. It was disrupting their mental models, imaginations and windows of tolerance that were still too flimsy. Their wineskins were not yet resilient enough to receive the beauty that was soon to be upon them. Perhaps this was why Jesus told them to wait and pray. They had to get ready for what was coming.

With the movement of the Holy Spirit at Pentecost, we get the next iteration of what the psalmist was referring to when it comes to dwelling in the house of the Lord all the days of his life. For if Jesus is the Temple, and he now dwells within us in the presence of the Holy Spirit, to dwell in the house of the Lord is to live intimately in the presence of other God-followers. As it turns out, *we* are the house of the Lord, something that at Pentecost would have fully upended the disciples' notion of the temple, not least because it would eventually include Gentiles as well. St. Paul picks up this theme in 1 Corinthians where he writes of how Jesus' followers are the body of Christ, each being an indispensable part (1 Corinthians 12:12). Jesus' body is the temple (John 2), and we are Jesus' body. Hence, we are the temple in which we are to dwell. Paul further reflects on this notion in Ephesians when he claims, "In him the whole building is joined together and rises to become a holy temple in the Lord. And in him you too are being built together to become a dwelling in which God lives by his Spirit" (Ephesians 2:21-22).

This progression from tabernacle to temple to Jesus to us reaches its zenith when, in the Revelation of John, we read these words from Jesus: "I am coming soon. Hold on to what you have, so that no one will take your crown. The one who is victorious I will make a pillar in the temple of my God. Never again will they leave it. I will write on them the name of my God and the name of the city of my God, the new Jerusalem, which is coming down out of heaven from my God; and I will also write on them my new name" (Revelation 3:11-12).

What I want to invite you to imagine—and what each member of a confessional community must imagine as well—is the movement within the biblical imagery: tabernacle → temple → Jesus → Holy Spirit → us as Jesus' body → each of us as a pillar of beauty in the temple in the city of God. We move from encountering the beauty of something outside of us (the tabernacle and temple), to the beauty of the person of Jesus and our interaction with him, to the beauty that we ourselves become, first as members of Jesus' body and then as the very structural supports within the holy city.

What does this have to do with the disintegration that Aaron, Tara, Hudson, or any of the others were facing? When Tara first began to work in the group, she would frequently remain silent until someone else "came to find her," as it were. Eventually she was able to reveal how anxious she had been about saying anything at all. She had done meaningful, hard work in individual psychotherapy to address much of her history of trauma. But despite the healing and confidence she had developed in that effort, upon being exposed to seven people she didn't know, the prospect of revealing her story felt overwhelming, and old feelings of shame and panic returned.

Later she would report how "amazed" she was at the ease with which other group members shared with each other the most difficult, painful, and shaming parts of their narratives. Initially, it was as if she were watching "an utterly beautiful dance" (her words) emerging before her very eyes—but one she was too uncomfortable to join. This is not unlike what it means to dwell in a tabernacle or temple. You "occupy" the space of beauty, you witness it as others participate in it, but it initially feels overwhelming. One certainly wants to live an integrated life, and Tara had discovered what it meant to come closer to that in her individual therapy work. But to "dwell in the house of the Lord" meant the beauty she witnessed in the relationships among the others in the group required that she join it, that she become part of it. As fearful as she was to take her first tentative steps of vulnerable revelation to the other members, they were even more eager for her to do so. They didn't want her to miss out on any part of what it meant to be loved in the way they had been coming to love each other.

In this way, the community gently but insistently coaxed Tara to move from dwelling in the house of the Lord as if she were separate from it to becoming part of the house of the Lord in which God and all the other members were also dwelling. She learned, in a deeply felt, right-hemispherically mediated fashion, how to move from tabernacle to temple to Jesus to Pentecost. After being part of the group for about nine months she reported, "I never knew what it meant to be known until I was known in this community. And now, I take everyone in this room with me everywhere I go." Which, of course, is the point. We Christians assert that "the earth will be filled with the knowledge of the glory of the Lord as the waters cover the sea" (Habakkuk 2:14). It is not too much to say that God's "glory" is the very wellspring of all beauty that exists in any fashion, not least the beauty Tara saw in the group as people came to know healing and recommissioning in an embodied fashion. It is this beauty, this glory of which Jesus speaks in John's Gospel, that, as Lesslie Newbigin reminds us, is the glory of the love between the Father and the Son (John 17:1). It is the glory of the Son hearing his Father's voice telling him how much he loves and is pleased with him and of the Son loving his Father by trusting him even when the evidence would suggest strongly that he do otherwise.[8] It is the glory, the love that is made manifest in the room of participants when they are dwelling long enough to behold each other's beauty, not least in those parts of their stories that each would say they hate the most.

When a toddler who is securely attached goes off to preschool, she takes her mother and father with her—not that they physically accompany her into the classroom, but she takes them with her in her mind. She of course is not aware of this; at this developmental stage, this takes place implicitly and nonconsciously. She does not think to her three-year-old self, "Don't forget to take Mom and Dad with you in your mind today." But this is essentially what she does, and this is what attachment is all about. She forms sensed, imaged, felt, thought, and embodied responses of awareness of the presence of her parents and their love for her in her mind, and she forms an awareness of *her* being in *their* minds as well, carrying her with them wherever they go. In this way our toddler is mimicking what the writer of another psalm is referring to when he asks,

"Where can I go from your Spirit? / Where can I flee from your presence?" (Psalm 139:7). Our securely attached toddler simply assumes this is so. And it is crucial that we pause to recognize this: unless and until we have had the sensed, imaged, felt, and embodied encounter of secure attachment, it will be virtually impossible for us to appropriate in our lives the reality of the words of this psalm. It will not happen just because someone tells us to "believe" them.

Likewise, the participants in our confessional communities enter into the same process our toddler does, with an important difference. Our toddler is securely attached. Many of our patients are stepping onto the path of co-creating secure attachment in a community of people for the first time, bringing with them the remnant memories of insecure attachment that still await renewal. Some have already begun that process in the context of their individual psychotherapy work or in spiritual direction or with a wise mentor. But expanding that attachment process in the context of a community places substantial demands on one's interpersonal neurobiological architecture, and at the same time it requires the actively engaged presence of that very community. This is not an easy task as the members are widening their windows of tolerance, integrating the nine functions of their middle prefrontal cortices, and strengthening their social engagement systems. All of these mental functions work in concert to move them toward earned secure attachment.[9]

For Aaron, Carmen and Graham, Tara, Hudson, and Charlotte, the persevering work of dwelling led each of them on a journey of transformation from the first through the third stage of development in the life of the community, as described earlier. This progression corresponds to the maturation of their imaginations as well, with each member gradually strengthening their ability to hold the others in their minds—as our toddler holds her parents—while also sensing that the community holds them in its collective mind as well. As this becomes an increasingly accessible state of mind for each patient—"I am holding the group in my mind, and they are holding me in theirs"—it takes on a particular sense of permanence and continuity that reflects what it means to dwell in the house of the Lord "all the days of my life." The "house of the Lord" goes with you everywhere your life takes you in the same way that our toddler's parents go with her everywhere she goes.

In this way, the body of Christ no longer remains an abstract theological motif, nor is it simply a metaphor for those whom we attend church with or who are part of our small group Bible study. It literally becomes something, interpersonally and neurobiologically, in which we dwell and that dwells within us, providing ballast, confidence, and joy even in the most challenging parts of our story. With the deep dwelling in which members of the confessional communities participate, much of the biblical narrative moves out of the recesses of their brains' left hemispheres into their right brains, taking up residence in the nooks and crannies where before only their shame lived.

All of this, like a beautiful Dickens novel, unfolds over time, weaving together those threads of their stories they once were convinced represented only trauma and disintegration but now, standing as they are on the ancient paths, they see as the very place where the good way lies.

GAZE

To gaze on the beauty of the L ORD.

P SALM 27:4

"I'M HAVING A REALLY HARD TIME SAYING THIS."

Brendan had been a member of one of our confessional communities from its inception. Now, more than a year into the formation of that group, he had grown in his capacity to hold the stories of others as well as his own—to dwell with them. He had on many occasions spoken with compassion, not least into the narratives of some of the women in his community whose interactions with men had too often been harsh, condescending, or sexually exploitative, and those women noticed and their stories were changed—made more beautiful—because of him. He had also received the mercy of the kindness of the eye contact and tone of voice of the other members, the messengers of God, sent to deliver him from crippling elements of shame that he had long carried.

But Brendan was now standing on a precipice, about to reveal something he had held in secret from the community up until this moment. He fumbled with his hands as he paused, trying to find the courage and the words. Sarah, another member, said softly, "Take your time. We're not going anywhere."

"That's the thing, right? I'm actually a little worried that you will go somewhere when you hear what I have to tell you."

His angst was physically palpable, and the tension in the room was thickening by the second. But being as this was the "house of the Lord," the room waited.

Haltingly, he began. "Eight years ago . . . Man! I don't know why . . . no, that's not true. I do know why . . . I'm having such a hard time with this . . . okay. Eight years ago, I fathered a child, a daughter. I was making business trips to Europe pretty frequently, and I had an affair that lasted about six months. I eventually told my wife, and we began a painful process of reconciliation that has led to healing. But about a year after I broke off the affair, and after my wife and I had started marriage therapy, I got an email from the woman . . . and she told me she had become pregnant with my child and had the baby. But she didn't want to reconnect with me, nor did she want the child to have anything to do with me.

"My wife and I discussed it at length and agreed that I should follow up on it, but the woman has never returned any of my emails. I had met the woman in one country, but she lived in another, and I have no idea where either she or the child is. It's like this blight that I carry around that always reminds me of a choice I made that I regret and that I just can't seem to escape. . . . I know how much harm men have done to some of the women in the group—to you, Jill, and you, Sarah. And I'm really ashamed of what I did. I worry you'll think I'm that guy who's just like all the men who have mistreated you.

"So, there you have it." He finished with a sigh, like someone bracing for impact.

The group sat in silence for probably thirty seconds, holding the moment. For Brendan the silence felt like a lead curtain. It was Sarah who came to his aid. Sarah, whose husband had also had an affair that ended in divorce when he would not pursue reconciliation, leaving her and their three children for a life on the West Coast. Tearfully Sarah spoke of her gratitude for Brendan's transparency and acknowledged his seemingly genuine remorse. Then she named the palpable shame he was displaying in the presence of his cloud of witnesses, stating that she did not want him to remain there. She wanted him to look at her—which he found excruciatingly difficult to do—and be free of it.

But she also confessed that his words evoked in her ancient, sharp feelings of betrayal, shame, and despair as images from the story of her own husband's perfidy began to rush into her consciousness. Along with her desire for Brendan to be unburdened from his shame, she also sensed anger welling up quickly within her. Anger at Brendan, anger at her ex-husband. Anger at so many men who had betrayed so many women and children, including other women in the group. I witnessed Brendan's nonverbal responses to Sarah's words, one phrase at a time: initially the first hints of relief, then the secondary wave of distress as she named the painful emotion his story was evoking in her. Nonetheless, she restated what she most wanted him to hear from her—love in the face of his and her pain.

Not surprisingly, the rest of the community members were beginning to feel and express a range of feelings, connecting those emotions to Brendan's, Sarah's, and their own individual stories. Men and women alike found themselves overwhelmed by multiple layers of emotion, mostly finding it challenging to contain it all. One woman, Gwen, began to quietly sob. Another man, Tom, first expressed gratitude to Brendan for sharing such a vulnerable part of his narrative, but one could tell, given his cool tone of voice, that more was coming. Tom went on to describe how furious he was upon hearing this news, realizing that as he himself had not been a paragon of virtue in his own life, he still wanted to know there were other men he could trust to model for him what it meant to create beauty in the world. He had thought Brendan was one of those men, and now Tom felt the ground moving under his feet. He wanted to believe he could trust Brendan, but at the moment his own anger and fear were very much getting in the way of that.

This community, which had over many months become a dwelling place, a house of God for those who came week after week, was feeling for the first time less stable, less predictable, as the most tender parts of each member's stories were revealed and as they each felt tempted to mobilize their defensive postures. One could almost see the doors closing and the windows being shuttered. If this was true of Brendan, who else was hiding things that could mar the beauty of what the community was building? What else would happen to undermine the trust and confidence everyone had worked so hard and for so long to co-create? How were they supposed to navigate being present with this level of pain and brokenness in the very location that was intended to be one of comfort and confidence? Where was beauty to be found in the middle of all this? Who in their right mind would sign up to be in the space where this community's members found themselves the day of Brendan's revelation? Who would want to touch the third rail like that?

As it turns out, it is in these very moments that the biblical narrative turns everything on its head.

■ ■ ■

In May and June of 1992, the cellist Vedran Smailovic played Albinoni's Adagio in G Minor in the ruins of Sarajevo for twenty-two days uninterrupted after a mortar shelling killed twenty-two people in a market in the besieged city. He played in the crosshairs of snipers and artillery gunners amid the rubble of his town. When all around him tragedy and affliction were the only daily story—with no end in sight—his response was to create and offer beauty. Not anxiety. Not fury or revenge. And not despair. Beauty. And the beauty he offered changed everything.

I don't mean it stopped the shelling. The siege would continue for nearly four more years, and many more would lose their lives. One could argue that nothing changed at all. But what Smailovic's commitment to beauty did was change the direction and trajectory of people's attention and action. And this is what it did for Brendan, Sarah, and Tom. And it is what it will do for us.

Our desire for and encounter with beauty could be described in terms of wonder, welcome, and worship. When asked to imagine beauty, our minds turn to Yosemite's Half Dome, the Chartres Cathedral, Dvorak's *Symphony No. 9 in E minor*, Henry Tanner's *Annunciation*, or the Trek Domane SL6 road bike (even if you're not a cyclist, you will immediately want to become one when you see this bicycle). We would approach any of these with eager anticipation and an uptick in heart rate. We would view, listen, or ride paying full attention to the beauty we are encountering. All else would fade away as we were swept up in the moment, compelled and captivated by what we were sensing and perceiving. And we would want the moment to travel into the next and the next.

The beauty embodied in all of these examples implores us, in a word, to gaze. We don't glance at beauty. We gaze at it. It captures our attention and holds it. We catch our breath—and breathe again—and then ponder. And here, to gaze upon beauty refers not only to our visual senses but to all the ways we sense the world. For indeed we are able to engage the world only as we first sense it in a kaleidoscope of ways.[1] We listen to beauty in the drumming of the pileated woodpecker. We taste it in the black raspberry pie (and believe you me, my wife's is the best). We touch it in a cashmere sweater. We smell it in the scent of a lilac. Beauty reveals itself to us of its own free will; we do not demand that it do so, for if we did, the very essence of the beauty would be diminished. We are not its owner but rather the recipient of a gift we do not deserve.

To be aware of beauty in this way compels us to gaze. In this posture we do not leer, gawk, ogle, or glare at beauty. To do so reflects disintegrated and disintegrating responses that emerge out of shame, responses that are clutching, hoarding, fearful, condemning, consumptive, and, ultimately, violent. The shame that ignites these responses to beauty is itself the nidus of all sexual lust, abuse, and violence. A man can be aroused by the presence of a woman; that arousal can take less than three seconds to mobilize. The question is what he does then: Does he gaze, or does he commit violence?

To gaze on an object of beauty is to be present and look upon it on its terms, not on our own. We allow beauty to enrapture us and carry us to peaks and troughs of what it means for us to be human. We long to linger with it, to remain with it as long as it will remain with us (hence our yearning to stop the clock on that spectacular sunset), sensing ourselves being mysteriously transformed by it. In fact, if asked to imagine beauty in any fashion, we would likely expect to gaze upon it, nonconsciously anticipating doing so. It is not difficult to see, then, how our poet of Psalm 27 expresses his longing to gaze upon God's beauty, beauty that is an expression of God's very essence, an essence from which all other imagined notions of beauty emerge.[2] Beauty that would swallow us up, that we might become that upon which we gaze.

Moreover, if we are the dwelling place of God, if we are the body and face of Jesus, then, by extension, we reflect the very beauty of God upon which we gaze. We must work to imagine how, just as our poet longed to gaze upon God's beauty in the tabernacle, we do the same in the progression from tabernacle to temple to the body of Jesus to pillars in the temple of our God in the new heaven and new earth. And we encounter that very beauty of God no more powerfully than by gazing upon each other. I am not equating us with God in some pantheistic sleight of hand. Rather, I am inviting us to imagine how, being sisters and brothers created by the Holy Trinity in the love of our Father, rescued by our older Brother the King, and nurtured and empowered by the Spirit as we dwell together, we see the resemblance of our Father in each other's faces, hear our Brother's delight in each other's laughter, and revel in the Spirit's joyful transformation of us as individuals and as a community in each other's stories of new creation. In this way, as we gaze upon each other, we gaze upon God's beauty.

But we don't go looking for beauty in a war zone. We play the cello in a concert hall, not the rubble that remains in the wake of a mortar shelling. It would not ever occur to us to search for beauty in a minefield; no one would enter such terrain expecting to discover, embrace, and be transformed by beauty. How would it be possible? We would be too distracted by the fear of the obvious danger. Moreover, it would be sheer lunacy to consider that same minefield as a construction site for an outpost of beauty. No one knowingly walks into the ruins of one's dwelling place and the crosshairs of sniper fire with the expressed purpose and expectation of creating beauty and putting it on display. But as it turns out, this is exactly what God has done in the incarnation. And whether he knew it or not, the incarnation is what Smailovic was echoing in Sarajevo. And this is what was taking place in the confessional community when Brendan revealed what he did.

The beauty of a giant sequoia or Wendell Berry's poem "The Peace of Wild Things" is self-evident. Not so much Brendan's story—or the emotion it evoked in the room. It is not the sort of thing we would long to gaze upon as we would the Milky Way, its luminosity traveling light years to find us in the night sky. It is here, once again, that I invite you to do the work of stretching your imagination and widening your window of tolerance. It is hard enough for us, as it was for Brendan, to look at our own shame, let alone invite others to look at it in our presence. It can be so repulsive that we don't even want to consider it, let alone look at it, moreover gaze at it. Gaze at Van Gogh's *Wheatfield with Crows*? Yes. At Brendan's or Sarah's or Tom's anguish? Hardly. At our history of sexual abuse? Addiction? Racism? Shaming self-accusation? We practice avoiding these at all costs.

It's risky enough to reveal our own shame in a community. But we also carry an additional fear that Brendan was now realizing. It is one thing for me to endure the moment in which I see you seeing my humiliation; it is quite another when the awareness immediately dawns on me of how my shameful action is also wounding and shaming another, activating painful implicit and explicit memories of their own narrative. Brendan had at one time potently offered empathy to Sarah when she told of her husband's infidelity. Now, in the moment that he admitted his own affair, he sensed, ever so subtly, that he was adding to her sorrow, shaking her confidence not only in men but in a good and beautiful God.

How on earth would one imagine beauty emerging out of this minefield? How could one possibly pick up one's cello and offer such vulnerable beauty in the rubble of one's place of dwelling, in full view of sniper and mortar fire? But again, this is exactly what this community was doing. To enter into and become this confessional community, the members are ultimately, intentionally (however consciously aware of it they are) inviting others to gaze upon their shame, fear, and affliction.

Each is asking the others to look upon them and keep them in their sight-lines. And in the very gazing, what once was horrific, grotesque, and hideous is transformed into beauty.

The transformational power of gazing and being gazed upon with intention and love in the very presence of our hideousness becomes the solid ground on which the community stands, creating beauty in the middle of bomb craters. This requires perseverance and dwelling of the nature I have described, both of which enable enlargement of the members' imaginations and widening of their windows of tolerance. It was with this hard-fought and hard-won embodied confidence that, even in the turmoil of the rupture that emerged as Brendan made his confession, the group as a whole, with help from my colleague and me, drew upon their memories of having been loved deeply by each other. They each remembered what it had been like to experience moments in which their shame dissolved in the facial expressions, tone of voice, and body language of kindness that flooded over them. As a group, the community gathered itself, with various people telling Brendan, Sarah, and Tom (along with Gwen, who was still sobbing) that no one was leaving the room. Telling each other that as hard as this moment was, they were still going to look upon each other and breathe. Gaze upon each other's torment while quieting their own brainstem activity that was screaming at them to run out of the room in a fight-or-flight moment.

How were they able to do this? What was going on that enabled the community to remain, continuing to dwell, continuing to gaze even in the harsh light of the shame of new revelation and old wounds?

■ ■ ■

Beauty and goodness emerge only in the presence of God, regardless of our awareness of it. No beauty or goodness ever materializes apart from the vitalizing work of the Spirit. This is the story we repeatedly tell in the confessional communities, reminding each other that if anything good or beautiful is happening, God is in the room and on the loose. We must not only be aware of the mechanics of the mind and apply them to its healing but also integrate the biblical narrative that undergirds those very mechanics and leads to the creation of beauty, not least in the setting of trauma and shame. This Christian anthropology and IPNB are what provide guidance for Brendan, Sarah, Tom, and the others to discover that there is no greater beauty we create than that formed out of the parts of us that lie crushed under the rubble of our artillery-shelled lives. It is to IPNB and the biblical narrative that we turn, then, in our exploration of confessional community so that we might extend that experience to the systems we occupy as humans in order to bear the image of our Creator in the world.

THE GAZE OF INTEGRATION

Psychotherapy provides a setting in which shame is deconstructed through and in the presence of a properly boundaried, empathic relationship and in which movement toward secure attachment is initiated and sustained. As we've seen, patients often try to outflank the therapist in their attempt to avoid what the therapist is actually trying to discover. This is usually an implicitly remembered reaction that the patient mobilizes to remain camouflaged, to protect against the feeling of shame inherent with the fear of being seen in their brokenness, not unlike Adam and Eve hiding from God as he asks where they are.

But in the context of a community, given the sheer number of minds in the room paying attention to the stories being told, it is far more difficult to hide. Shame cannot as easily fade into the woodwork. With more people looking for us, we will more likely be found, sometimes when we want to be and sometimes when we very much would rather remain invisible.

Moreover, the payload of shame we each carry is great enough that it requires a countermanding force, one that can both absorb the shame and push back against it with a story of renewal. I would have little trouble stopping a toy wagon that was moving toward me at a velocity of two miles an hour. But a train moving at the same speed would pancake me. It is not the speed but the mass of the train that makes it unstoppable.

The same is true of our shame. It has the emotional mass effect of a
locomotive, not a toy wagon. As such, we need more mass working on
our behalf to move our shame in a different direction. This is what
being in a community provides for our brains. And it is the gazing and
all that it represents that provides the mechanics for this process. It is
virtually impossible for any of us to look upon our own shame with
compassion. We need someone else to gaze upon it empathically. But
to stop a train, no matter how slowly it is moving, we need multiple sets
of eyes gazing upon it, and we need that gaze for extended periods of
time to provide the mass effect of healing.

Gazing is an integrating process. Shame disintegrates the mind and
relationships and overwhelms our window of tolerance, yanking us out
of our social engagement system (with which we effectively co-regulate
difficult emotions) and into our sympathetic nervous system, with its
fight-or-flight options at the ready, or further, into our dorsal vagal
nervous system, shutting down our ability to connect completely and
leaving us to wander alone in the dark. In like fashion, shame discon-
nects our middle prefrontal cortex from our brainstem and limbic circuitry, rendering us to live more like lower mammals or reptiles that find
themselves under threat.

Gazing, on the other hand, integrates our mind. Being seen, soothed,
safe, and secure in the presence of our shame and trauma gives us the
opportunity to literally sense, image, feel, and think and our bodies the
chance to behave in a completely different way in response to the shame
we have carried for so long. The willingness of the community to dwell
with each other as a means of gazing—not least upon that which we find
repulsive, as did Brendan—enables Brendan's, Sarah's, and Tom's middle
prefrontal cortices to move to a place of integration, a state of connection
between the anterior cingulate gyrus and the brainstem and limbic circuitry. It leads to the capacity of each to experience greater connection
between their right hemisphere and their body, enabling greater physical
composure, and it connects the right and left hemispheres more helpfully, with each person able to cognitively reflect on what they are sensing

in their bodies. The nine functions of the middle prefrontal cortex are strengthened and fortified—they become integrated.

Our challenge is that our experience of shame can be so great that we need the heft, if you will, of an entire community to speak, both verbally and nonverbally, to our shame. It is the physical presence of many people in the room that provides the ballast for shame to be healed. This requires perseverance (Have I mentioned this?). Especially when shame is trying to commandeer multiple members of the group at the same time, as it was attempting to do in the wake of Brendan's announcement. My colleague and I reminded the group of the importance of pausing long enough to name, even in the face of evil's attempt to co-opt the moment, what they were feeling and where in their bodies they felt it. We invited them to literally breathe into those parts of their bodies that felt tense or felt like fleeing or fighting and to picture in their minds their awareness of the voices and faces of those in the room who loved them and wanted them to be there.

Only then did I ask Brendan, "What do you want—for Sarah?"

I did not initially ask him what he wanted for himself but for her—for the one he was sure he had wounded. And he was able, through tears, to say to her directly, "Sarah, I'm so sorry for how what I did has hurt you too. I have no excuse. But I don't want to grovel—I'm not getting the impression you want me to do that. I want you to be safe and confident. I want you to be whole and joyful. I want you to be treated right by men. And I want to be one of the men who does that. And I would love for you to let me do that. Let me be that. I know you may not be able to, given what I've just said; I don't know. But that's what I want. For you. For both of us."

Gwen, the woman who had been sobbing, stopped. Everyone noticed. And waited. And now they gazed at her. She slowly looked up and around at everyone, then said directly to Brendan, "I have never heard a man apologize for much of anything, let alone for this. I can't speak for Sarah, but I want you to know that what you just did has been healing for me."

Gwen went on to talk briefly of her father's dismissive harshness, of which the community was already familiar. A hallmark of this was that he had never apologized for any of the times when he had hurt Gwen or her siblings, had never taken responsibility for his actions. What Gwen witnessed in Brendan's actions literally initiated new neural network activity—new creation—in her brain. This new creation was made possible explicitly because people were willing to gaze at each other's trauma and affliction. It was one thing for Gwen to have experienced empathy from her therapist, the one she claimed was "paid to pay attention to me." It was quite another to be caught off guard in an act of healing she didn't see coming while watching her peers repair a rupture of their own. This is the power of the body of Christ embodied, literally, in men and women who are committed to telling their stories more truly.

Essentially, what the members of this community were doing in telling their stories more truly was loving each other. They were vulnerably taking risks of revealing and giving parts of themselves to others without guarantee they would be received. But they were received, and beauty filled the room. As Jeremy Begbie reflects, "If beauty is to be ascribed primordially to the triune God, and the life of God is constituted by the dynamism of outgoing love, then primordial beauty is the beauty of this ecstatic love for the other. God's beauty is not static structure but the dynamism of love."[3] As the members of the group love one another in this sacrificial way, their collective community bears God's image and thus, like him, is beauty in the way Begbie describes.

GOOD FRIDAY, EASTER, AND THE BEAUTY OF A CRUCIFIED LORD

When we gaze upon the beauty of the Lord in a confessional community, we do so in light of the precedent that has been set in the biblical narrative. We call Good Friday "good" because of Easter—because of what happened after that particular Friday in history. Apart from the Easter resurrection, there would be no Good Friday. If not for the empty tomb, it would have been just one more forgettable Friday in which a forgettable person was crucified—and we would know nothing about it. We likely would be far less aware that such a thing as crucifixion even existed; to the degree that we were, we would likely understand it only to be a horrible method of torture and execution.[4] We certainly wouldn't wear crosses as jewelry or as symbols that say to the world that death, in the end, is not the end. Given what we do know it to be like, we would hardly be expected to think about it, let alone ponder it, let alone gaze upon it. Who would do that on purpose?

The Romans intended crucifixion not only as a means of killing someone but of maximally humiliating the victim, along with the entire society in which it took place.[5] It was intended as a knockout punch to beauty. What could be uglier than for the religious, political, and social structures—whose very institutional existences are intended to make possible the creation and stewardship of beauty and goodness in the world— to converge to torturously execute an innocent man, a man who had himself been only a conduit of beauty over the course of his life? Instead of curating beauty, they moved to destroy it in an act of horror, one that was seemingly equal and opposite to the beauty it attempted to devour.

But Easter changes what is grotesque about a Roman crucifixion. In light of the resurrection, we no longer see the crucifixion as a symbol of all that is awful. Instead, paradoxically, we see it as the gateway to life. For we do not look on it on evil's terms. We look on it on God's terms. To gaze on a crucifixion for its own sake and apart from resurrection would be macabre. But we do so through the lens of Easter. In this way, resurrection gives us a hope not only about our future but also about our past. This is crucial when it comes to the notion of what it means to gaze upon the beauty of the Lord and thereby, in essence, to gaze upon our own trauma, shame, and the disintegrated minds that result. Here it is not too much to say that, in light of the resurrection, there is nothing more beautiful than a crucified Lord.

However, it is not enough to merely articulate this as a rational, abstract, theological expression about the nature of the world. Interpersonally and neurobiologically speaking, we begin with experience, with how the brain works: bottom to top and right to left. Theology and anthropology shape and inform that very experience. They are necessary as guides when our sensing brain is confused by other elements of our story in which shame and fear have grabbed the talking stick. But unless we sense theology in our physical experience, it has not yet been made fully real to us.

This is why beauty is so critical to healing. Beauty is God's presence being sensed, and until that is the case, God is only ever an abstraction devoid of any power to transform my life. Which is why the stories of the Gospels are so important. Not just because they teach theology (which they do) but because they model for us ways to sense, image, and feel the beauty of the gospel as well as think about its truth in just the order in which our minds are made to receive it—bottom to top (spinal cord → brainstem → limbic circuitry → prefrontal cortex), then right brain to left brain. Gazing, as a function of sensing, precedes thinking.

In John's Gospel, we are drawn into intimate contact with gazing upon Jesus at his crucifixion when we read of those who remained with him at the cross (John 19:24-27, 37). The text indicates that they continued to look upon him and he on them—can you imagine?—over the course of at least six hours. How many of us would want someone to remain with our nakedness and shame in that way and for that long? But look upon him they did. And even in his pathos, Jesus was attuned to his mother's grief. He introduced her and the disciple he loved to each other in a new mother-son relationship. Again, even in the middle of a brutal execution, new creation is dawning as Jesus looks beyond his death to a future in which he is resurrected and ascended—but in which Mary will still require protection in the absence of his physical presence. All of this required that those at the cross pay attention, remaining where brutality was taking place before their very eyes.

Later, Nicodemus and Joseph of Arimathea would care for Jesus' body, which required intimate contact with his wounds, all while experiencing deep grief (John 19:38-42). It appears that, although handling a corpse was not their day job, they did not hesitate to take on the task of being present with Jesus in this way. They, too, were required to gaze upon the work before them as they wrapped his body in linens and spices.

Easter enables us to encounter these stories with hope rather than despair; however, we are drawn into them also because the anguish we find there we find in ourselves. We are called to the creation of beauty, but this often requires Herculean effort on the part of our imaginations because of what we witness in our world and in ourselves. The members of the confessional community believe in resurrection, but at the same time they have to contend with adultery and abuse and addiction—and being hurt by others across the room who were ostensibly there to be their friends.

Apart from the resurrection, we have no sustainable answer for our anguish and are thereby more likely to keep it buried where it festers and eventually emerges in the form of an infinite array of psychiatric conditions, the expression of disintegrated interpersonal neurobiological states. Easter is a message of the creation of beauty in the very face of crucifixion. The hopeful beauty Sarah had been creating out of the pain of her broken marriage (and in no small part because of the empathy Brendan had offered her over many months) was at risk when Brendan made his confession. But the work they and others together had done up to that time in healing the trauma of many of their stories provided a buffer for the rupture of Brendan's admission. It sustained not only Sarah and Brendan but others, including Gwen, who was able to support Brendan in the middle of his own shame while others did the same for Sarah. The healing the community experienced was new creation. It was beauty that emerged in the face of brokenness.

The patients in our groups gaze upon each other's wounds not on shame's terms but on the terms of the Holy Trinity. They look upon each other's trauma with the intention and anticipation of creating beauty out of the very thing that was meant for affliction. We enter into the rubble of a bomb crater with our cellos and begin to play. We do so not in the absence of fear but in the face of it. And we do so because we are imagining the presence of the Holy Spirit being in the room orchestrating the entire symphony. Who would have imagined that Brendan's shame, Sarah's trauma, and Gwen's history of emotional barrenness and scorn would become the very places where beauty would emerge in the presence of witnesses who actively supported the process?

ART: FACILITATING THE CREATION OF BEAUTY IN THE PRESENCE OF TRAUMA AND GRIEF

Our imaginations can be more fully drawn to the implication of what it means to find beauty in trauma if we spend time gazing upon artistic expressions that speak not only to our agony but also the beauty that emerges from it. Gazing upon beauty requires practice; practice, then, enables us to be more aware that we are seeing beauty when we do. For this reason, we encourage people to use art to heighten their ability to notice beauty in places and moments that before would have escaped them. I now want to draw our attention to three such works as examples of how putting ourselves in the path of oncoming beauty expands our ability to look for and see the possibility for beauty to emerge in the places we would least expect it to do so.

The first is *Crucifixion* by Georges Rouault (for this and other works described in this section, I invite you to find a representation online and refer to it in connection with our discussion). Rouault was one of the most important artists of the twentieth century, a painter who, as a Christian, worked out the grappling of his inner life through his art, pressed as it was between the world and the kingdom of heaven.[6] It surprises, then draws us in. It bids us dwell and gaze and allow all that emerges within us emotionally to come forth. It is expressionistic and thereby does not allow us to dismiss it too quickly, as if we know what it's all about, just as the crucifixion itself, should we allow it to hold our gaze, catches us off guard—what god would grant us the freedom to torture him to death on the way to creating a new and beautiful world? Like the crucifixion, Rouault's work takes us to places in our own hearts that we often dare not go, much like what happens in the context of our confessional communities.

Another artistic work is the great hymn "O Sacred Head, Now Wounded." It originated from a medieval Latin poem, *Salve mundi salutare*, whose verses direct attention to numerous parts of Christ's body during the crucifixion.[7] The hymn itself represents the last stanzas of the poem, focusing on and drawing our attention to Jesus' head. Listening meditatively, or singing this together with others, opens our imaginations—our capacity to image—to gaze upon the beauty emerging in the very presence of Jesus' suffering. The music and words together evoke within us an awareness not only of Jesus' affliction but of our own as well. By putting ourselves in the path of the oncoming beauty of this hymn, we open ourselves to the possibility of transformation; as we are immersed in the hymn's beauty, it draws forth the emotional states related to our stories, both the joys and sorrows, desires and griefs. When we do this in the company of others, as happens in our confessional communities, we speak of what the music evokes and in so doing are enabled to gaze at each other's trauma and shame but always in the light of the wonder and welcome of the community, which leads on to worship.

Lastly, I invite you to consider the *Pietà*, Michelangelo's sculpture depicting Mary, the mother of Jesus, holding the body of her Son after the crucifixion. To see it in person is to be held rapturously, even as Mary holds Jesus. We gaze upon it and remain captivated. If we allow it, our attention will be gripped by the sheer magnitude and depth of what is before us—remembering that we must dwell with it long enough to actually gaze upon it rather than glance at it. The splendor of the sculpture merges with the agony of the story it tells. The story and the marble are told and seen through the prism of Easter, which calls to the grief of our own narrative, making hope possible because it is being pulled out through and into beauty. When trauma and the shame that energizes it are exposed to beauty that is unwilling to be moved (as manifested in the sheer weight of the *Pietà*—6,700 pounds), healing commences. As fragile as Smailovic and his cello were, they filled the empty, war-torn space in Sarajevo with a beauty whose density resiliently withstood the violence of mortar rounds.

A confessional community that perseveres in dwelling together enables its members to gaze upon each another's shame and, through the lens of Easter, first imagine and then see the emergence of beauty. In so doing, the community bears witness to atonement: to God's *at-one-ment* (the Old English phrase from which we acquire the word) with human-kind, not least in the depths of our trauma. What the group accomplishes is exactly what Yahweh, speaking to the people of Jerusalem through the prophet Ezekiel, declared was required: that the people would neces-sarily have to "be ashamed and bear your disgrace" (Ezekiel 16:52) as part of their redemption. They would, in other words, need to look upon, to grapple directly with the shame of their behavior so as to ultimately ex-perience what it meant for their shame to be absolved and made pow-erless over them (see Ezekiel 16:35-58). Likewise, during the exodus, upon sustaining lethal attacks from venomous snakes as a result of their complaining, God instructed the Hebrews to look upon the raised bronze serpent, a symbol of their disease of sin, as the means of healing. They were to direct their attention back to God and away from the source of their pain—but not without looking upon that very source (Numbers 21:4-8). As much as we don't want to look at an abscess, only by doing so can we lance and clean it for healing.

Gazing at Rouault's *Crucifixion* or Michelangelo's *Pietà* or listening to "O Sacred Head, Now Wounded" places us in the path of oncoming beauty, expanding our imaginations to see beyond our trauma and shame to the next new thing God is calling us to create with him and each other. We do not deny or minimize our trauma, our grief, or our shame. Rather, by gazing at it—by listening to each other's stories in all of their interpersonal, neurobiological weight in the light of resurrection and the presence of the Holy Trinity—we make way for beauty to be imagined and created.

But to fully enter into that new creation process, there remains an-other step: inquiring of the Lord in his temple. It is to that inquiry that we now turn.

9

INQUIRE

And to inquire in his temple.

Psalm 27:4 NRSV

"**What do you imagine will happen?**" asked my colleague Courtney. The rest of us in the group waited.

"The same thing that always does," Carmen answered. "We'll just end up in a fight." She was referring to her husband, Graham, who was not present, as he was part of a different confessional community.

Courtney pressed in gently. "Do you mean that if you tell Graham you want to be closer to him, you both will end up in a fight? How will that happen?"

"I don't know. I just know it will." Carmen gave a sigh of resignation. But my colleague was not to be deterred.

"No, I want to check something with you. Tell us exactly how this conversation will go, step by step."

With that, Carmen began the detailed work of role-playing, Courtney standing in for Graham.

Through this conversation, Carmen was able to articulate her version of how an interchange with Graham would proceed, all in the presence of the group that was bearing witness to Carmen's life. At each turn, my colleague kept her engaged in the present moment, keeping her from jumping ahead to a catastrophic endpoint in the story without including the details of how she got there. Courtney gently and firmly prevented Carmen's mind from being diverted by anxiety or shame. Whenever Carmen tried to truncate or stop the interchange, Courtney would ask, "What are you feeling? Where in your body are you feeling it?" After answering these questions, Carmen practiced breathing deeply, relieving those parts of her body that were carrying her tension. As she did so, her anxiety diminished, and she was able to answer my colleague's next question, one that everyone in the group becomes accustomed to.

"What do you want now? What do you want with Graham?"

"I really want to be closer to him," Carmen responded.

"And what are you afraid of?" Courtney responded.

"I'm afraid that he doesn't want to be closer to me. I'm afraid that he's going to leave me."

"I'm so sorry you find yourself feeling this. That has to be really hard," Courtney replied.

As the clinicians in our practice have worked together shepherding these confessional communities, we have developed, through a great deal of practice, a rhythm and an unspoken understanding of how to play in concert with each other, passing and receiving the baton, complementing each other's efforts in supporting the group as it creates the space for beauty to emerge. At this point in the conversation I did something we often do when one of the members of the community has found themselves in a hard emotional place. Receiving the baton from Courtney, I asked the group, "What are others feeling?"

This is not simply an attempt to acquire information. It is primarily an invitation for the group to enter the conversation by doing at least two things simultaneously. First, each member will speak to what he or she feels (not what they think)—what emotional states are being evoked by what they are witnessing in the exchange between Courtney and Carmen. They will become more aware of parts of their own stories, naming them and how Carmen's is speaking to them. But second, my hope is that they will mobilize as a single body on Carmen's behalf. By this I do not mean that they are lining up on her side against Graham—this is not about one or the other of them being right or wrong. Rather, in validating her feelings of shame and fear of abandonment, they are connecting deeply with her, and in so doing, healing comes to her collectively, as the temple of the Lord.

Community members voiced feeling protective of Carmen. Of longing for her to be confident and at peace. They validated that the work she was doing was hard. With this, Carmen's anxiety dwindled. Not only was she more comfortable, but her heightened comfort spoke to the other members, indicating to them that they indeed had agency to be conduits of healing. Sculptors of beauty and goodness.

Carmen's body visibly relaxed. Her voice strengthened. She sat up straighter in her chair. She talked about how she felt more confident in her body and said she could even imagine telling Graham she wanted to be closer to him. As she envisioned that conversation with him in her future, which now seemed very different, she was unafraid of what his response might be. Even if his words were not immediately what she wanted them to be, she could now sense herself being confident, composed, and kind. Moreover, she said what many of our community members say in such moments: "I can see you all being with me, standing right next to me as Graham and I talk. I'm going to take you with me."

And with this, beauty was created out of the very substance of shame and fear. We were all playing cellos in the rubble.

The above exchange at first glance might seem to be something distinctive to a group psychotherapy setting, something you would never expect to witness in a board room or a faculty meeting or a football coaches' staff meeting. And in terms of the content of the interaction, that may be accurate. But among many things that were taking place in the room, one of the most important features was not unique to a confessional community but is in fact germane to all systems that seek to create beauty and goodness. (And if you don't think that's exactly what football teams are doing, just ask Joe Ehrmann, who in his tenure at Gilman School taught his players—while winning state titles—that their primary purpose in playing football was to learn to love one another.)[1]

I'm talking about curiosity, and, naturally, curiosity finds its voice in the form of questions. Questions of a certain kind are an important, fundamental element of how we create and curate beauty. This is the culmination of what our poet in Psalm 27 is expressing. We dwell. We gaze. And we do so in order to inquire in the Lord's temple. It's in inquiring that we take the necessary next steps of creating beauty and goodness out of the traumas and tragedies of our lives. This is what the message of the gospel is about.

From gazing, then, we move to inquiring in the temple of the Lord. To inquire is to be curious, not only of others but of ourselves, and to allow others to do the same. To inquire of anyone, not least the Lord, is to live as his image bearers, for God is an inquiring God. He doesn't sit around typing out missives telling us what to do; rather, he engages us, and as often as not, he does so with questions. These questions are not simply an attempt to acquire information. Nor are they offered with the expectation that we have the right answers or that we should be ashamed when we don't. They are the initiatives of a God who is genuinely curious about us, in the same way parents are (hopefully) curious about their child.

In the process of creating, we are first curious. Curiosity necessarily leads to questions. We inquire as a means to gather information, but even that is ultimately in the service of strengthening our sense of being seen, soothed, safe, and secure—essentially, to regulate our emotional states. At times, what on the surface appears to be an attempt to gather information is, underneath, a way to protect ourselves.

Sometimes we ask questions to defend ourselves from our fear and shame. For example, at the conclusion of many of my speaking engagements there's a time for questions. Once an audience member asked me, "What can I do to get my friend to want to get help?"

This was not an unreasonable inquiry. We all want to properly encourage people to do the next right thing. And we all at times deeply long to help someone who seems unwilling to help themselves. This person had tried all sorts of things in attempting to convince her friend to give up drinking. But underneath her query was something else. Instead of answering her question directly, I asked her a question instead. "What do you suspect will happen to your friend if she doesn't get help?"

"I'm afraid her husband and their kids will leave her," she answered. "And she'll end up in even more trouble. Maybe homeless."

"And what will you feel if that happens?" I asked.

"I will feel sad, really sad. And I'll feel responsible that I didn't do something to stop it. I'll feel ashamed that I didn't do enough."

I pointed out to this compassionate, well-meaning woman that her original question was really a safer, more protective way of saying, "I have a friend whose life is revealing to me how much sadness and shame I carry around with me. I am afraid that those feelings are going to come roaring through my front door if she doesn't do the work she needs to do to change her life. I want her to do her work so that I can do my work on my own shame and sadness."

As sometimes happens, even in public settings such as this one, I (hopefully tenderly enough) took one more tentative step forward. I asked, "How long have you felt responsible for making sure important people in your life are okay?"

"All my life," she responded.

This brave woman, who may have thought she was asking a "functional" question, one whose answer would tell her plainly what she should "do about my friend," discovered that her question was really a statement about herself disguised as a question—as many of our questions are. And as she revealed her fear and shame, she also became aware that her friend's resistance to "getting help" was as much about her sense that she herself had not "gotten enough help" to heal her own shame and fear. Her question was much more about herself than it was about her friend. But the point was that in asking a question, she discovered something about her own life that was important for her to know. She discovered that her shame and fear were lurking in places she had not seen, and now they were in the open (in front of two hundred people, no less), accessible to be addressed. In essence, her inquiry led to the possibility of discovering beauty in her story, whereas prior to our interchange she was barely thinking of it, so well-hidden was it by the story of her friend.

This woman was asking for information, but I was curious about *her*. I wanted to speak with her rather than about her friend's problems. And as it turned out, her question led to my question. This way of being curious begins in childhood. As a parent, even if there are things I know about my son or daughter, I am still curious about their experience of what I know to be true. Moreover, I want them to sense my curiosity, my desire for them to have the experience of being known—in their beauty and in their brokenness—and so come to believe in their very bodies that they are truly loved. I want them to sense my interest—my curiosity—so that they become persuaded that they are interesting and worthy of attunement. In my interchange with my audience member, I didn't just want her to leave with data about what to do; I wanted her to have the experience in that very place that *she* was the center of the conversation, not her friend who wasn't there.

This is how the experience of the group setting begins to transform people. They become increasingly aware that whenever they ask or answer questions (as above, with Carmen talking about her marriage), they are doing so with someone else who is as interested in *them* as they are in the topic at hand—if not more so.

I and the others in our confessional communities pursue curiosity imperfectly. But as Christians, we do this out of the conviction that we are image bearers of God. We seek out others with curiosity and ask questions as a means of fostering the experience of being known, known in the sense St. Paul speaks of it in his letters to the Corinthians and Galatians (see 1 Corinthians 8:2-3; Galatians 4:9). To be known in this way is to have the stage set for the development of secure attachment. And an integral part of developing secure attachment is the meaningful deployment of questions in the service of creating beauty and goodness in our lives.

But that is not always our experience. In our insecure attachments, curiosity is often so intertwined with shame that we downgrade or eliminate it from our experiential diet. We either stop asking certain kinds of questions (of others or ourselves) or we begin to use them to protect ourselves instead of naming what we want or what we feel. We in fact practice *not* naming those things or asking for what we truly want, and often we are not even aware *that* we desire, let alone what we desire.

A great deal of the work of confessional communities—and any system that seeks to create beauty in the world—consists of inquiring of others. The process of asking questions unearths shame from its hiding place, where we have bound up energy so that it is not available to us to create in the way we have been made to create. Beauty eludes us because we have tied our own hands behind our backs interpersonally, neurobiologically, and institutionally. But when we understand—through the prism of Easter—that beauty is to be found in, even created out of, the very substance of our trauma, we also discover that every question offered in the genuine spirit of curiosity with the intention of finding beauty and goodness becomes a launch point for new creation. This new creation comes in the form of community members' willingness to take the risk necessary to make a new thing, be that a garden, a marriage, a piece of software, a nonprofit enterprise, a church fellowship, or a parent-child relationship. Such new creation begins in the mind and in conversation but quickly congeals and extends into the material world, not unlike what happened to Ryan when he was commissioned to start his microloan project after so many years when all he felt in thinking about that venture was shame.

God is in the business of new creation, and when he is doing something new, he often begins by asking questions. Yes, to acquire information (our theology of his omniscience notwithstanding—that is another story). But usually it is to make the information he seeks available to us. He asks questions to engage and draw us out of ourselves and toward him, into deeper intimacy and love. But given that our traumas are often forged in experiences of relational intimacy, we can find God's questions threatening, often without even knowing why. But the Holy Trinity has no intention of shaming us. He is in the business of loving us in order to expand our desire to love him, ourselves, and others in response. And the expansion of our love is measured in terms of our joy in being who we were made to be, people who long to be known and to know—for the purpose of creating beauty, not least in the places where we would least expect it to emerge. It all begins with God's inquiry.

The Lord asked questions of Adam and Eve, of Cain, of Job, of Moses, of Elijah. Jesus asked questions in virtually every situation in which he found himself. We are in relationship with a curious God. And we must remember: God does not use questions merely to educate us. He's not inquiring of us just to teach us where we're wrong. He does so in order that we can experience what it's like for someone this beautiful, this good, and this authoritatively true to be deeply curious about us. It is not just the explicit nature of the question that matters; it is that *God* is asking it.

Carmen's mother, it turned out, had never been curious about Carmen like Courtney was. Courtney's curiosity, her eagerness to build a bridge of intimacy with Carmen in public before witnesses, gave even more heft to the healing power inherent in her question. Courtney was not just asking for herself; she was speaking for the group, many of whom nonverbally expressed their affirmation of the question as Carmen received it. And in sensing their support, Carmen was able to engage in the role-playing work that allowed her to re-envision her conversation with Graham. Moreover, she was beginning to neurobiologically rewire her embodied sense of what it meant for God to be curious about her, for Jesus to ask her questions without condemnation.

Hence, we persevere to dwell in a confessional community in order to gaze upon the beauty that is present in the midst of our grief and shame. In so doing, we create the space to ask important questions of each other, questions that lead to the liberation that commissions people to create beauty in all of the domains of life they occupy. For others to be curious about our lives leads to new creation in our friendships, marriages, churches, schools, and places of work. And this creation of beauty is not

John—In the Beginning, Makoto Fujimura

Golden Sea, Makoto Fujimura

Charis—Kairos (The Tears of Christ), Makoto Fujimura

New Wine, Makoto Fujimu‸

limited to relationships. We create beauty in the very products we make in whatever endeavor we find ourselves, be that our garden, our warehouse, or the family law courtroom.

The last line of Psalm 27:4 is translated in various ways: "and to seek him in his temple" (NIV), "and to meditate in His temple" (NASB), "and to inquire in his temple" (NRSV). In this chapter I am using the latter, which emphasizes more directly and explicitly how seeking and meditating reflect curiosity—we do these things out of our longings. To inquire is to shift our curiosity directly to our left-hemispheric language centers and, as his image bearers, begin to ask questions, even as he asks us. But to "inquire in his temple," given what we have envisioned the temple to be in actuality, is to inquire of others in the confessional community. It is to speak with curiosity with each other. It is to open ourselves to being questioned, even as we question them, even as Courtney and I questioned Carmen. As I inquired of my audience member. We inquire not only to acquire information, nor to expose the shame of others or protect ourselves from our own. Rather, we inquire in order to help everyone—ourselves included—tell our stories more truly and, in so doing, make possible the creation of beauty and goodness in the world.

In one respect, there is no end to the kinds of questions we can ask (just ask the parents of a three-year-old).[2] But let us turn our focus to just four questions the Scriptures tell us God and Jesus asked of others. With each of these four questions, God is moving to heal and recommission. He is acting with curiosity, intending not just to elicit an "answer" but to build, to construct, to create a relationship while at the same time revealing things that are unknown to the person of whom he is inquiring. These questions, as I will present them, move in an intended direction, each building on the one that precedes it. As you will see, we have previously explored elements of the first two questions in chapter seven. There they served the purpose of elucidating what it means to dwell. Here we will extend our exploration even further, tying them together with the two that follow.

From an IPNB perspective, these four questions can be understood as a developmentally advancing means by which God moves over the course of the biblical narrative, creating ever-increasing states of integration as he does so. These questions are both invitational and demanding at the same time. Invitational in that God invites his hearers to draw closer to him, demanding in that he expects a response and the response itself both reveals and mobilizes. Our answers to these questions don't just tell us the facts; they comfort and convict us. They mobilize our lives toward a greater capacity to co-create outposts of beauty and goodness with God in every domain of our lives.

The questions we will explore here are not the only ones God asks in the biblical narrative, nor are they necessarily the most important ones he asks. They are, however, cardinal questions: fundamental queries with which we must engage in order to become who we were made to be. Each represents a category, if you will, of questions that pursue curiosity from a distinct direction, with a different intention in mind. This particular collection provides a framework, a way of mindfully engaging each other in the community.

And not just a confessional community. I would suggest that these questions represent a collective way of being curious that any system can appropriate to advance its members' capacity to create beauty and goodness in any domain of life, be that education, business, the arts, or the church. For indeed, Psalm 27:4 is a model for how all of creation can respond to our Maker with love and creativity, doing so out of the very trauma and shame that evil expects to be the end of our stories. My hope is that in exploring these questions, we will develop the embodied habit of being curious without condemnation and in so doing be stewards of the expansion of beauty wherever our feet fall.

Before we launch into the questions themselves, I want to highlight one last feature they hold in common. As all questions do, they seek information. But their purpose is transformation. The words that are embedded in the questions point to places in our souls that do not barter first in words; rather, they trade, as St. Paul writes in Romans 8, in the groans of the Spirit that are both pre- and postverbal. The Spirit longs for us to realize our longings—but does so by transforming them into the beauty we long to become so that our desires become as good as they are beautiful. Those groans come not from our rational left hemisphere but from our lower and right brain; they precede our language and extend beyond it. As such, they answer the call of those things in our world that approach from the direction of beauty. Beauty that we find in nature, art, and worship.

In this way, the questions function as artistic expressions, speaking to both our desires and our griefs, intending to sculpt them all through the process of lament and hope into the artistic beauty God intends for us to become. Recall that we often approach our lives as problems to be solved rather than beauty to be created, lodged as we are in their quagmire. As such, our answers to these questions can be limited and superficial at best. But when seen as works of art in whose path we now place ourselves, they become something else altogether. Many of our longings and griefs feel inaccessible to us, but artists come to our rescue by giving shape and color and cadence to them in a way that our logical, linear wordsmithing has not yet caught up to.

As we explore the questions that follow, I will refer to the work of Makoto Fujimura, an artist whose work has been and continues to be transformational for many. I invite you to be open to the questions and to Fujimura's paintings as they reflect and direct what God is doing to make all things new in and through the beauty of our lives.

FOUR QUESTIONS TO CONSIDER

Where are you?

We begin with this question because it was God's first query of the human race, and I would daresay it is a question he asks us anew each day. We cannot begin to know the path of our journey—what and how we will be creating beauty today—unless we have a sense of where we are to begin with. Found in Genesis 3:9, this question reminds us that God has early and often been in the business of seeking us out. He is a curious God, one who invites us to "come now, let us reason together" (Isaiah 1:18 ESV). He takes us quite seriously. Far more seriously, in fact, than we take ourselves.

When we are children, we have no way of knowing how seriously our parents take our welfare; they take it far more seriously than we do. A three-year-old doesn't understand why his parents get upset when he runs into the street. Neither are we able at times to grasp how seriously God takes us, in all of our contexts with all their complexities, and that he does so with great delight and longing for us as his motivation. When God asks Adam where he is, he is not merely looking for a response of, "I'm over here, in the woods. The guy covered in greenery." There are multiple layers to "where" Adam and Eve are. Yes, they are in the woods. But they are also hiding—from God and each other. They are ashamed. They are afraid. And they are telling stories in their heads about God and each other.

"If she didn't have to talk so much, that conversation with the snake wouldn't have lasted so long and we wouldn't be in this mess!" says Adam.

"If he only talked more, he could have said something and we wouldn't be in this mess!" says Eve.

"We're going to die," say both of them.

Our immediate context shapes and guides us, but that context is not just our current, visible, surface-level circumstances. Had God come walking up to ask his question in the middle of the conversation between the woman and the serpent, perhaps a very different dialogue would have ensued. With God in the conversation, she might have turned to him to tell him she was uncomfortable and confused and, possibly, beginning to feel ashamed. She could have used God as a co-regulator (since Adam apparently wasn't up to the task) to reduce her shame and make a different decision about the fruit. When God asks us where we are, given what we now know about the nine domains of integration, the nine functions of the middle prefrontal cortex, and the window of tolerance, our answer to him would, to say the least, be more nuanced. What I am sensing, imaging, feeling, and thinking and how my body is inclined to act—and then the story I tell to make sense of it all—shape whether in this moment I will be an agent of creativity or destruction. Of integration or disintegration. Whether or not I will tell my story more or less truly. (Adam: "I'm here hiding, and I have screwed up." Or, "I heard you. . . . I was afraid. . . . I'm naked. . . . And, by the way, the woman? . . . The one you gave me? . . . It's her fault.")

As we discussed briefly in chapter three, Makoto Fujimura is a contemporary artist whose paintings are in the tradition of *nihonga*, or traditional Japanese painting. Fujimura has deepened and expanded the technical definition of this form.[3] He describes this style of painting as an "ecosystem" that is composed of many mineral materials; multiple people are involved in producing the pigments and glue necessary for creating the paint and multiple eras and cultural stories contribute to the spirit and beauty of *nihonga* as Fujimura conceives of it. The first of his paintings I invite you to immerse yourself in is titled *John—In the Beginning* (this painting, along with the three other pieces from Fujimura that I discuss, can be seen in the color insert).

Embedded within our first question is God's desire for us to offer him a response that details our "ecosystem," not give him a flat answer. In the example above, Courtney was pursuing a line of questions that presumed Carmen's story to be multidimensional, not flat. It holds many minerals, multiple people, and many generations. Courtney was, like Fujimura with *John—In the Beginning*, collaborating with Carmen to do the slow work of life in community so that she could continue to do it with Graham even more confidently. It's with good reason that we often refer to our communities as art studios for lives that are being transformed into new creations.

But evil hates this artwork of new creation, and it will use shame to ruin it. This is what shame does as evil's proxy. It colors how we read people's intentions, and how Adam read God's. From where we sit, reading the text after the fact, we have no reason to believe that God was doing anything other than asking a direct question, seeking to engage Adam. But from where Adam found himself, and indeed where I often find myself and the community members do as well, that sort of question can evoke a sense of peril within. Much like our first parents, we shudder from answering it, given that it can activate shame as much as it is a bid for love and intimacy. When a member seeks out another in the community, we can sometimes feel the tension as the recipient of the question initially pauses, then gathers his or her courage to answer as truly as they can. Over time, the community members become increasingly comfortable asking and answering this question. But, as we saw with Brendan in the last chapter, there are parts of our stories that take time and courage to reveal. Not surprisingly, be it consciously or unwittingly, we sometimes avoid telling our stories as truly as we could in these moments.

During a session in one of our groups, I inquired of one member who had been silent. "Ella, where does today find you?" I asked.

Ella paused, then spoke of how she had been considering for some time talking about a topic that was troubling her but had resisted because she found it embarrassing.

"What are you afraid would happen if you began to talk about it?" I asked.

"Oh, I don't know," she said. "I would just feel really ashamed."

I assured her that we loved her, that we wanted to help her use whatever she was holding to create beauty in a way she couldn't yet see. I reminded her that we wanted to be in the room with her and were not going to leave.

Ella hesitated while the room waited. Slowly, she began to describe how she had begun to feel uncomfortable around her boss, Eric, a man she respected in many ways and who was equally well-respected in their industry. The work they did together was in an area where she was passionate and experienced.

The other group members asked her to give an example of what she was trying to put into words. They were, in essence, asking her to tell them where she was, as God had asked Adam so long ago.

Ella said flatly that there was no hint of Eric ever making direct sexual advances toward her. But on occasion he would send her an email about something he found interesting and thought she might enjoy as well— something that had nothing to do with their work together. A piece of artwork. An intriguing essay. A recipe (Eric was an accomplished cook).

Immediately, Joy chimed in. "I feel uncomfortable, too, when I hear you tell your story. I feel tense in my chest and hands, and I want you to just leave your job. It sounds like your boss is making a bid for intimacy with you. What does your husband think?"

"I've tried to tell Steve, but I don't feel like he listens to me. He seems to think I'm making more of this than there is. But I also know that Steve needs me to have this job. Besides, he's too busy with his own work, and his dad's terrible health has been taking up a lot of his time."

Ella had spoken of her marriage often. She loved and admired Steve deeply, and he was, she believed, deeply committed to her. But he was not as accessible to her emotionally as she desired. He was an engaged father and worked hard to provide for their family. Still, she wanted more. She wanted the subtle signs of interest her boss was showing her. After all, who wouldn't want someone to send you emails about things that might interest you? But it wasn't merely the content of the messages that was captivating; the emails indicated that Eric was thinking about her. Ella longed for Steve to think about and be interested in her in that same way. What troubled her even more was her awareness that she enjoyed being sought after and at times was even aroused—then she felt ashamed for feeling that way. All the more reason she was reluctant to speak about this in the community.

■ ■ ■

When God asks, "Where are you?" he is directing his question to our entire mind. If we are called to love God with all of our mind, and our mind is an embodied and relational process, then to tell him where I am means I describe not only everything I sense, image, feel, and think, along with how my body wants to act, not only what I am doing in terms of the nine domains of integration, not only the narrative I am constructing about the story I believe I am living, but also where I am in relationship to other people. God was not just asking for Adam's individual whereabouts. He was seeking Adam in relationship to Eve as well. For, as it turns out, I *am* my brother's keeper (see Genesis 4:9), and my brain won't let it be any other way.

In her line of questions to Carmen, Courtney was gently seeking an intimate foothold in a tender place in Carmen's soul. Implicitly woven into the fabric of the exchange was the ongoing question of Carmen's whereabouts. Courtney wanted to know what she sensed, imaged, felt, and thought and how she was feeling compelled to act with her body. Moreover, she was exploring what Carmen was experiencing in relationship with and response to the others in the community. For instance, when Courtney asked Carmen about her marriage, Carmen's response was not limited in scope to her relationship with Graham. It was also a reflection of her relationship with Courtney. Even as Carmen talked about her marriage, she was working out her fear and shame in her relationship with Courtney in that very moment. The fear and shame she felt about her relationship with Graham was being absorbed in the embodied interchange in which Courtney pursued her and in how the group held her even as she spoke about her life. In no small way, then, her marriage was being changed by the interactions she was having with the community. And all this began with asking, "Where are you?"

Where Carmen "was" was a place of fear and shame as she imagined her relationship with Graham as it was shaped by attachment patterns formed in her developmental years and by her experience with her husband. But all of that was being transformed in her interactions with Courtney and the rest of us as we pressed Carmen to say more. With each of her answers we drew her closer to us and further away from her fear and shame. Not by providing her with information or insight about her marriage or about Graham (whom no one else in this group knew) but by being present with her where she "was" in order to take her someplace else.

Doing so presses into grief along with joy. In the context of our confessional communities we can name the grief of our shame and sadness because we are with people who are not going to leave the room when we do. We immediately give the group permission to shape and change not only our answers but our felt experience of our shame and the trauma associated with it. This enables us to unlock the energy bound up in our efforts to contain our shame and use it to create the next good, beautiful thing God longs to co-create with us.

What do you want?

From "Where are you?" we move to "What do you want?" This order is intentional, for what we want is a function of where we are. "What do you want?" These first words of Jesus in the Gospel of John (see John 1:38) bring us to a place where we can name our desires. As we learned in chapter seven, we often do not name them because we fear they may be too much or fall outside the boundary of what God or others see as proper. Sometimes we cannot name them because we do not even know what they are, so bound up are we by years of dismissing or denying desire. In either case, in not naming what we want, we neurobiologically burn energy containing it, only to have it leak out often in unproductive or even harmful ways.

We have limited practice naming our longings to be seen, soothed, safe, and secure in most domains of our lives. Perhaps we have more experience naming them in marriage, but even there we can find ourselves longing to experience the four s's in ways we don't, only to languish emotionally, engage in affairs, or journey toward divorce. We have so elevated marriage as the holy grail of relational aspirations that friendship takes a back seat and is rarely given the opportunity to be a place where we can be known. And in our jobs? In our educational endeavors? The notion of naming what we want in any of these settings in terms of the four s's would never occur to us. But in not naming our longings or our desire to pursue greater creativity, we become bored and depressed. Similarly, we do not admit that we want more from our relationship with God, a longing that becomes bound up in a lifetime of anger because we fear that God cannot tolerate us in our emotional turmoil—and so we wilt on the vine that is Jesus rather than take nourishment from him.

We do not name that we want to generously give our lives away without fear of scarcity and thus continue to hoard our time, money, and relationships. In so doing we refrain from generously pouring into others what they need in order to be recommissioned in life and become a blessing to the world. It is here that we pick up Ella's story once again.

During a lull in the conversation, another member, William, said to Ella, "I'm pretty sure your boss is interested in you. I don't know that he even knows it, but he's definitely interested." He didn't say this with anger or fear. He just said it. We immediately felt the air thicken in the room.

"How are you so certain?" Ella asked.

"Well, it's not hard to see why he would be attracted to you in that way," William said. "You're attractive. You're smart. You're funny, and you're kind. You've been especially kind to me on a number of occasions. Besides," he hesitated, "I can imagine he's interested in you because I'm attracted to you."

If we'd thought the air was thick before, now we could cut it with a lightsaber. Suddenly, what had begun as a discussion of Ella's life outside the group transformed into something altogether different. The community moved swiftly from contemplating something outside its perimeter involving one of its members to engaging in something between two of its members and involving everyone in the room.

What the community did not know was that William and I had been speaking about this in his individual sessions for some time. He and I were meeting monthly as a way to process what was happening for him in the community, and at one point he had said, "You know, the thing I told you I was afraid would happen in the group has happened."

When I had first invited William to join, one of his primary concerns what that it was a coed group. He was worried that, given the level of intimacy he (rightly) presumed would develop, he would become attracted to a woman, and this would threaten his marriage. And now that attraction had emerged with Ella. But his marriage was not in trouble because of it, precisely because he began to talk about his experience instead of keeping it hidden.

"Tell me what you mean when you say you are attracted to her," I had said in our individual session.

He responded with a blank look, as if to ask, "What do you mean, 'Tell me what you mean'?" As if it was self-evident. William assumed being "attracted" was reducible to some homogenous physical-emotional "thing" we call "attraction," and if you are married and are attracted in this way to someone who isn't your spouse, that's wrong and poses danger. William was astute enough to admit to me that he'd known he would be attracted to other women after he was married, but his standard operating procedure was to assume his sense of attraction was a signal to turn away from the feelings and from the woman in question—if he didn't, trouble would soon find him. I affirmed that, indeed, setting proper boundaries in such instances was necessary, but I also said that if we ignored the feelings, they would eventually emerge somewhere, if not in outright infidelity.

I pressed him. "What exactly do you feel when you are interacting with Ella in the group?"

He began by indicating that she wasn't hard to look at. And that she was smart, insightful, and kind.

I redirected him, asking again, "Yes, but what do you *feel*?"

He said that when Ella addressed him, he felt seen and cared for in a way that was rare for him. He did not doubt that his wife loved him; in fact, she had actively, enthusiastically encouraged him to join the group even as he told her his fears because of the presence of other women. But he felt understood and even emotionally protected by Ella in a way he didn't always feel with his wife.

He and his wife had worked on this element of their marriage, but it was still imperfect. He carried a memory of being deeply wounded by his mother in early childhood and an equally deep longing to be comforted in a primal way by his wife. When he had spoken about his sadness in relationship to his mother, several members offered empathic responses. Ella, though, had expressed compassion in a particular way that had captivated his attention. Moreover, he admired her calm, tempered response to others' agitation when it emerged in the group and was aware that this enabled him to feel more comfortable and confident himself. This kind of response was far different from what he had known as a young boy, with his mother either screaming at him or leaving him to fend for himself while she locked herself in her bedroom.

He admitted that he had for some time been afraid to speak of any of this even to me because to name it might bring it out of the dark and into the light. What if in naming it he was unable to keep himself from acting on it?

"Act on it how?"

The community groups hold high confidentiality standards. No one has contact with anyone else outside of the group, and they often don't even know each other's last names. William and I both were confident he would not contact Ella apart from the group. How, then, did he fear he would "act" on his feelings?

"What do you want from her?" I asked him. "What do you want *with* her?"

William paused. Would he be able to name exactly what he wanted? I again focused on what he felt. "Do you feel arousal to any degree?"

"Yeah, to some degree."

I crossed the Rubicon. "To the point that you want to have sex with her?"

"No!" he exclaimed. "And why would you put that thought in my head? You see, this is what I was afraid of!"

I paused to slow down the process, then reapproached him.

"Afraid of what?" I asked.

"Afraid I would have thoughts about a woman—"

"Ella, you mean—not just any 'woman' but this one in particular," I interrupted.

"Okay, sure, Ella. Thoughts about her sexually. And that's not what I want! I don't want to have any sexual thoughts about any woman other than my wife."

"Okay—that's what you don't want, and I understand that. But what *do* you want?" I inquired again.

And there again was the question. "What do you want?" I'm not sure where you, the reader, find yourself at this point. You may be thinking any number of things, not least that I should never be trusted to conduct psychotherapy with anyone ever again. Who would ask such things?

But as we continued to maneuver around this question, we were able to eventually see that, beyond arousal, beyond the hollow promise of fantasized orgasm (which, by the way, William was not thinking about), was the much deeper longing housed within his soul. What William ultimately wanted wasn't sex with Ella. He wanted to be wanted. He wanted to be confident. He wanted to be found interesting. He wanted to be admired by someone he admired. William wanted beauty and goodness in the form of being seen, soothed, safe, and secure, such that he could comfortably and confidently direct his spiritual energy toward creating beauty with others without fear of diminishment in any way.

Ronald Rolheiser describes this as the eros, the energy, of our spirituality.[4] William wanted this energy in ways he had heretofore buried but that being in this community revealed. Yes, he had attempted to address this with his wife, but when that endeavor was only partially successful, he more or less white-knuckled it, transferring his desire to be seen by her to other endeavors. But then along came the community, with Ella as part of it, and he could no longer hide his desire from himself or the others.

William and I processed this over a period of several weeks, until I finally made the big ask. "So, what do you think about the idea of saying all of this in the group? Saying it to Ella?"

William nearly fell out of his chair. Once again we revisited what he wanted. What he wanted was to be able to say all of these things and not have anyone shame him because of it. I wondered with him what that might be like, to be able to name these things, these longings, and to imagine no one running out of the room. What would it be like, I asked, for him to name what he wanted in a room where the community itself would protect both him and Ella from hurting each other (or anyone else in the group) in the process?

William began to imagine the possibility that this might even provide him the courage to engage his wife more effectively on the issue. We laid out a plan. He agreed that at some point he would, with my help, open one of our group sessions by asking to talk about this, and he would do so by first naming his fear of being shamed for what he was about to say.

But all of that planning went out the window on the day Ella told her story. Before I knew it, William was letting the cat out of the bag. And oddly enough, when he did, no one died. As I said, the air was suddenly thicker, but it wasn't poisonous. After everyone caught their breath (including me, who was as surprised as anyone that he chose this moment to make his announcement), I simply asked William to say more about what he meant by being attracted to Ella.

He reiterated what he and I had discussed, namely that he felt understood and protected by her in ways he didn't always feel in his marriage, and he did not refrain from naming that he found her to be physically attractive—but that he was afraid she and the rest of the group members would shame him for even feeling these things.

He didn't mention sex explicitly, because, as he and I had discussed, this was about much more than sex. It was about his longing to be seen and how he had felt invisible to his mother. He went on to say that the most important thing it highlighted was his desire to be seen by his wife, and he intended to redouble his efforts to work toward that end. As he spoke, eventually his words found the feelings, and the feelings found the tears. Many in the group validated not only William's feelings but his courage in saying what he had.

Of course, everyone was waiting to hear from Ella. She spoke of feeling cared for and not objectified by William and of feeling flattered. Given the community's common commitment to strengthening marriages, she also expressed her confidence and surprising lack of anxiety that anything untoward would happen between them.

What's more, it turned out that this event was not just between Ella and William. Cora, another woman who lived in a committed but challenging marriage, entered the conversation by saying, "You know, for a long time, I just figured I would have to live with my marriage the way it is. And I had come to terms with that. But you all are making that difficult. I realize now how much energy I have been burning just containing my resentment that my husband won't be more emotionally engaged. And now I'm all worked up. I think this means I'm going to have to do some work on my marriage I didn't think I was going to do. The genie is out of the bottle, and there's no putting it back."

■   ■   ■

As William's story reveals, there is much we desire that we aren't even aware of—we do not have because we do not ask, as the New Testament letter from James indicates (James 4:1-3). We either don't ask for what we want or ask in a way that reveals how consumptive we are in our asking because we have not taken the time to explore the depth and intensity of our desire to be seen, soothed, safe, and secure. To name the degree to which we long for those experiences and to have those longings validated is to provide the space to create beauty. William and Ella were able to do this because they named what they wanted at the most primal levels of their minds' activity. As they each remained in contact with the sharpness of their longings to be seen, soothed, safe, and secure, they were able to receive those very things from the community. And the more they practiced taking them in, the more they sensed them even when they were not in the room. After that point they were less distressed when they did not receive everything they wanted from their spouses even as they continued to press into their marriages.

The four s's are relational in nature. They are not so much something we acquire as something we share with others. Most of what I want, I want to keep. I want to clutch and hoard. I want it to be mine so that I can guarantee that it won't leave me and remind me of how ashamed I am. And so we find that William and Ella and Cora were creating beauty not only with each of their respective spouses. No—they were creating beauty in the room that day with each other and with other members of their community. That was beauty in the making. It was not something anyone could grasp and keep for themselves. They would have to remember it in their minds, just as one has to recall a beautiful sunset—you can't hoard it or bring it home and put it in your family room. When Jesus asks John's disciples what they want, he is coaxing them not toward acquiring something. He is coaxing them toward himself. Toward relationship. Toward the beauty and goodness he longs to draw us into as well.

Here I draw your attention to the second of Makoto Fujimura's paintings, *Golden Sea*. The expensive pigments involved in Fujimura's work are layered upon each other and refract the light differently over time. Each pigment affects how all the other pigments are experienced by the viewer. Our desires are much like this, layered under so much other material that we cannot easily distinguish them well or perhaps even see them at all. In *nihonga,* each layer of pigment, once applied, requires a lengthy time to dry. This layering process can take days or even weeks. Once the painting is finished, the viewer needs time to "unlayer" them in order to appreciate the depth of the beauty of the work. In the same way, we move slowly and at a layered pace to name our most primal longings, a pace that enables us to name them in the earshot of others who will hear and validate them—but not without demanding of us that we name those desires right at the very doorstep of God. For if it is true that God is ultimately what we are longing for, we will be unable to rest until we have found that to be true in our embodied experience.

Naming where we are enables us to pause long enough to observe the nine domains of integration of our minds in the absence of condemnation. This further facilitates our capacity to name what we want, which leads us to hope—but also to the hard work of coming to terms with the idea that God is in the business of refining even what we want in order to create the possibility for us to become beauty—his poetry—in ways we cannot yet see (Ephesians 2:10). Jesus introduces us to that hard work in our next query.

As an aside, when it comes to being people of desire and our longing to create and interact with beauty, no dimension of our lives speaks more deeply, more tenderly, and at times more powerfully than our sexuality. And likewise, no dimension contains and represents our grief more painfully than our experience of sex in all its forms. We do not have enough space here to consider how our sexuality affects and is affected by the interactions that take place in confessional communities. But the community's experience, with William and Ella at center stage, demonstrates that sexuality is always in the room. Just as it is in every room, and it doesn't matter if the group is single-sex or male-female.

What is important is that we become aware of and name what is being channeled through our sexuality. Our shame would have us tell

INQUIRE   199

an incomplete narrative about what we want, as William was tempted to do. We will think that because our sexual desires are aroused, our desire is really—and only—about sex. And in our culture, that means "having sex," no matter the form. When we fail to name this, we miss the opportunity to do the work William and Ella were able to do. With the assistance of the group, they were able to diffuse their fear of what they felt by going beyond what culture told them they ultimately wanted. Culture told William he wanted to have sex with Ella. The biblical narrative told him he wanted to be seen, soothed, safe, and secure and that, although these desires were being activated by his interactions with Ella, they had their origins in early developmental events and would find their consummation in God. But what to do in the meantime?

We humans have tacitly (as well as consciously and with intention) understood, approached, and manipulated our sexuality for as long as we have been fully sentient. We posture ourselves before it as that one thing, should we be able to take and hold it, that will, like the fruit of the tree of knowledge of good and evil, provide knowledge, power, and beauty. We imagine this knowledge, power, and beauty as ends in themselves rather than as byproducts of relationship. (We actually do this with many things. "If only I can have *this thing*," we think—"this job, this marriage, this church, this body." We know the drill.) However, if we are truly seen, soothed, safe, and secure, our desire will not be so much for our own wishes to be fulfilled (although they are not to be dismissed) but rather to see joy in the face of the other as a result of our delight and generosity of love for them.[5]

I was asking William, ultimately, the same thing Jesus was asking John the Baptist's disciples: "What do you want?" His attraction to Ella was real in and of itself, but even more than that, it represented what William really wanted, and what he wanted was beyond sex. He wanted to be deeply seen, soothed, safe, and secure, and his "attraction" to Ella involved much more than Ella herself.

In the setting of the confessional community, in which men and women gather together, "sex" is happening in the room all the time. No one is taking their clothes off. But we are asking people to become naked in the same way Adam and Eve were naked before they ate the fruit that gave shame the authority to ruin everything instead of creating beauty and goodness in its absence.

Can you drink the cup?[6]

The mother of Jesus' disciples James and John came, with her sons, to Jesus with a request. As he does in the opening scene of John's Gospel, Jesus asks her, "What is it you want?"

She starts right in. "Grant that one of these two sons of mine may sit at your right and the other at your left in your kingdom" (Matthew 20:21).

Can you imagine? This has to be one of the most presumptuous requests recorded in the Bible. Whose idea was this? Was it a Jewish mother making sure her boys got what they deserved, given how they had left her husband to clean all the fishing nets by himself? Maybe she figured that if they were going to wander around the countryside without getting paid, they deserved a pension. Being first lieutenants of the king wouldn't be too bad—it might even get her husband a new fishing boat. Perhaps it was James and John's idea in the first place, but they didn't have the courage to ask. Mom got tired of all the whining around the dinner table and decided to take matters into her own hands.

But I must be careful. This mother is an easy target to condemn, but I am very much like her. I want the best things for my children and my marriage and my friends. I want the best for my colleagues and patients. I want beautiful and good things to be easy to come by for everyone. And who knows? Perhaps James and John's mother felt comfortable with Jesus and believed her boys had the skills to rule next to Jesus. Besides, she knelt, she was polite, and she had the courage to ask for what she wanted in the first place. All of which counts for something. Perhaps I wish I had the courage to ask Jesus this directly for what I want, and my judgment of her presumptuousness is really my shame talking.

Whatever it was that James, John, and their mother wanted, and whoever's idea it was to ask, the center of gravity of the exchange swiftly shifts to Jesus. "You don't know what you are asking," Jesus says to them. "Can you drink the cup I am going to drink?" (Matthew 20:22).

With this pivot, Jesus introduces them to the process they must endure if they are to realize what they really want. Shame has so tainted our desires that they themselves are at the center of what God intends to transform on the way to creating beauty with and out of us.

If we want to be this close to Jesus—if we are willing to enter into a confessional community and ask the first two questions—we must be prepared to suffer. Naming where we are and what we want invariably leads to discoveries that bring us great comfort but also demand that we be present to the brokenness of our own lives and that of others—and that brokenness does not disappear with one conversation. Often our griefs remain with us for much longer than we think we can bear them. We long for our brokenness to be transformed, but we know this takes time.

As Gerald May argues, we are all addicts—or what the Bible would call "idolaters."[7] And as addicts, our recovery is a lifelong process. Many of our desires have been hijacked by behaviors that short-circuit our longings in the direction of hollow promises. Once we have tasted the dopamine rush of whatever our coping strategy offers us, it is difficult to believe that it cannot, will not, ultimately save us. But it won't, and when it doesn't, we suffer with all that Eve and Adam suffered in the wake of betrayal by the serpent and each other. Just ask Tara, whose husband's return to his pornography addiction extended the suffering she had experienced in her church as a young girl.

Most suffering occurs, somewhat counterintuitively, not as a function of pain but of isolation—one of shame's premier attributes. This happens when our failed attempts to clutch and hoard beauty leave our hands and arms empty and our lives barren and detached. This is what our coping strategies lead to. But a second form of suffering follows us when we decide to swim against the current of our traumas, our shame, and our addictions, the current pushing us to pursue what we want at all costs, even the cost of our souls. To flourish in this world—not a pretend one— is to suffer. For it means honestly answering the questions, "Where are you?" and "What do you want?" repeatedly, acknowledging that the answers we offer and receive are bridges to a deeper relationship with God and each other. We may or may not receive what we long for in the way we think we want it—James and John certainly didn't know what they were asking for—but in the process of dwelling, gazing, and inquiring, like gold from which the dross is sifted, our deepest, purest longings are more perfectly realized as we are more deeply known in the context of proper boundaries. For indeed, as people of desire and grief, we must learn to live in the space between them. When we do, joy and creativity find us, not as replacements for our suffering but in the presence of and despite it, transforming it and changing our brains along the way.

As St. Paul reflects, and as we hope in the glory of God—God's utter, dazzling joy at being in our presence—"we also glory in our sufferings, because we know that suffering produces perseverance; perseverance, character; and character, hope. And hope does not put us to shame, because God's love has been poured out into our hearts through the Holy Spirit, who has been given to us" (Romans 5:3-5). It is the hope of God's glory to which we bear witness, glory the hint of which we gaze upon in this, his temple, this confessional community. As we do, we learn not only to name what we want but also to suffer without shame, and in so doing, we discover that the suffering itself leads to even deeper connection, driving us as it does to those with whom we "participate in the sufferings of Christ" (1 Peter 4:13).

This brings us to the place of boundaries in our lives. In the garden of Eden, God provided for the first couple an almost infinite "yes!" But in the center of this "yes" was God's "no." "No" is as much a part of God's love, as necessary for completing it, as is his "yes." And in our saying "no" to each other, we create the space for growth, as we do when pruning a tree. We must say no to our addictions. We must say no to sexual behavior outside the boundaries of marriage, and here I don't just mean "having sex." I mean what Jesus meant when he said that to look upon a woman— in person, on a screen, or in your mind—with the intention to lust after her devours the souls of everyone involved.

We must say no to the impulse to lose our temper. We must say no to food. We must say no to the narratives shame has formed and the very self-condemnation we use to protect ourselves. We must say no at times to those appetites that, in the moment, we believe we cannot live without. We must, if we desire to create and become living breathing icons of beauty, drink the cup.

Saying no to our idols, our addictions, can be excruciatingly painful, depending on the depth and degree to which we still need to be seen, soothed, safe, and secure. But in so doing, we open the door to life. As with any integrating discipline, to say no to our impulse to clutch, to hoard, and to consume, we say yes to everything else in which beauty is stored, waiting to be released. And we must remember that the difficulty or pain of setting boundaries for our appetites is not something we should be ashamed of, despite our shame attendant's commitment to making us believe so. Instead, the community waits to hear us speak of the sensations, images, feelings, thoughts, and bodily impulses we experience in the presence of saying no to our addictions and helps carry and refine all of it, creating beauty we cannot imagine where before we could see only unrealized desire.

Somewhat counterintuitively, of the four s's, being safe is most closely related to the "no" of boundaries. We often think of safety as being protected from something outside ourselves that might cause us harm. We want to be safe from others or outside circumstances hurting us. This is one way the community works to provide safety for its members. But, as it turns out, the force in the world that most threatens our safety is . . . us. We are the ones who continually repeat the self-condemning mental activity that leads to our need for those things that end up exploiting us and wounding others. The biblical narrative is plainspoken when it tells us that the only thing in the universe that won't end up exploiting us, won't abuse us, won't devour us is God himself. But it is difficult for us to see that, what with all of our longings being fueled by a culture that tells us to self-identify, to ask for and expect to get what we want. Hence, to say "no" to any of our wants in this sense is actually a way to protect ourselves, to keep ourselves safe. And so in our confessional communities, we learn to say and hear "no."

At the same time that William was naming what he wanted from and with Ella, he was also naming what he would not do, just as Ella was saying that she would say no to her boss, even though she felt arousal when she read his emails that had nothing to do with work. For Jesus to drink the cup was for him to say no to a path that was far easier in the short run, a path that was broad and had a much wider gate, one that had easy access and many traveling it. There may be no harder work than that of saying no to our desires once they have been awakened, which is why they have remained in hibernation for so long in the first place.

Just as Jesus' disciples did not know what they were asking, neither do we. We easily settle for life's surface desires of money, sex, and power—and any of their infinite array of offspring. As with Fujimura's *Golden Sea* or Rothko's *No. 61*, these desires are what we in our inattentiveness initially see only superficially on the surface or at a glance. But to see all of the beauty, all of the refraction, we must recognize that we do not see things easily or clearly. We do not know that what we seek is not the right job, friendship, spouse, or church. What we long for is to be seen, soothed, safe, and secure. And we find this in confessional communities. It is not found only here. But many have born witness that they have found it here as truly and faithfully as anywhere. It is in this space that we speak not only of our longings but of our griefs—a grief that Cora, for instance, was able to articulate because her longing was exposed in the exchange between William and Ella.

But Cora's journey was to be an extended one. Her husband was faithful. Flexible? Not so much. It would still be months before she saw the first sign of willingness to be more emotionally available. And Ella? The conversation she had with the community eventually led to strong arguments with her husband—which led them to marital therapy. It was hard work. But not as hard as the work that led to Ella leaving her job against the protests of her boss and, at the time, her husband as well. The community became the hard deck on which she stood to move to where she wanted to dwell—in a marriage that was as life-giving as the group was.

We must not forget that shame, one of trauma's most disintegrating affects, has a way of behaving like the cells of a germ layer. In embryology, these are cells from which various differentiated parts of the body arise: the gastrointestinal tract, the central nervous system, the musculoskeletal system. All of these systems emerge from cells that originally look similar and appear to function similarly. Eventually, different cells in a germ layer give rise to different parts of the body. In like fashion, shame arises out of its germ layer to present itself in particular ways depending on the differentiated experience or relationship, such as in Tara's traumatic adolescence. To the degree you have experienced it in that context, you will move to address it as she did. And when you do, you will think you have learned how to address shame in general. And, to be sure, you will be more integrated. As Tara was.

But evil fades into the woodwork in its effort to remain hidden, and a new line of cells develops from shame's germ layer, and it shows up in a different situation, perhaps in our work setting or our body's decline. In Tara's case, it showed up in her husband's renewed viewing of pornography. Shame shows up in a new suit of clothes, and we are tempted to be ashamed that we still struggle with shame. Didn't I already deal with my shame? And on and on it goes. Because evil does not intend to go quietly into the night. In this way, we will suffer; we will drink the cup that represents our resistance to evil as we swim against its current in our moving to create outposts of beauty and goodness.

In the context of a confessional community, we suffer, we grieve together, and as such our suffering itself is transformed. For when I repeatedly bring to my community my deepest and longest-lasting grief, over which I have seemingly no agency (my spouse's drinking; my father's narcissism; my friend's chronic tendency to take me for granted; my grief over my multiple miscarriages; my divorce; my son's suicide), I practice sensing, imaging, feeling, and thinking about their presence while I simultaneously encounter my grief. And in so doing, I learn to hope. I hope not in receiving exactly what I thought I wanted in the way I wanted it, but more. I hope in being seen, soothed, safe, and secure, all in the face of my grief and affliction. I see in the faces of the group members the face of Jesus seeing me and confidently reminding me that he is my older brother who loves me and is not leaving the room no matter how hard it gets.

For some, it is too hard to remain. At times members have stopped participating in groups without saying goodbye or providing good reasons for leaving. They just stopped coming and no longer communicated with us. This is rare, but it happens. It will happen to anyone who is serious enough to turn their gaze toward the beauty of the Lord. People also left Jesus and stopped following him (John 6:66). But to be seen demands that we reveal ourselves in our most vulnerable places, something not everyone is prepared to do, no matter how convinced and convincing they are that they're ready to dwell in the house of the Lord all the days of their lives.

Remember Brendan? Over the course of the time he was (and continues to be) in the community, he remained estranged from the daughter he longed to know. You see, to dwell in order to gaze upon the beauty of the Lord such that we can inquire of him—ask him anything—means we have to be up close. And the closer we get, the more lovingly demanding he becomes. He will winnow our shame until its voice is barely audible to us. But along the way, we will discover that far more important than our receiving everything we want is knowing *that* we want it is valid, even when we don't receive it. This process points to the four s's, all of which are what children receive in secure attachments.

It is, moreover, the essence of what it means for us to hear our Father's voice telling us, repeatedly, "You are my daughter." "You are my son." "I am so very pleased that you are on the earth." "I cannot believe I get to be your Father!" Brendan practiced hearing that voice in the presence of the voice of shame, which attempted to remind him that his story was marked by infidelity and dishonor. Every time it did, he practiced bringing the voices of the group to his consciousness, and what was once only sadness became a mission of confident prayer for the daughter who, as of this writing, he has never met.

To be close to Jesus is to be drawn in by him to answer his question, "What do you want?" And when we tell him, there will be times when he says, "You don't know what you're asking. You want to be close to me. And so you shall, because you don't really want anything more than that. But you need to know, on the way to becoming beauty, I will take away everything about you—including your desires—that have even the hint of shame lurking around the edges."

In the work of *nihonga*, the pigments that are eventually mixed with glue to become the paint have their origin in precious minerals. Azurite. Malachite. Ruby. Silver. Gold. Oyster shell. Each of these is hand-pulverized by experienced artists in Japan. The brilliance and refractory nature of the paintings when completed depend on the pulverization of the minerals and the paper-thin shavings of gold or silver. As Fujimura describes it, beauty necessarily requires pulverization. It is out of our trauma, our griefs, and our shame—even our longings that are at times painfully unrealized—that the most powerful acts of the creation of beauty emerge.

In *Charis—Kairos (The Tears of Christ)*, Fujimura portrays in an array of colors the beauty that emerges from Jesus' tears—and that emerges from our own. To sit with this painting is to sit with the reality of unrealized, legitimate desire. It is to put ourselves in the path of oncoming beauty such that it finds our own griefs that we can then share within a community, the members of which don't leave the room when we do. To press on to beauty is to be pulverized, is to be formed, is to be joined with other colors that are so very different from us but that together create beauty the likes of which we cannot imagine unless we are willing to drink the cup that Jesus drank. Indeed, many tears have been shed in our confessional communities, all of which have been bottled by God, honored by God who is the source of living water for all of us. In the face of our suffering, we look upon the beauty of the Lord in the faces of those who gaze upon us and see Jesus' gaze, one that never shames us, always comforts us, always helps us see that even though we do not know what we're asking for, he is the answer we seek.

Do you love me?

We come now to the final of our four questions. This question has its source in one of the final scenes of Jesus' life as recorded in John's Gospel (see John 21:17). Here I want to focus on Jesus' question to Peter, which is as much about recommissioning as it is about revelation.

As the disciples are in the middle of the breakfast Jesus has prepared for them, he begins a sort of inquisition—at least that's how it might appear to one observing the scene casually. Jesus asks Peter, repeatedly, "Do you love me?"

This was not Jesus' attempt to shame Peter but rather to draw his attention to his shame in order to redirect Peter's attention simultaneously to himself. He was saying to Peter, "We both know that we both know what you did. Everyone sitting around the breakfast fire knows. You are tempted to remain in your shame and so return to fishing for fish. I want none of that. I want you fishing for men and women. I have work for you to do—and do in the very face of the shame you feel so that you can watch it be transformed into something so beautiful that it will become unrecognizable to you. It will become confidence and comfort. And you will become both for others.

"Where your bluster was once your coping strategy for your deep insecurity and fear, you will know joy and humility instead. You will be seen. Soothed. Safe. And now, secure. You will know, by looking at me looking at you and remembering this meal, that your betrayal will be known not for my death but for your liberation to fish for men as I said you would. To create the beauty you were born to create."

The question "Do you love me?" accomplishes two things. First, it subsumes the first three questions. Jesus personally yet publicly, in the context of community, pursued and joined Peter—an example of heaven coming to earth. Second, it sets up Jesus' next command: "Feed my sheep." Jesus has work for Peter to do. He has new things for Peter to make. New acts and artifacts of goodness and beauty to create and curate. And so it is for us. But these acts and artifacts begin—as they do for us from our beginnings—as relationships. Attachment research reveals that parents and children first establish a secure base in order for the child to venture out into the world. Upon doing so, they return from their adventures to "re-member" their attachment—in order to once again venture out, this time even further. These ventures are ultimately ventures of creativity as a function of secure attachment.

It was in each of their respective confessional communities that Graham and Carmen found other members pursuing them in their heretofore insecure attachments. Each had their particular way of expressing where they were, what they wanted, and the terror they feared would find them in their future together. But each began to practice taking their respective communities with them as they worked on their marriage, to remain in difficult, frightening emotional states for the sake of the other—in essence, to suffer, to drink the cup. The process took at least nine months as they found their footing in their separate communities, which provided the ballast they each needed. Over time they were each able to name, without my prompting, how amazed they were at the beauty that was emerging in their relationship. Creating beauty had been the last thing they imagined in our very first conversation. They were also able to bear witness that the work they were doing on their marriage was shaping all of their other relationships in redemptive ways.

This venturing will naturally lead to ruptures. Messes will emerge as a direct result of our creating beauty. Paint gets on our clothes. The kitchen requires cleanup after a long day of baking. Relationships absorb pain, wounding, and disruption as we connect and create with others. Relationships, like art, are messy. But confessional communities place us in position to ask, "Do you love me?" at the very place where the ruptures happen. And when we have the attention of the one we ask the question of, we can then, like Jesus, say, "Good. I'm so glad. I have new creation work for you to do. Work to create and become an outpost of beauty and goodness."

Some time ago, a number of us gathered and watched over several days as Makoto Fujimura began what would eventually be a several-week-long project creating the painting *New Wine*. We witnessed him making the pigment from a combination of pulverized mineral dust and glue; we saw how he took the thinnest of gold sheets and, using a specialized tool, transformed the sheets into gold flecks that veritably floated onto the surface of the canvass. Over time the azurite, malachite, ruby, gold, and other materials were carefully layered in such a way that, depending on which angle you viewed the painting from, the refraction of the light returned to you differently.

To see the painting now in all of its splendor while holding the memory of what it was in its early stages—along with the memory of Makoto's careful attention to each moment of creation—provides a vision for what Jesus was doing in his conversation with Peter and what we encounter in the confessional community. In inquiring, "Do you love me?" we seek out where shame lurks for the purpose of its healing. This is the curation of the minerals, in which they are mined, chosen, and pulverized and purified by hand. Once Peter's attention is turned away from his shame and toward Jesus, Jesus further directs it by saying, "Feed my sheep"—in essence, "I have work for you to do. I have new beauty for you to create and curate." Jesus says the same to each one of us. Like Makoto applying the mixture of mineral or oyster shell powder and watery glue, Jesus takes the essence of our traumas and its attendant shame and creates New Wine.

There is beauty to be found everywhere. But never is beauty more poignant than when we see it through our trauma and shame. We see Good Friday through the lens of Easter and everything about its brutality, its pulverization of God in the person of Jesus, is transformed into the beauty of the resurrection. This is what it means to fully answer the question, "Do you love me?"

10

PRACTICING
for HEAVEN

A People of Beauty

*"But I tell you that everyone will have to give account
on the day of judgment for every empty word they have
spoken. For by your words you will be acquitted, and
by your words you will be condemned."*

MATTHEW 12:36-37

TO GAZE UPON BEAUTY while being gazed upon as beauty reorients
our shame at the level of the middle prefrontal cortex, integrating the
nine domains of our mind's landscape, widening our windows of tolerance, and moving us into and strengthening our social engagement
systems. All of this further enables us to inquire of each other, in ever-
expanding and deepening ways, where we are, what we want, if we can
and how it is to drink the cup of suffering, and if we love one another—
such that we are then recommissioned to further create the works that
God has planned for us to create (Ephesians 2:10).

But our imaginations need to expand yet beyond this. All of the above
is to enable us to practice for what is coming—to practice for heaven. We
are getting ready to "give account on the day of judgment for every empty
word [we] have spoken" (Matthew 12:36).

Jesus and the New Testament writers referred to heaven—that domain of reality that God occupies[1]—coming fully together with the earth. This, God's kingdom dwelling on earth as it does in heaven, was referred to as "the age to come." They often compared it to "this present age," the long period that the biblical writers understood to be the time-space world between Eden and the new Jerusalem (Mark 10:30). We Christians believe that God has, in raising Jesus from the dead, ushered in the early stages of the "age to come." Abraham, Moses, David, and the prophets, right up to and including John the Baptist, were all doing what they could in their respective wildernesses to

> prepare
> the way for the LORD;
> make straight in the desert
> a highway for our God. (Isaiah 40:3)

They were doing the hard, beautiful work to make possible that

> every valley shall be raised up,
> every mountain and hill made low;
> the rough ground shall become level,
> the rugged places a plain. (Isaiah 40:4)

The age to come has begun, overlapping with this present age from the time of the resurrection. We believe that the age to come will arrive in its fullness at the parousia, the appearance of Jesus. To many of us moderns in the twenty-first century, with all of our sensibilities, the idea of a resurrection, let alone a new heaven and earth, sounds a bit ridiculous. And indeed, compared to every other story offered about where we came from and what will happen to us at the end of the world, the Christian story is ridiculous. St. Paul said it well: to religious folk who are more committed to their religion than to telling their stories as truly as possible, the gospel is a stumbling block; it's painfully confusing. And to nonreligious folk who are just as wary of telling their stories truly, the gospel is utterly foolish; it's painfully threatening.

But "we preach Christ crucified" (1 Corinthians 1:23). We believe that beauty is to be found by looking at the crucifixion with the eyes of resurrection, and in gazing at our trauma and shame this way, beauty emerges out of that which has been pulverized, out of that which has been crushed. Moreover, the more finely the mineral is pulverized, the greater the refraction of the light and the more expansive the beauty will be. We practice "preaching Christ crucified" in our confessional communities. Not in order to check some theological box that verifies unsullied belief but to speak truly of our lives, which in all of their desires also carry great grief. This grief is then transformed by our lament in the presence of others and by the faithfulness of those who will not leave the room.

The age to come—the new heaven and earth—will be many things, most of which I cannot begin to imagine. We know that heaven will involve a mysterious transformation in which we suddenly find ourselves fully mature (1 Corinthians 15:52), but is it possible that it will be more? Is it possible that heaven is where our story will actually begin?[2] Is it possible that each of our stories will begin with a conversation with Jesus, one in which he inquires, and requires, as he has before—patiently, kindly, unflinchingly—that we provide an account of every word, careless or otherwise? And would this not follow what our poet of Psalm 27:4 has asked for, now that our dwelling is eternal and we gaze directly upon God's beauty in his presence? Is it possible that our work in these confessional communities, in this present age that overlaps with the age to come, prepares us for a greater conversation that will, by necessity, given how many empty words there are to account for, require eternity? A conversation that leaves no stone unturned but, in the turning of every pebble, does so in the absence of shame?

Imagine the moments of anger you have to account for. The moments of envy (for me, those aren't moments; that is my life). The moments in which you agreed with your shame attendant that you were not merely unwanted but unwantable. The moments when you mentally undressed the woman who was not your wife. The moments when you condemned the person of another ethnicity. The moments when you held in contempt the person with a different political perspective. The moments you entertained hate for your spouse. The moments you took advantage of an employee because the power gradient between you made it possible. The moments you chose to wear a mask to help prevent the spread of a virus, or chose not to, but thought less of those who did what you weren't doing. You get the picture.

Now imagine Jesus inquiring of you what was behind each of these moments. Imagine the physical location where this conversation is taking place: what you are wearing, what you sense in your body as the conversation proceeds. But imagine as Jesus frames each question that he first wants to know where you were—as he wanted to know of Adam—when you uttered or thought each empty word, each sensation, image, feeling, thought, or bodily impulse. Imagine his unhurried follow-up question, inquiring what it was you really wanted in that moment. And what suffering you were avoiding such that you uttered it or thought it or imagined it in the first place. As this whole conversation unfolds, you eventually discover, like Peter, that Jesus is taking you somewhere.

He eventually asks you if you love him. Love him? If it weren't Jesus asking it, you would think the question silly. The answer seems patently obvious. Is not your being in this new heaven and earth evidence that you do in fact love him? Yes. And even though Peter was a witness to the age to come, having been with the resurrected Jesus at least twice before eating breakfast with him on the beach, it was not enough to keep him from returning to his old fishing habits. Jesus had no intention of leaving him there, and he has no intention of leaving us there either.

Where is "there"? "There" is where we are unable to imagine the beauty of new creation because we still carry shame in hidden interpersonal neurobiological spaces. It is where we, like Peter—like Carmen and Graham and Ella and William (before they gazed upon the beauty of the Lord as it pierced through the trauma and shame of others' stories so as to find and liberate them from their own)—cannot imagine our lives being any different than they are, so we return to fishing for fish instead of men and women. Might not Jesus then also, in his demand that you give an account of your every idle word—every single sensation, image, feeling, thought, and embodied impulse—ask you if you love him, exposing every instance when you didn't in order to disallow that moment from ever again requiring you to divert energy to contain or manage it? Might not this all take place on the way to getting you ready to do the work—the acts of creating new beauty in the age to come, even as it overlaps with the age that is passing away?

I suggest that in and through a confessional community, we practice living in the age to come while maintaining a firm foothold in the present. In these communities we are practicing for heaven. We practice vulnerability with others with whom we have great difference and in the absence of shame. These are the fundamental relational conditions required for the emergence and creation of beauty, both in terms of who we are relationally and what we sustainably create materially in the world. All the while we grow in our awareness that relationships and the material world are not categorically different realities; rather, they are differentiated forms of the heaven and the earth that are destined to come together on the last day.

Our final excursion into the world of art is the Japanese art form *kintsugi*. *Kintsugi* is the tradition of mending broken vessels by putting the pieces back together with an adhesive that is then overlaid with a precious metal such as gold, silver, or platinum. The word *kintsugi* is composed of, literally, *kin* (gold) and *tsugi* (to join together).[3] It originated between the fourteenth and fifteenth centuries when, as the story goes, a Japanese shogun shattered his favorite tea bowl. He sent it to China for repair, only to have it return in an unacceptable fashion. The shogun was deeply distressed and planned to discard the bowl. When his craftsmen heard this, they repaired the bowl, but instead of hiding the fracture lines, they highlighted them, giving the bowl a beauty that outshone its appearance before it was broken.[4]

Kintsugi represents the work we do in confessional communities. We do not attempt to hide the fracture lines. Rather, we pay close attention to them, bringing the pieces of a shattered life together, bonding them in the depth of new relational connection, and overlaying them with gold in the recommissioning of each person's life as an even greater source of beauty than it was before trauma and shame overtook them.

EXPORTING BEAUTY

Beauty is something to which artists draw our attention, but its locale is not limited to art, nature, or religious experience. It is ubiquitous if we have eyes to see it, emerging in the context of our desire and grief, our longings and our trauma and shame. Moreover, it is something we are called to create in whatever domain of life we occupy. In the confessional communities, beauty not only emerges in the groups themselves; it also becomes something members create in their lives outside the community as a direct result of the work they do there.

Graham and Carmen, who attended separate groups, were able to use what they did in the communities to strengthen their marriage; they shared with their pastor what they were doing, and the pastor invited them to facilitate a group for couples in the church that was based on the principles of telling stories more truly, holding people's desires as well as griefs in the mission of healing trauma and shame. The pastor did not stop there. He invited our staff to join him and the elders of his church in an exploration of how the work we do in our groups could be propagated, with the elders training small group leaders to use this material in the same way.

Francine, another member, had in her younger years dabbled in painting. She had last put acrylic to canvas in her midtwenties; by the time she was in our group, she was in her late thirties. She had grown up in a family that had a generational fear of scarcity. She had wanted to major in art in college, but her parents worried that she wouldn't be able to make a living as an artist. In their anxiety, they nudged her—not subtly—into business and finance, fields in which, as it turned out, she was also gifted, though she had little interest in them. After college she took a job in an accounting firm where she excelled, but internally, she languished. Single, she had long desired to be married. And although she had been pursued by multiple suitors, marriage had never been the result.

She entered psychotherapy to address her growing depression, which she thought was mostly about her marital status. And to be certain, that was an important part of her story. But underneath this lay a deep sense of not being seen, soothed, safe, or secure that had begun with her parents and continued in her dating life. What was even more exasperating was her experience in the two church fellowships she had been part of in the last fifteen years. She heard much well-intentioned advice about how one's identity needed to be grounded in relationship with Jesus, but when she looked around at how the congregations actually lived, it seemed they believed that the holy grail of life was finding the right person to marry. For all the theology they offered about single people being valued as highly as those who were married, that wasn't what she experienced.

When she joined our group, she casually mentioned her interest in art and how she had stopped paying attention to it. Andrew, another member, didn't forget her comment, and over several months he continued to re-visit the topic, being curious with Francine about what she was doing with her painting. He told her he longed for her to get out her palette and easel because if she did, it would give him the courage to return to playing the piano, something his wife had been begging him to do for most of their marriage. Andrew's patient, persistent prodding eventually led to Francine walking into the group one day with a small painting that took our breath away.

Its beauty was striking, but just as striking was the story Francine told of how, in Andrew's pursuit of her, she felt seen in a way she had not experienced in her entire life. Moreover, she spoke directly of how Andrew's attunement (and that of other men in the group) had helped heal the wound of being unseen by her father and the leaders in her church, many of whom were men. She went further, revealing how she had begun to feel more comfortable in her own skin, given the welcome and wonder offered to her in the group. She reported how much less often she was thinking about being single and framing it, as she had for so long, as a blight on her life. We all were able to acknowledge that the painting, in all of its beauty, reflected the beauty of the work that

Andrew (and others) had done to encourage her. It was in their delight in her that so much beauty in her life had begun to emerge.

Eighteen months later Francine had stepped fully into her gifting as an artist, producing multiple paintings that had been discovered by an important local art critic. At the time of this writing her work is being shown and purchased in multiple cities around the country. She has reduced her work at her accounting firm to part time. She has not yet met a man she is interested in marrying, but the lens through which she considers that part of her narrative has shifted, given the love she continues to know in her confessional community. The beauty that emerges out of trauma and shame has extended far beyond the walls of our small practice and is now gracing the lives of others in faraway cities through the beauty of Francine's art. Beauty will indeed save the world.

These examples show that the confessional community framework is not primarily about psychotherapy. We are practicing for heaven. If we take the biblical narrative seriously, we are to be practicing for heaven every moment of our lives. But, as with all vocational disciplines, to become effective at what you do, you must have a primary place to practice. You don't practice Bach's Suite No. 1 for cello at Carnegie Hall. No, you need a place to sweat, and repeat, and make mistakes in order to play at Carnegie Hall. You need a laboratory in which to experiment, a crucible in which to be tested, a studio in which to start your painting—and start over again.

In some respects, this is what weekly church fellowship is intended to do. It is supposed to provide a lab, a studio, a crucible in which we are formed into the image of Jesus by looking at him in the face of others. A space where everyone remains in the face of our mistakes and where people are committed to repairing ruptures. But that doesn't happen for everyone. I have often said that, given what happens in most ninety-minute sessions of our confessional communities, we would just need two or three worship songs at the beginning, a homily in the middle, and the Eucharist at the end, and we would have church. To be clear, the church gathered each Lord's day necessarily finds its life in the preaching of the Word and in the sacraments, life that extends into the rest of our lives and, in this case, the work that emerges in these communities.

We too often—and nonconsciously—experience our more explicit worship and congregational gatherings as separate from the rest of our lives, in the same way modernity has provided the most recent version of how mankind separates "god" and "spirituality" from the "real" and "material" world. However, unlike Las Vegas, what happens in church shouldn't stay there. What happens in church should by all means leave the church and go everywhere else. And in no place should we be more committed to dwelling in order to gaze upon the beauty of the Lord as found in the pathos of his people, having our shame swallowed up (as was Francine's), and being recommissioned as creators and curators of beauty in the domains of our lives than we are in the church.

From there, in whatever vocational domain we occupy—families, schools, churches, businesses—there is beauty to be created. In the same way we name where we are, what we want, if we are able to drink the cup of suffering, and if we love one another in our groups, we should have those conversations in contextually appropriate fashion in every sphere of life, expecting to witness God and us co-creating outposts of beauty and goodness as a result. Outposts of beauty that will save the world.

And this beauty, necessarily, in God's economy is always a herald of justice. Justice not least in all the realms of human existence that have anything to do with money, sex, or power. Justice that is the evidence of God putting things right. Hence, as much as this work includes the question of where are you anticipating that you will create beauty in your school? Your law practice? Your accounting firm? Your farming? Your composition of music? Your parenting? Your microfinance venture?—it also includes the question of how are we looking to create beauty in our deepest places of systemic and institutional trauma? The list is endless of how and where what we do in confessional communities becomes what we do in all domains of our lives—and in each composition, justice is what will follow in its wake.

In any creative endeavor we undertake, in every nook and cranny of life we occupy, naming our longings and griefs (and developing a practice of hopeful lament for what it means to live in between them both) paves the way for beauty to emerge in the presence of our trauma and shame. This means, practically, that no matter what venture we aspire to, beauty is waiting for us. Of course, typically there are no trained psychotherapists in charge of the long-term work in other vocational domains, but there are basic methods of practice that can be put into place that generally follow the ideas highlighted in this book.

The following are some concrete steps to consider taking as part of any system, be that your family, church, school, business, or explicitly creative endeavor. These ideas can be honed more specifically to your particular setting and are a way to live hopefully, creating outposts of beauty and goodness, playing the cello in the middle of whatever war zone you find yourself in.

We begin by affirming that the biblical narrative is the story in which we believe we are living, and as such, the anthropology we find there is the hard deck on which all else is constructed. We go on to acknowledge that whatever system we are engaging exists to create and become an outpost of beauty and goodness in the world for the purpose of human flourishing.

As a direct extension of this, we acknowledge that we are people of desire, that we long to be known in relationship, and we long for those relationships to energize us to create the beauty that we also long to become.

We also understand that we are people of grief and our longings live side by side with brokenness and afflictions that make it difficult for us to imagine, let alone see, the beauty we long to create and become.

We next help people begin to shift from understanding their lives in terms of problems to be fixed or pathologies to be treated to a way of imagining their lives in terms of being curious about what the next new artifact of beauty is that they want to create.

We next invite people to tell their stories to each other. (In our communities, initially, to begin the process, we allot each person twenty minutes. This can certainly vary from system to system.) You might be surprised to find how much can be revealed when a person is given twenty minutes to tell their story. But this is just the jump-start for telling our story, as we will see.

We especially focus attention on people's experience of trauma and shame, providing particular exercises to name and respond to both.[5]

We ask members to explore Psalm 27:4, much as we have in this book. We begin with acknowledging that life is hard and the creation of beauty requires perseverance or, as Nietzsche wrote, "a long obedience in the same direction."[6] We proceed next to what it means to dwell, to gaze upon beauty that is to be found in our trauma, and then to inquire. We use the four questions I described earlier as a template and framework for many other, equally helpful questions, all of which are intended to help identify shame in order to recommission group members to create as they want to create in the presence of necessary boundaries.

From the beginning and throughout this process, we continually name and apply the precepts of IPNB, that is, the features of the created world, as a helpful way of understanding and employing the mechanics of the mind for the purpose of integration, of loving God and others with our whole selves as we are loved, of being whole as our Father in heaven is also whole.[7]

We emphasize the significance of putting ourselves in the path of on-coming beauty in as many different forms as possible in order to strengthen our anticipation of and capacity to engage beauty when it presents itself. Two questions that can be helpful here are the following: First, in whatever domain of life you occupy (occupation, student, parent, friend, etc.), how are you explicitly including beauty as part of the landscape of that particular endeavor? Second, how specifically are you committing to put yourself in the path of oncoming beauty on a regular, cadenced basis (e.g., viewing visual art, listening to music that has proven to be enduring, encountering the creation, spending time in a beautiful place of public worship, etc.)?

Throughout all of the above, the primary activity of the group is to live out the gospel's mission to deepen their relationships with each other, telling their stories more truly before a committed cloud of witnesses who will remain in the room no matter what. In so doing, they are loving one another in the way Jesus spoke of when he told his disciples, "By this everyone will know that you are my disciples, if you love one another" (John 13:35). In this respect, the stories that each begins to tell in their allotted twenty minutes goes on to be told, as in Makoto Fujimura's paintings, in textured layers of precious minerals; the more finely pulverized they are, the more gloriously refracted the light is. Moreover, each person's story and the story of each community we inhabit can become its own expression of *kintsugi*.

At the moment when I write the final words of this book, we are a year into a pandemic and at a heightened moment of a call to make right the injustices of racial bigotry and discrimination in the United States. We are polarized politically, with great acrimony mushrooming. We are worried and we are afraid, largely unaware of how evil is wielding shame to do its best to disintegrate us not only as individuals but as communities.

In light of all the chaos and rigidity that surrounds us, it is here that I invite you to consider that God is asking us where we are. He deeply wants to know what we really want, for his desire is that we desire all that is beautiful and good and true and also that the way we desire is as good and beautiful and true as what we long for. Moreover, he asks if we are willing to drink the cup of suffering that we will experience along the way, so that we know he knows that suffering is a necessary part of the journey—and he is with us in the very center of it.

And he is asking us these questions to prepare us to answer him when he inquires of our love for him. When we answer, knowing that our love is imperfect, he will remind us that, despite evil having no intention of going quietly into the night, it will still eventually go. In the context of the communities in which we are being transformed, Jesus will draw our attention away from our trauma and shame and direct it to his gaze—his gaze of beauty as he sees the beauty in us and as he imagines the beauty he longs for us to create and become together. And we will hear him say, "Come on! Bring your cello and let's get to the bomb crater! I have beauty for us to create—and it's waiting for us just around the corner."

ACKNOWLEDGMENTS

I DON'T DESERVE MY LIFE—and not least in terms of those people (far more than I can count to list here) who have been agents of beauty and goodness for me and who have encouraged me to continue to complete this project when I was struggling in my attempt to do so.

I will begin with my friends at InterVarsity Press, who have patiently waited until the ideas for this book finally crystalized and my writing began in earnest. In no small way, my editor, Ethan McCarthy, provided needed guidance but even more so, the encouragement to risk imagining that the ideas herein were not only worth writing but were necessary for people to read. I am ever so grateful for Ethan's even, unflappable presence and his willingness to push me to deliver the ideas that were rattling around in my head in the manner in which you find them.

Moreover, I am also grateful for IVP's willingness and effort to create a book that I trust you will find to be every bit as much an object of beauty itself, if only in a small way, reflecting in its material presence that to which it has been my intention to point the reader. It was my hope that the book's very physicality would reflect the beauty that God intends for us to create and become. And so, thank you, thank you to all the folks at IVP who have made that beauty possible.

Not surprisingly, the highlight of this expression of beauty is the inclusion of the four paintings of Makoto Fujimura. My deepest gratitude extends to him and his wife, Haejin Fujimura, for their kindness and enthusiasm in supporting this project and making it possible for those who do not know of Makoto's work to be introduced to it here, and inspired by it to even further see the beauty that can be discovered in the most unexpected places in our lives and in our world.

Over the last five years in particular, my colleagues in our practice have sustained me and my work and have on many occasions, sometimes without being aware of it, blown fresh air into the embers of this book that at times felt like they were not going to make it to flame. They have provided the necessary curiosity, comfort, and critique that are all required for any work of art, let alone this writing project, to emerge. They have not merely supported me. They have loved me in ways for which I have no words to properly express my gratitude.

There is nothing like having a literary agent who has the patience of, well, even more than, Job. That role falls to Leslie Nunn Reed, who over the past thirty years has become in many respects the curator of much of the work I do, not least that work that is in print. I am so grateful to have the benefit of her steady hand of guidance, in particular as she shepherded this project to its culmination.

Lastly, I want to thank my wife, Phyllis. No one has more graciously or more deeply been with me over the course of what has become this book. No one has had to sacrifice more or has provided more mercy or more necessary prodding than my wife. But mostly, it is Phyllis who, by God's grace—in her dwelling with me, gazing upon me, and inquiring of me—has been *the* agent of beauty and goodness in my life and has been *the* one by and with whom God has most intimately, kindly, and clearly awakened my imagination to what he intends for us and the world to become. It is *she* that, like no other, has enabled me to name my deepest longings and my saddest griefs and has drawn my attention to the joy of new creation that is approaching, for which we are practicing together. Of all the things in this life of beauty and goodness that I do not deserve, she sits in the highest place of honor. Honor that it is my utter joy to bestow upon her.

NOTES

INTRODUCTION

[1]Quoted in Caitlin Smith Gilson, *Subordinated Ethics* (Eugene, OR: Cascade Books, 2020), 78.

1. DESIRE: A PEOPLE OF LONGING

[1]Ronald Rolheiser, *The Holy Longing* (New York: Random House, 1999), 3-5.

[2]Augustine, *Later Works*, ed. John Burnaby (Philadelphia: Westminster John Knox, 1995), 290.

[3]René Girard, *Things Hidden Since the Foundation of the World* (Stanford, CA: Stanford University Press, 1987), 283-98.

[4]James K. A. Smith, *Desiring the Kingdom* (Grand Rapids, MI: Baker Academic, 2009); see also *You Are What You Love* (Grand Rapids, MI: Brazos, 2016).

[5]Smith, *Desiring the Kingdom*, 46-55.

[6]Smith, *Desiring the Kingdom*, 46-55.

[7]Smith, *Desiring the Kingdom*, 28-30.

[8]Augustine, *The Confessions of Saint Augustine* (New York: P. F. Collier & Son, 1909), 5.

[9]Walker Percy, *Love in the Ruins* (New York: Picador, 1971), 6 .

[10]René Girard, *I See Satan Fall Like Lightning* (Maryknoll, NY: Orbis Books, 2001), 7-18.

[11]Curt Thompson, *The Soul of Shame* (Downers Grove, IL: InterVarsity Press, 2015).

[12]Michael Lewis, *Shame: The Exposed Self* (New York: Simon & Schuster, 1992), 91-94.

[13]John Donne, "Batter My Heart," in Malcolm Guite, *The Word in the Wilderness* (London: Canterbury Press, 2014), 70.

[14]Gerard Manley Hopkins, "God's Grandeur," in *Gerard Manley Hopkins: Poems and Prose* (New York: Penguin Classics, 1985).

[15]John O'Donohue, "For Longing," in *To Bless the Space Between Us* (New York: Doubleday, 2008), 35-36.

[16]Peter Berger, *The Sacred Canopy* (New York: Anchor Books, 1969), 45-47.

[17]Girard, *I See Satan Fall*, 7-18.

[18]Smith, *You Are What You Love*, 1-2.

[19]Girard, *I See Satan Fall*, 9-10.

[20]Allan N. Schore, *Affect Regulation and the Repair of the Self* (New York: W. W. Norton, 2003), 37-42.

[21]Schore, *Affect Regulation*, 37-42.

[22]Peter Fonagy, Gyorgy Gergely, Elliot Jurist, and Mary Target, *Affect Regulation, Mentalization and the Development of the Self* (New York: Other Press, 2004), 3-4.

[23]Diana Fosha, Daniel J. Siegel, and Marion F. Solomon, eds., *The Healing Power of Emotion* (New York: W. W. Norton, 2009), 148-51.

[24]Daniel J. Siegel, *The Developing Mind,* 2nd ed. (New York: Guilford Press, 2012), 146-49.

[25]Sanjay Salgado and Michael G. Kaplitt, "The Nucleus Accumbens: A Comprehensive Review," *Stereotactic and Functional Neurosurgery* 93 (2015): 75-93.

[26]Siegel, *The Developing Mind,* 104-11.

[27]NEEDTOBREATHE, "Wasteland," *Rivers in the Wasteland,* Atlantic Records, 2014.

[28]See AT&T advertising campaign, www.ispot.tv/ad/weeB/at-and-t-tv-and-internet-services-more-for-your-thing.

[29]Daniel J. Siegel and Tina Payne Bryson, *The Power of Showing Up* (New York: Ballantine Books, 2020), 5-6.

[30]Siegel and Bryson, *Power of Showing Up,* 5-6. The four s's as I have outlined them here are different in that my description of "secure" entails not only an integrated internal sense of the self but also the capacity to move outward into the world in a way that takes proper, necessary risks.

2. BEAUTY: DESIRE MADE MANIFEST

[1]Daniel J. Siegel, *Mindsight* (New York: Bantam, 2010), 64.

[2]Siegel, *Mindsight,* 71-75. The nine domains of integration are consciousness, vertical, horizontal, memory, narrative, state, interpersonal, temporal, and transpirational.

[3]Daniel J. Siegel, *The Developing Mind,* 2nd ed. (New York: Guilford Press, 2012), 395.

[4]Stephen W. Porges, *The Polyvagal Theory* (New York: W. W. Norton, 2011), 11-19.

[5]Porges, *The Polyvagal Theory,* 269-71.

[6]Pat Ogden, Kekuni Minton, and Clare Pain, *Trauma and the Body* (New York: W. W. Norton, 2006), 27.

[7]Ogden et al., *Trauma and the Body,* 28-38.

[8]Roger Scruton, *Beauty* (Oxford, UK: Oxford University Press, 2009), 1-33.

[9]John O'Donohue, *Beauty* (New York: HarperCollins, 2004), 2, 12.

[10]Aidan Nichols, *A Key to Balthasar* (London: Darton, Longman & Todd, 2011), 1-9.

[11]Nichols, *A Key to Balthasar,* 2-3.

[12]Nichols, *A Key to Balthasar,* 17.

[13]James R. Hart, "Re-Enchanting Worship: Beauty, Heavenly Participation, and Worship Renewal," Robert E. Webber Institute for Worship Studies, 2018, www.iws.edu/wp-content/uploads/2018/08/JHart_Re-enchanting-Worship.pdf.

[14]Makoto Fujimura, *Culture Care* (Downers Grove, IL: InterVarsity Press, 2017), 15-21.

[15]Barbara A. Somervill, *Michelangelo: Sculptor and Painter* (Minneapolis: Compass Point Books, 2005), 80.

[16]Alice M. Ramos, *Dynamic Transcendentals: Truth, Goodness, and Beauty from a Thomistic Perspective* (Washington, DC: Catholic University of America Press, 2012), 71.

[17]C. S. Lewis, *The Weight of Glory* (New York: HarperCollins, 1949/1976), 42.

[18]Thomas S. Hibbs, *Rouault-Fujimura: Soliloquies* (Baltimore: Square Halo Books, 2009), 8.

[19]"Felix Mendelssohn: Reviving the Works of J.S. Bach," Library of Congress, www.loc .gov/item/ihas.200156436.

[20]Roger Fry, *Transformations: Critical and Speculative Essays on Art* (New York: Doubleday, 1956), 235-36.

[21]Iain McGilchrist, *The Master and His Emissary* (New Haven, CT: Yale University Press, 2009), 209-13.

3. BEAUTY: BECOMING WHAT WE CREATE

[1]Pat Ogden, Kekuni Minton, and Clare Pain, *Trauma and the Body* (New York: W. W. Norton, 2006), 29-33.

[2]John H. Walton, *The Lost World of Genesis One* (Downers Grove, IL: InterVarsity Press, 2009), 23-37.

[3]Alice M. Ramos, *Dynamic Transcendentals: Truth, Goodness, and Beauty from a Thomistic Perspective* (Washington, DC: Catholic University of America Press, 2012), 71.

[4]Pope Francis et al., *Not Just Good, but Beautiful* (Walden, NY: Plough, 2015), 86-88.

[5]Makoto Fujimura, *Art and Faith* (New Haven, CT: Yale University Press, 2020), 17.

[6]Curt Thompson, *The Soul of Shame* (Downers Grove, IL: InterVarsity Press, 2015), 88.

[7]Ned Bustard, ed., *It Was Good* (Baltimore: Square Halo, 2006), 18-20.

[8]John O'Donohue, *Beauty* (New York: HarperCollins, 2004), 12.

[9]C. S. Lewis, *Mere Christianity* (London: Collins, 1952), 202-3.

[10]David Wilcox, "Covert War," *Home Again*, A & M Records, 1991.

[11]Miguel A. De La Torre, *Genesis* (Louisville: Westminster John Knox, 2011), 8.

4. TRAUMA AND SHAME: A PEOPLE OF GRIEF

[1]*The Lord of the Rings: The Two Towers*, directed by Peter Jackson (Burbank, CA: New Line Cinema, 2002).

[2]Marion F. Solomon and Daniel J. Siegel, eds., *Healing Trauma* (New York: Norton, 2003), 285.

[3]Peter A. Levine, *Healing Trauma* (Boulder, CO: Sounds True, 2008), 9.

[4]Substance Abuse and Mental Health Services Administration, *SAMHSA's Concept of Trauma and Guidance for a Trauma-Informed Approach* (Washington, DC: US Department of Health and Human Services, 2014), 6-7.

[5]Ed Khouri, "Understanding Trauma," ISAAC International, August 2015, www.isaac -international.org/wp-content/uploads/2015/08/UnderstandingTrauma_EdKhouri.pdf.

[6]Khouri, "Understanding Trauma."

[7]Lenore C. Terr, "Childhood Traumas: An Outline and Overview," *American Journal of Psychiatry* 148, no. 1 (1991): 10-20.

[8]Iain McGilchrist, *The Master and His Emissary* (New Haven, CT: Yale University Press, 2010), 37-49.

⁹McGilchrist, *The Master and His Emissary*, 389-93.

¹⁰Lesslie Newbigin, *The Gospel in a Pluralist Society* (Grand Rapids, MI: Eerdmans, 1989), 8-11, 53.

¹¹Curt Thompson, *The Soul of Shame* (Downers Grove, IL: InterVarsity Press, 2015), 100-107.

¹²David Wilcox, "Show the Way," *Big Horizon*, A&M Records, 1994.

¹³Tom Holland, *Dominion* (New York: Basic Books, 2019), 2-4. Holland notes that there is little recorded about crucifixion in Roman history, as it was a deep, horrific embarrassment for the Romans, who preferred to ignore or deny it for that reason. It would rarely if ever be acknowledged, despite its documented, widespread use to control enslaved and subordinated populations.

5. CONFESSIONAL COMMUNITIES: TELLING OUR STORIES MORE TRULY

¹Andy Crouch, "The Three Callings of a Christian," Andy Crouch (website), http://andy-crouch.com/extras/the_three_callings, accessed March 10, 2021.

²We often read Matthew 5:16 with a deep sense of personal responsibility (and we should) but without a sense of God's delight in our being a conduit of our Father's glory. If, upon seeing our good works, others would look at us and say, "Wow, your dad is amazing," we would feel joy that others' attention on our Father necessarily is a reflection on us.

³Throughout the rest of this book I will use the terms "group," "community," and "confessional community" interchangeably.

⁴Curt Thompson, *The Soul of Shame* (Downers Grove, IL: InterVarsity Press, 2015), 133-34.

⁵For our purposes, I am here using the terms "psychotherapy," "therapy," and "counseling" interchangeably.

⁶Various additional interventions and therapy models include, but are not limited to, cognitive behavioral therapy, psychodynamic psychotherapy, interpersonal therapy, emotion-focused therapy, internal family systems, eye movement desensitization and reprocessing, neurofeedback, dialectical behavioral therapy, pharmacologic intervention, transcranial magnetic stimulation, electroconvulsive therapy, or other community-based and body movement interventions.

⁷Jim Wilder, *Renovated: God, Dallas Willard and the Church That Transforms* (Colorado Springs: NavPress, 2020), 3-4.

⁸See Louis Cozolino, *The Neuroscience of Psychotherapy* (New York: W. W. Norton, 2010).

⁹For example, interpersonal psychotherapy. See Myrna M. Weissman, John C. Markowitz, and Gerald L. Klerman, *The Guide to Interpersonal Psychotherapy* (Oxford, UK: Oxford University Press, 2018).

¹⁰Daniel J. Siegel and Mary Hartzell, *Parenting from the Inside Out* (New York: Tarcher/Penguin, 2003), 197-201.

¹¹Daniel J. Siegel, *Pocket Guide to Interpersonal Neurobiology* (New York: W. W. Norton, 2012), 31-1–31-7.

¹²Karl A. Menninger, *Bulletin of the Menninger Clinic* (Volume 48, Issues 4-6, September 1, 1984, 457).

6. IMAGINE THAT: LOOKING AT WHAT WE DON'T YET SEE

[1]N. T. Wright, *Surprised By Hope* (New York: HarperOne, 2008), 29.

[2]Robert Alter, *The Book of Psalms* (New York: W. W. Norton, 2007), 91-92.

[3]Walter Brueggemann, *The Prophetic Imagination* (Minneapolis: Augsburg Fortress, 2001), 1-6.

[4]Eugene Peterson, *Run with the Horses* (Downers Grove, IL: InterVarsity Press, 2009), 71-77.

[5]Peterson, *Run with the Horses,* 48-52.

[6]Søren Kierkegaard, *Purity of Heart Is to Will One Thing* (New York: HarperOne, 1994).

[7]In *The Soul of Shame* I describe our experience of shame by saying it's like having a personal attendant, albeit one whose intention is to devour us. See Curt Thompson, *The Soul of Shame* (Downers Grove, IL: InterVarsity Press, 2015), 93-96.

[8]J. B. Recknor and S. K. Mallapragada, "Nerve Regeneration: Tissue Engineering Strategies," in *The Biomedical Engineering Handbook,* 3rd ed., ed. J. D. Bronzino (Boca Raton, FL: CRC Taylor & Francis, 2006).

[9]These include at this point proper diet, proper sleep habits, aerobic exercise, mindfulness practices, creative novelty, humor, deep reading, and securely attached human relationships. This list is not exhaustive, as it continues to grow. The common feature throughout is the frequent, repetitive practice of each of them.

[10]Curt Thompson, *Anatomy of the Soul* (Carol Stream, IL: Tyndale, 2010), 51.

[11]Daniel J. Siegel, *Mindsight* (New York: Bantam, 2010), 110.

[12]Chuck DeGroat, *When Narcissism Comes to Church* (Downers Grove, IL: InterVarsity Press, 2020), 18-24.

[13]N. T. Wright, *Paul for Everyone—Romans: Part One* (London: SPCK, 2004), 140-41.

[14]Bessel van der Kolk, *The Body Keeps the Score* (New York: Penguin, 2015), 7-21.

[15]C. S. Lewis, *The Screwtape Letters* (London: Collins, 2016/1942), ix.

[16]For a guided experience centered on a Rothko work, see Curt Thompson, "No. 61," CurtThompson MD (website), https://curtthompsonmd.com/reflections/no-61, accessed March 16, 2021.

[17]Kierkegaard, *Purity of Heart,* 98-103.

7. DWELL

[1]J. R. R Tolkien, *The Return of the King* (New York: Ballantine, 1955/1983), 147-62.

[2]N. T. Wright, *Following Jesus: Biblical Reflections on Discipleship* (Grand Rapids, MI: Eerdmans, 1995), 33-41.

[3]We will explore both of these questions in additional depth and purpose in chapter nine.

[4]In one sense, loneliness is not so much a "thing" as much as it is a word we use to describe the convergence of sensations, images, feelings, thoughts, and behaviors that shape the narrative we tell about ourselves and the world and that are, collectively and ultimately, a function of our not being known. We are unaware of what we are

experiencing below the surface of what we call loneliness because no one asks us, "Where are you?" and "What do you want?" in the way God and Jesus asked the people they were engaging. Even in our church communities, in which we ostensibly gather in the Spirit of Jesus to create deeply committed relationships, we often find ourselves, to our great surprise, feeling more estranged than we would have expected.

[5]Anthony Lane, "The Hobbit Habit: Reading 'The Lord of the Rings,'" *The New Yorker*, December 10, 2001, www.newyorker.com/magazine/2001/12/10/the-hobbit-habit.

[6]Nicholas Carr, *The Shallows: What the Internet Is Doing to Our Brains* (New York: W. W. Norton, 2011), 5-16.

[7]Richard Nordquist, "A Guide to Deep Reading," ThoughtCo, accessed February 11, 2020, www.thoughtco.com/what-is-deep-reading-1690373.

[8]Lesslie Newbigin, *The Light Has Come* (Grand Rapids, MI: Eerdmans, 1982), 225-27.

[9]Daniel J. Siegel and Mary Hartzell, *Parenting from the Inside Out* (New York: Tarcher/ Penguin, 2003), 143-47.

8. GAZE

[1]Aidan Nichols, *A Key to Balthasar* (London: Darton, Longman and Todd, 2011), 20.

[2]Jeremy S. Begbie, "Created Beauty," in *The Beauty of God: Theology and the Arts,* ed. Daniel J. Treier, Mark Husbands, and Roger Lundin (Downers Grove, IL: InterVarsity Press, 2007), 21.

[3]Begbie, "Created Beauty," 22.

[4]Tom Holland, *Dominion* (New York: Basic Books, 2019), 2.

[5]Holland, *Dominion,* 2-3.

[6]Thomas S. Hibbs, *Rouault-Fujimura: Soliloquies* (Baltimore: Square Halo Books, 2009), 8.

[7]Hugh Henry, "Salve Mundi Salutare," *The Catholic Encyclopedia,* vol. 13 (New York: Robert Appleton Company, 1912), www.newadvent.org/cathen/13408a.htm.

9. INQUIRE

[1]Dave Sargent, "Lessons from Athletics: Joe Ehrmann," MaxPreps.com, www.maxpreps .com/news/yZ63uKp3kUKGhk6OjCUYIw/lessons-from-athletics--joe-ehrmann.htm, accessed March 22, 2021.

[2]In the English language we have at least six interrogatory words, five of which are most useful in acquiring information: who, what, where, when, and how. The sixth, why, certainly can be used to gather data (why did the car slide off the road?). But as often as not, "why" is used as a substitute for making a statement about what we feel or what we want. "Why won't you work on our marriage?" might appear to be a reasonable question (indeed, it seemed so for Sarah, whose husband left her for another woman). But when "why" is posed in this way, no answer will suffice. ("I just don't love you anymore" surely didn't cut it when Sarah's husband offered it to her.) In this sense, "why" is used as a substitute for naming what Sarah was longing for. In asking "why," she was really saying to her husband, "I want you to *want* to be with me! With us!" She

was using a question to make a statement. But questions can often serve the purpose of protecting us. From an IPNB perspective, it is far more vulnerable to tell someone what you want ("I want you to *want* to be with me") or what you are afraid of ("I am afraid you will leave me") than to ask, "Why won't you work on our marriage?"

[3]Makoto Fujimura, "Live (Almost) from Mako's Studio: What Is Nihonga?" YouTube, June 14, 2020, www.youtube.com/watch?v=54Lpl7Jbx40.

[4]Ronald Rolheiser, *The Holy Longing* (New York: Image, 2014), 6-12. Rolheiser notes that the Greek word *eros* primarily connotes the energy that is created by God within each one of us. And although we often reduce the meaning of *eros* to sex or sexuality, its meaning is broader—and deeper—than that. None of us comes quietly into the world. We come screaming and demanding and longing. The question for each of us—and for William—is what we will do with the longing, the energy, the *eros* with which we are imbued.

[5]For a further exploration of this theme, see Wesley Hill, *Spiritual Friendship* (Grand Rapids, MI: Brazos Press, 2015). Hill helpfully describes friendship in a deeper biblical sense, a reflection of much of what emerges in the context of these confessional communities.

[6]I attribute the proper use of this question to Terry Wardle, founder and president of Healing Care Ministries (www.healingcare.org), who, over the course of several personal conversations, highlighted it as a crucial step in the process we are exploring here.

[7]Gerald G. May, *Addiction and Grace* (New York: HarperOne, 1988), 3.

10. PRACTICING FOR HEAVEN: A PEOPLE OF BEAUTY

[1]N. T. Wright, *Following Jesus* (Grand Rapids, MI: Eerdmans, 1995), 100.

[2]C. S. Lewis, *The Last Battle* (New York: HarperCollins, 1956/1984), 228.

[3]Makoto Fujimura, *Art and Faith* (New Haven, CT: Yale University Press, 2020), 43-45.

[4]For an example, see Paul Blais, "Kintsugi and Hope | Makoto Fujimura | Episode 620," *The Potters Cast* (podcast), April 11, 2020, www.thepotterscast.com/620.

[5]Two such exercises are (1) completing a trauma egg and (2) completing a shame inventory. See Eli Machen, "Understand How to Do the Trauma Egg," YouTube, January 22, 2016, www.youtube.com/watch?v=D2xU1O18ZnY; and Curt Thompson, *The Soul of Shame* (Downers Grove, IL: InterVarsity Press, 2015), 139-41.

[6]Friedrich Nietzsche, *Beyond Good and Evil*, trans. Helen Zimmern (London: T.N. Foulis, 1907), 106-109.

[7]For a deeper dive into IPNB, see Curt Thompson, *Anatomy of the Soul* (Carol Stream, IL: Tyndale, 2010).

ALSO BY
CURT THOMPSON

The Soul of Shame
978-0-8308-4433-3